PARTIES!

Also by Melanie Barnard and Brooke Dojny

Sunday Suppers

Let's Eat In

PARTIES!

Menus for
Easy Good Times

Melanie Barnard
and
Brooke Dojny

Photographs by Randy O'Rourke

HarperCollins*Publishers*

The authors are grateful to *Bon Appétit* for permission to reprint the following recipes:
Cranberry–Pecan Pound Cake © 1990, *Bon Appétit;* Double Corn Minimuffins © 1990, *Bon Appétit;*
Apricot Almond Tart © 1991, *Bon Appétit;* Brown Sugar Almond Wafers © 1991, *Bon Appétit;*
Spiced Peach Lattice Pie (Marianne's Spiced Peaches and Cream Pie) © 1991, *Bon Appétit;* Ginger Carrot
Bisque (Autumn Bisque) © 1991, *Bon Appétit;* and the entire menu
for "A New England Thanksgiving" © 1991, *Bon Appétit*

HarperCollins books may be purchased for educational, business, or sales promotional use. For information,
please write: Special Markets Department, HarperCollins Publishers, Inc., 10 East 53rd Street,
New York, NY 10022.

FIRST EDITION

Designed by Hans Teensma
Produced by Jeff Potter and Impress, Inc.

Library of Congress Cataloging-in-Publication Data
Barnard, Melanie.
    Parties : menus for easy good times / Melanie Barnard, Brooke Dojny. — 1st ed.
       p.   cm.
    Includes index.
    ISBN 0-06-016596-0
    I. Holiday cookery.   2. Entertaining.   I. Dojny, Brooke.   II. Title.
TX739.B34 1992
642'.4—dc20   92-52582

92 93 94 95 96 ❖/RRD 10 9 8 7 6 5 4 3 2 1

For our families, who love parties as much as we do!

Acknowledgments

INSPIRATION for this book comes from our families and the many friends who have given some very special parties and have come to ours. Laurel Gabel and Mary Bevilacqua are the founders of the Wellesley Cookie Exchange, which has gained national acclaim. Toni and Dale Burmeister are both extraordinary party-givers, as are Joy and Bill Schmitt.

We have said right from the beginning that Randy O'Rourke, ably assisted by Chuck May, was just the right photographer for *Parties!* His experience, his flexibility, and his creativity have combined to produce photographs with exactly the feeling and beauty that we had hoped for in this book. And Hans Teensma has put words and pictures together in a lovely design.

Many people have very generously offered their houses for locations, their possessions for props, and their talents and services to contribute to the photographs. Thank you especially to Stephanie Whitney-Payne and to Ingrid Pettricone, who helped to style some of the loveliest shots. And thank you to Judy and Bob Kamerschen, Mary and Howard Maynard, Danielle Vignjevich, Susan Maloney, Edna Yergin, Beverly Cox, Hester and Henry Maury, Ben and Jane Schmitt, Martha, Alexis, and Natalie Coleman, Jennie and Hannah Wolkwicz, Ryan Russell, and Robert Palladino, and Chris Powers.

Several Connecticut shops very kindly lent beautiful props. Our thanks, in New Canaan, to The Whitney Shop, The Studio, Bon Fleur, Canyon Road, Beval Saddlery, Franco's Liquors, and The Linen Shop. In Westport, we are grateful to Ed Mitchell's, Gallery Linens, The Family Album, Kayne & Co., Silver of Westport, Greens Farms Spirit Shop, Hay Day, Daybreak Florist, Artafax, Pier I, Kitchen Shoppe of Westport. Thank you also to Pat Guthman Antiques, Southport.

And thank you, once again, to our wonderful editor Susan Friedland, to art director Joseph Montebello, and to all the other great people at HarperCollins. We are grateful, as always, to Bob Cornfield and to Janet.

Contents

Introduction

THIS BOOK has been simmering on the back burner for quite a while. Long before we took up cooking as a profession, our idea of a good time was planning and throwing a party. We can both look back to some early disasters (the Christmas party that was top-heavy on potent punch and much too light on food; a dismal, stiff formal dinner party two weeks in the making) and realize we've learned a lot along the way.

Like many people who started entertaining in the sixties, we spent our early years dabbling in the game of culinary one-upsmanship, attempting high-risk, time-consuming, elaborate creations designed to startle and impress.

Some of those parties, though, were tremendously successful, for we were also discovering that the right formula includes more than just food and drink. A party is a total event. An energetic host who has done the right behind-the-scenes planning will make it all seem effortless to the guests. From the initial guest list to festive decorations, lively music, memorable toasts, and friendly introductions, every element should be strategically planned, timed, and initiated by the host.

But of course parties still do start and finish with the food. Our menus have become much simpler and more realistic over the years. Food styles in general, and ours in particular, have moved away from fussy and complicated to a liberated stylish but easygoing standard. Yes, we know that every party, of whatever size, takes some time. And periodically we still make a tiered cake for a wedding anniversary or a beautiful mosaic terrine for an elegant picnic, because certain occasions inspire the grand gesture. But we are comfortable with knowing that store-bought ingredients such as good breads, refrigerator pie crusts, and pâtés and condiments from a high-quality take-out establishment are not necessarily a compromise. Thus, we always think carefully about alternatives to homemade and give you some ideas for each menu in "If Time Is Short...."

Also, these days we pay a lot more attention to healthier eating. For almost all parties, we offer plain, cut-up vegetables as an hors d'oeuvre and a bowl or platter of unadorned fresh fruit as a dessert choice.

Our menus can be made by one person alone, and our "In Advance" section gives you very specific guidance on how to organize each one by yourself. (But we never refuse an offer to help!)

Freezers are a real boon, and we rely on ours, especially for big parties. However, our recommended freezing times are relatively short because, in our opinion, quality suffers if food is frozen too long. Also, remember that at large parties people eat less, so our yields are gauged accordingly.

The key to menu planning is to be flexible. If the strawberries for a tart don't look so great in the market, use raspberries instead. If you have a favorite recipe to insert into one of our menus, by all means do it. If you only use one of our recipes and build your own ideas around it, feel free. Allow yourself options and be open to your own creativity.

That's how this book came about. These are real parties for real people in today's real life-styles. The menus span the seasons from the dead of winter to mid-summer, detail anniversary and graduation celebrations for our own kinfolk, re-create homecomings and reunions, and remember get-togethers with friends planned for absolutely no reason at all. There are big, lavish cocktail parties and easy little spur-of-the-moment dinners. From an Easter egg brunch to a Christmas cookie exchange, and from a bridal tea to a Valentine tête-à-tête, the occasions are limited only by our imaginations.

So let's party!

WINTER

Christmas Open House

Wellesley Cookie Exchange

New Year's Day Buffet

Super Bowl Party

Mid-winter Brunch

Valentine's Day

CHRISTMAS OPEN HOUSE

A Multigenerational Holiday Party

FOR 50

White Christmas Fruit Punch—Orange Ice Ring   6
Youth Soft Bar (NO RECIPE)
Adult Hard Bar (NO RECIPE)

~

Cherry Tomato and Broccoli Crudités with Russian Dip   7
Lox on Small Bagels with Lemon–Scallion Cream Cheese   8
Roasted Chestnuts   9

~

Currant Sage-glazed Corned Beef   10
Whole Smoked Turkey on a Bed of Kale   11
Wild Thyme Honey–Mustard Sauce (PAGE 94)
Anadama Bread   12
Poppy Seed Pan Rolls (PAGE 208)
Chopped Green Cabbage and Red Apple Salad   13

~

Cranberry–Pecan Pound Cake   14
Gingerbread Persons (PAGE 28)
Sugar-crusted Christmas Cutouts (PAGE 29)
Mamie's Famous Fudge   15
Pyramid of Winter Fruits and Nuts   16

~

Coffee (NO RECIPE)

BROOKE HAS BEEN giving a big Christmas party for years, mostly for adult friends. One year, when both of her children were teenagers, she decided that instead of hiring them to pass platters and wash dishes, the kids were old enough to be invited, along with their friends and their friends' parents, as guests at the party.

The multigenerational party has evolved into an unstoppable tradition, expanding over the years to embrace the young peoples' visiting relatives as well as siblings. The only basic admission requirement is a familial connection to one of the teenage guests.

This open house is not a casual, drop-in event. The guest list is carefully negotiated and invitations are mailed early. Every visible room in the house is decorated to within an inch of its life. Every piece of silver is polished, and tables are covered with holiday cloths.

On the evening of the party, the house is aglow with dozens of candles. An adult bar (with bartender) stands ready, and the self-service youth bar, adorned with its huge centerpiece punchbowl, is set up in another room. Hors d'oeuvres are strategically placed around the house and are also hand-passed.

Sooner or later everyone gathers at the

dining room buffet, which is laden with lavishly garnished platters of meats, salads, breads, and spicy condiments. All the while the dessert table beckons, spilling over with a childhood fantasy of sweetmeats.

This party becomes more fun for everyone every year. The first year we were astonished that the younger generation dressed up, many brought hostess gifts, and even wrote thank-you notes! Now we all relax and watch with joy and pride the mingling of the generations.

In Advance

WITH THE BUSYNESS of the season very much in mind, this party is planned so that much of the food can be made well ahead, leaving ample time for the fun of decorating the house. Because of the size and scope of the event, we strongly recommend that you hire some assistance in the form of a bartender and a kitchen helper. Consider it an early Christmas present to yourself.

Several weeks in advance, take stock of your linens, china, and serving pieces. Plan your arrangement of the buffet and the bars to promote natural traffic flow.

The largest chunk of the cooking can be done early in December—which also gets you right into the spirit of the season. Make and freeze the breads, the pound cake, the fudge, and all of the cookies. Two weeks ahead, make and freeze the ice ring for the punch.

A couple of days before the party, set up all of the buffet tables and bars. Make the punch base and the mustard sauce. Assemble the pyramid of fruits and nuts.

One day ahead, make the lemon-scallion cream cheese and the Russian dip. Prepare the vegetable crudités. Cook and glaze the corned beef.

On the day of the party, thaw the bread and desserts. Make the cabbage salad. Carve and arrange the smoked turkey. Assemble the lox and bagels.

At party time, finish the punch and set out the food platters.

If Time Is Short ...

☞   Buy a prepared corned beef from a quality delicatessen.

☞   Use high-quality store-bought honey mustard.

☞   Substitute country-style whole-grain bakery bread for the Anadama bread and soft dinner rolls for the poppy seed pan rolls.

☞   Rely on a trusted bakery for some of the Christmas cookies and other desserts.

White Christmas Fruit Punch

If you wish to make a light alcoholic punch for adults only, replace one quarter of the seltzer and of the lemon-lime soda with white wine.

4	12-ounce cans white grape juice concentrate, thawed
½	cup lemon juice
2	tablespoons lime juice
4	quarts seltzer
3	quarts lemon-lime carbonated soft drink Orange Ice Ring (recipe follows)

1. Stir together the undiluted grape juice concentrate, lemon juice, and lime juice. (Can be done 2 days ahead and refrigerated.)

2. At serving time, pour the juice base into a punch bowl and pour in the seltzer and soft drink. Stir gently, then float the ice ring in punch.

Orange Ice Ring

This fruit-studded ring looks impressive floated in the punch bowl and, as it melts, the orange juice adds its flavor to the punch.

Makes 1 large ring

2	cups orange juice
2	cups distilled water
3	thin slices lemon
3	thin slices orange
3	thin slices lime
3	maraschino cherries, halved

1. Clear a place for a 6- to 8-cup ring mold in the freezer. Pour the orange juice and 1½ cups of the water into the mold, stirring to combine. Place level in the freezer and freeze for several hours until firm.

2. Cut the citrus slices in half crosswise and arrange them and the halved cherries over frozen surface. Pour remaining water around fruit, using enough to just barely cover the citrus slices, leaving the tops of the cherries exposed. Freeze again until firm.

3. To unmold, dip bottom of mold into warm water and turn out onto a sheet of foil. Wrap well and return to freezer. (Can be made 2 weeks ahead.)

Cherry Tomato and Broccoli Crudités with Russian Dip

This dip also makes a delicious spread for a corned beef sandwich, or a dressing for a green salad. You can also add other vegetables to the crudité platter, but the colors of broccoli and tomato strike a particularly seasonal note.

MAKES ABOUT 3½ CUPS

Russian Dip
- 2 cups mayonnaise
- ½ cup bottled chili sauce
- 1 teaspoon Worcestershire sauce
- 1 teaspoon lemon juice
- ½ teaspoon freshly ground black pepper
- ½ cup finely chopped green bell pepper
- ½ cup finely chopped celery
- ¼ cup finely chopped onion

Crudités
- 4 bunches broccoli (about 5 pounds total)
- 3 pints small cherry tomatoes with stems

1. Stir together all dip ingredients. Cover and refrigerate at least 1 hour, or up to 24 hours.

2. Trim the broccoli to make florets, each with about 1 inch of stem. Blanch the broccoli in a large pot of boiling, salted water for 1 to 2 minutes, until barely crisp-tender. Drain in a strainer, then refresh in cold water until cool to stop the cooking and retain the bright green color. Shake heads of florets dry or blot thoroughly on paper toweling. (Can be prepared 24 hours in advance and refrigerated, well wrapped.)

3. To serve, spoon the dip into a decorative dish and surround with broccoli and tomatoes.

Lox on Small Bagels
with Lemon–Scallion Cream Cheese

Lox, traditional with bagels and cream cheese for breakfast, is the saltiest and most intensely flavored of smoked salmon, so a little bit goes a long way. We have redefined this favorite to become a savory snack. If you can't find small bagels, cut up regular bagels or use toasted plain bagel chips. If you don't want to assemble these as canapés, simply put the components in bowls and invite guests to make their own.

MAKES 72 PIECES

16	ounces cream cheese, softened
4	teaspoons lemon juice
1	teaspoon grated lemon zest
¼	cup thinly sliced green part of scallions or chives
18	plain small bagels
12	ounces very thinly sliced lox or other smoked salmon
3	tablespoons small capers, drained and rinsed
	Coarsely ground black pepper

1. Beat together the cream cheese and lemon juice and zest. Stir in the scallions. Let stand at least 30 minutes at room temperature or cover and refrigerate up to 24 hours, but return to room temperature before spreading.

2. Split each bagel in half, then cut each half in 2 pieces to make 4 canapé bases from each bagel. Spread each piece with about 1 teaspoon cream cheese, then top each with a sliver or thin piece of lox; press 1 or 2 capers into the cream cheese, and then sprinkle lightly with pepper. (Can assemble up to 3 hours ahead. Arrange on a platter, cover with plastic, and refrigerate. Remove from refrigerator about 30 minutes before serving.)

Roasted Chestnuts

Chestnuts can be roasted in the oven, but if you have a fireplace, it is worth seeking out a chestnut roasting pan, for hearth-roasting is entertaining. At Melanie's house, everyone picks a chestnut and then minor side bets are placed as to whose will "pop" first—sort of a chestnut horse race.

Look for firm, shiny chestnuts as a sign of freshness and good taste. The only tedious and somewhat tricky part to the roasting process is making the crisscross in the nuts, but don't skip this step or the resulting nut explosion will be more appropriate for a July Fourth fireworks display than a Christmas party.

MAKES ABOUT 50 SERVINGS

5   **pounds chestnuts in the shell**

1. To prepare the nuts for roasting, use a small, sharp knife to make a crisscross cut on the flat side of each nut, cutting all the way down to the meat. This might take some practice. (Can be done a day ahead.)

2. Chestnuts may be roasted over an open fire or on the hearth by placing them in a single layer in a special chestnut roasting pan with a perforated bottom or in an old-fashioned popcorn popper with holes in the bottom. Roast, shaking the pan gently, for 10 to 15 minutes until the nuts are toasty and browned and begin to "pop." Peel and eat the chestnuts while they are warm.

3. For oven-roasting, preheat the oven to 425° F. Set prepared nuts in a single layer on a baking sheet. Roast, turning often, for 10 to 15 minutes as directed above. Pass in a napkin-lined basket.

Currant Sage-glazed Corned Beef

A glazed corned beef looks lovely on a buffet. When carved into thin slices, this lean, intensely flavored meat goes a very long way.

Corned Beef and Garnish

3	5-pound pieces corned beef brisket or round (see Note)
	Branches of sage for garnish
	Kumquats and their leaves for garnish, if desired

Currant–Sage Glaze

⅓	cup currant jelly
3	tablespoons white wine
¾	teaspoon prepared horseradish
1	tablespoon chopped fresh sage, or ½ teaspoon dried

1. Rinse the meat and simmer in water to cover for about 3 hours, or until tender when pierced with a fork. Do not let water boil. Keep beef in the cooking water until cool enough to handle, but still warm.

2. In a small saucepan, combine the jelly, wine, and horseradish. Bring to the simmer, stirring, and cook until jelly is melted and glaze is slightly reduced. Stir in the sage.

3. While corned beef is still warm, remove from cooking liquid. Trim the fat from the top of each piece and pat dry with paper towels. Brush glaze over the meat. Cool and refrigerate for at least 3 hours. (Can be prepared a day ahead.)

4. Cut meat across the grain into thin slices, leaving some beef unsliced to display its glaze. Arrange slices overlapping on a platter. (Can be sliced several hours ahead. Cover well and refrigerate. Bring to room temperature before serving.)

5. When ready to serve, garnish platter lavishly with branches of sage and kumquats and kumquats leaves if desired.

Note: Look for lean corned beef, avoiding pieces with a large streak of fat running through the center.

Whole Smoked Turkey on a Bed of Kale

A whole smoked turkey with its dark burnished skin looks beautiful on a buffet. We carve some meat off the whole bird and supplement with smoked turkey breast. Buy from a good local market or from one of the many reliable mail-order sources. Among its many virtues is the fact that smoked turkey needs no further cooking!

MAKES ABOUT 50 BUFFET SERVINGS

1	**15-pound fully cooked smoked turkey**
2	**3 to 4-pound smoked turkey breasts**
1	**large bunch kale**

1. Remove skin from half the whole turkey and carve meat into thin slices. Cut breast meat into thin slices.

2. Line a large platter with the kale and place uncarved turkey on the bed of greens. Arrange sliced meat around the turkey, banking it up around the bird. (Can be sliced a few hours ahead. Wrap and refrigerate.)

Anadama Bread

The story goes that Anna was the laziest of Yankee wives, whose only recipe was a gruel of cornmeal and molasses. One day, in frustration, her long-suffering husband uttered, "Anna, damn her!," and added whatever else he could find in the cupboard to improve that same old supper. Though we do think that, if asked, Anna may have had another side of that story to tell, there is no doubt that the resulting Anadama bread was a latent stroke of genius, for this easy batter bread with its golden yellow crumb and rich browned crust is certainly delicious.

For this party, we suggest making 2 loaves. If you have a large mixer or a strong arm, you can mix them together at one time.

MAKES 1 LOAF

½	cup yellow cornmeal
2	teaspoons salt
4	tablespoons (½ stick) butter, cut into 8 pieces
¼	cup molasses
1	package (2 teaspoons) active dry yeast (see Note)
¼	cup lukewarm water (105° to 115°)
3	cups all-purpose flour
1	teaspoon yellow cornmeal for sprinkling

1. In a large mixing bowl or the bowl of electric mixer, place the cornmeal, salt, and butter. Add 1 cup boiling water and molasses and stir until butter is melted. Let stand 15 minutes to soften cornmeal.

2. In a small bowl, dissolve the yeast in the lukewarm water and let stand about 10 minutes until bubbly.

3. Stir the yeast mixture into cornmeal mixture, then add 2 cups of the flour and beat about 3 minutes until very smooth. Add remaining flour and beat in to make a soft, smooth dough. (You may have to beat in the last of the flour by hand if your mixer is not very strong.)

4. Butter a 9- by 5- by 3-inch loaf pan and scrape the dough into the pan, smoothing the top evenly. Cover lightly and let rise in a warm place for 1 to 1½ hours until dough has doubled and reaches to within 1 inch of the top of the pan. Sprinkle the top with 1 teaspoon cornmeal.

5. Preheat the oven to 400° F. Bake the bread in the center of the oven for 10 minutes, then lower temperature to 350° and continue to bake for about 35 minutes more until top is rich golden brown and loaf sounds hollow when tapped. Remove from pan and let cool completely on a rack before slicing. (Can be made 2 weeks ahead and frozen.)

6. To serve for the party, slice thin, then cut each slice in quarters and place in a napkin-lined basket.

Note: Fast-rising yeast may be used. Rising time will be about half that for regular yeast.

Chopped Green Cabbage and Red Apple Salad

Look for cabbage with loose dark green outer leaves to use as a garnish for the serving bowl.

MAKES ABOUT 50 BUFFET SERVINGS

Creamy Dressing

2½	cups mayonnaise
1	cup sour cream
3	tablespoons wine vinegar
2	tablespoons sugar
¼	cup Dijon mustard
2	teaspoons salt
1	teaspoon freshly ground black pepper

Chopped Cabbage and Apple Salad

2	large or 3 smaller heads green cabbage (about 8 pounds total)
2	cups currants or raisins
1½	cups minced red onion
6	crisp red-skinned apples, such as Empire

1. To make the dressing, whisk together all of the ingredients in a bowl.

2. Remove any large unblemished outer cabbage leaves, wrap in damp paper towels and plastic wrap and refrigerate. Cut cabbages in half, remove cores, and shred. Coarsely chop shreds. Combine in a large bowl with the currants and red onion. Toss with the dressing and refrigerate for at least 1 hour. (Can be prepared 12 hours ahead.)

3. Core apples and coarsely chop. (You will have about 6 cups.) Stir into cabbage salad. (Can be added 3 hours ahead.)

4. When ready to serve, line a large shallow bowl with the cabbage leaves, if available, and heap salad in the center.

Christmas Open House 13

Cranberry–Pecan Pound Cake

Adapted from a recipe from Maine's renowned Bethel Inn, this buttery cake is studded with toasted pecans and tart cranberries. It tastes best if allowed to mellow for a couple of days before serving.

MAKES ABOUT 25 SLICES

1	cup chopped pecans
1½	cups cranberries
1¼	cups all-purpose flour
1	cup cake flour
½	teaspoon salt
1	cup (2 sticks) unsalted butter, softened
2	cups sugar
5	eggs
¼	cup sour cream
¼	cup orange liqueur, such as Grand Marnier
2	teaspoons vanilla extract
1	teaspoon grated orange zest
	Confectioners' sugar for top

1. Preheat oven to 350° F. Butter and flour a 10-cup tube cake pan or two 8¼- by 4¼-inch loaf pans. (If using flat-bottomed pans, line with parchment or wax paper.) Place the pecans on a baking sheet and toast in the oven until lightly colored and fragrant, about 10 minutes. Cool. Coarsely chop the cranberries.

2. Sift or stir together the flours and the salt. Set aside.

3. With an electric mixer, cream the butter and sugar together until light. Beat in the eggs, 1 at a time, stopping to scrape the sides of the bowl once or twice. Beat in the sour cream, then the orange liqueur, vanilla, and grated orange zest.

4. With mixer on low speed, add the flour, mixing just until blended. Stir in pecans and cranberries by hand.

5. Pour batter into prepared pan(s) and bake on middle rack of preheated oven until golden brown and a tester inserted in the center comes out clean, about 45 minutes for loaf pans and 1 hour for the tube pan.

6. Cool cake in the pan for 10 minutes, then turn out onto a rack and cool completely. Wrap and refrigerate for at least 1 day and up to 3 days before serving. (Can be frozen for 2 weeks.)

7. Sift confectioners' sugar over top of cake before cutting into thin slices.

Mamie's Famous Fudge

Mamie Eisenhower made it famous nationally, but when Brooke's mother-in-law, Mamie, prepared this foolproof and delicious fudge recipe variation for her family, she became famous too.

MAKES ABOUT 40 SMALL SQUARES

6	ounces (1 cup) chopped bittersweet chocolate
½	cup marshmallow cream
2	teaspoons instant coffee powder
1	teaspoon vanilla extract
	Pinch salt
1	cup sugar
½	cup heavy cream
1	tablespoon butter
½	cup chopped walnuts

1.   Lightly butter an 8- by 8-inch baking pan.

2.   In a mixing bowl, combine the chocolate, marshmallow, coffee powder, vanilla, and salt.

3.   In a heavy, deep 2-quart saucepan, bring the sugar, cream, and butter to a boil over medium heat, stirring until sugar dissolves. Cover pan and cook over medium heat for 1 minute to dissolve any sugar crystals. Uncover and cook, stirring almost constantly to prevent scorching, for 5 minutes.

4.   Pour hot syrup over ingredients in the bowl and stir until chocolate is melted and mixture is smooth. Stir in nuts. Scrape into prepared pan, using a spatula to smooth and flatten the fudge. Cool about 30 minutes. While still slightly soft, cut into squares. Eat when completely firm. (Can be stored in a covered container for several days or frozen for 2 weeks.)

Pyramid of Winter Fruits and Nuts

If you build this pyramid on a footed dish, it's even more spectacular.

MAKES 1 CENTERPIECE

A selection of some of the following:

> Small oranges
> Tangerines or clementines
> Lady apples
> Lemons
> Limes
> Kumquats
> Mixed nuts in their shells
> Shiny leaves such as kumquat, lemon, or
>   holly (holly is not edible)
> Starfruit

1.   You will need some plain wooden toothpicks and a footed cake plate or a 14-inch flat plate.

2.   Line the plate with doilies if you like. Begin building, using the larger fruits to make a 10- to 11-inch stable layer on the bottom. Make each subsequent layer slightly smaller in diameter. The result will be a variety of fruit piled into a tall conical shape. When fruits begin to be precarious, anchor them to each other with the toothpicks, pushing picks all the way into the fruit so they don't show.

3.   Add nuts around the bottom layer and set them into the crevices between the fruit where they will remain without falling off. Garnish with the shiny leaves. Top with a slice of starfruit. (The pyramid, all but the leaves, will keep for several days.)

Note: Craft shops also sell conical Styrofoam forms. If you use one, simply poke the toothpicks into the fruit and then into the Styrofoam.

Wellesley Cookie Exchange

A Delectable Christmas Tradition
For 16 to 20

FOR MORE than twenty years, a group of women in a quiet Wellesley, Massachusetts, neighborhood have been gathering every December to exchange Christmas cookies. But this is far more than a simple Christmas party. It has become a cherished tradition, and Melanie has been privileged to be a part of it. Her dear friends Laurel and Mary are the founders and permanent hostesses of this special Christmas event.

In the beginning, they simply invited the women of the neighborhood for an evening of good cheer. Each was asked to bring a platter of her favorite cookies as well as an empty plate. Both Mary and Laurel are accomplished bakers and they spent several days making not only their own favorite cookies but also an impressive array of classic holiday desserts. They had such fun at their own party that they decided to do it the following year ... and then the one after that.

The guests arrive, brush the inevitable New England snow from their boots, and place their cookie trays on a large, decorated table set up near the fireplace in Mary's living room. Another, smaller table holds Laurel's antique copper kettle filled with a spicy, warm wassail. After sipping a cup of good cheer, the guests are invited to sample the dazzling desserts set out amid glittering balls and sparkling tinsel on the candlelit dining room table.

Then, as everyone settles into the living room with cups of steaming coffee, the cookie exchange begins. Each woman rises to say a few words about her cookies—where the recipe came from and why she chose to bring this particular one to share. The platter is passed and each guest takes two or three cookies to place on her empty plate. Some cookies are elaborate and painstakingly decorated (and have stories to match), while others are simple and homespun (usually accompanied by a rather harried and humorous tale), but each holds an equal place of honor on the plate.

As the platters empty and the plates fill, the guests gather more than cookies from their neighbors—they glean insights into each one's family history, personality, and interests. They come to know one another just a little bit better. By the end of the evening, neighbors have become friends.

The magic of the Wellesley Cookie Exchange is, for all of them, the real spirit of Christmas.

In Advance

THIS PARTY is very flexible. The hostess prepares as many or as few desserts as she wishes and as her time allows. It's most fun when two friends get together, as Mary and Laurel do, to share the work. Though they always make at least two desserts, they usually round out the table with a spectacular gingerbread house from a favorite bakery. We do the same for our party. (Gingerbread houses, by the way, can be sprayed with varnish and stored, out of the way of mice, for several years.)

If you're starting the exchange tradition in your community, issue invitations early, and include rather specific instructions about how it will work so that guests will arrive with both their empty *and* full plates.

The right size glass bowl is very important for the trifle. Borrow or rent one if necessary. A large footed compote makes the most spectacular presentation. Also, make sure you have a tray at least 15 inches long for the bûche. A wood plank cut to size and covered with foil and doilies can substitute.

It's a good idea for the hostess to choose to make a type of cookie for the exchange that can be stashed in the freezer, freeing you up to decorate the house and the tables at your leisure.

A bûche de Noël is a perfect Christmas dessert, since the frosted cake can be made ahead and frozen. The festive log can be decorated a few hours before serving. The meringue mushrooms will keep for several days.

Prepare the base for the wassail two or three days ahead, finishing it up on the day of the party.

The components of Laurel's winter berry

trifle can be prepared a day in advance, and the entire dessert can be assembled ahead of serving.

If Time Is Short …

☛ Limit the desserts to a single showpiece, but double the recipe. Then buy a few others from the best bakery you can find.

Our Personal Cookie-baking Tips

☛ We make virtually all cookie doughs in the food processor because doughs can be mixed very quickly in the single container, with no preliminary softening of butter or sifting of dry ingredients necessary. Almost all recipes can be adapted to the food processor method. First, process butter and sugar until smooth, then add egg and flavorings and use long pulses to mix. Measure flour into the work bowl, then leaveners and spices, giving a quick stir with a spoon to begin to mix. Use shorter pulses to process until dough just begins to clump together. (Overmixing can make the dough tough.) Gently pulse or stir in by hand optional additions such as chocolate chips, nuts, raisins, and the like. A standing mixer is also just fine for making cookie dough.

☛ We use unsalted butter and regular bleached all-purpose flour for best-tasting and most consistent results.

☛ When refrigerating a batch of dough, wrap in plastic, then use the plastic to help flatten into a rough disk about 1 inch thick. The dough chills more evenly and you have a head start on rolling.

☛ When making more than a couple of types of cookies, we make doughs and chill on one day and bake and decorate on another.

☛ Most cookie doughs may be frozen, well wrapped.

☛ Refrigerator doughs should be well chilled. Work with half or a quarter at a time, keeping remaining portion in refrigerator.

☛ Dip cutters in the flour that's on the board to prevent sticking.

☛ Keep rerolling of scraps to a minimum. Cookies tend to toughen slightly with each reroll.

☛ Know your oven. Check temperature with an oven thermometer and allow for variances when baking. Even a few degrees and/or a minute or two can be the difference between browned and burned cookies.

☛ If baking two sheets in the oven at one time, alternate positions halfway through to ensure even baking.

☛ Let sheets cool between batches. A quick rinse under cold water will speed this up.

☛ If storing two kinds of cookies in the same tin, be sure they are of like (hard or soft) consistency.

☛ Most cookies, except the very soft or the very delicate, freeze beautifully.

Spiced Cider Wassail Bowl

The wassail bowl, or "loving cup," is an ancient symbol of holiday hospitality. While many older recipes call for making wassail with spiced and sweetened ale or beer, we definitely prefer this version, which uses cider. Its fragrance wafting through the house signals unmistakably that this is indeed a special party.

MAKES 20 SERVINGS, ½ CUP EACH

8	cups good-quality cider
2	cinnamon sticks
10	allspice berries
8	whole cloves
¼	cup dark brown sugar
2	cups orange juice
1	tablespoon lemon juice
1	cup dark rum
½	cup brandy or Cognac
	Quartered orange slices for garnish

1. In a large saucepan, combine the cider, whole spices, and sugar. Bring to a simmer over medium heat and cook gently for about 5 minutes, stirring to dissolve sugar. (Base can be made 2 or 3 days ahead. Refrigerate.)

2. Stir in orange juice, lemon juice, rum, and brandy. Heat gently. When ready to serve, float orange slices in wassail. Ladle hot wassail into small punch cups or demitasse coffee cups, serving directly from the stove or placing pot on a warming tray in the dining room.

Mocha Bûche de Noël

Bûche de Noël is probably the easiest "fancy" cake in the world. Decorating it (even with the whimsical meringue mushrooms) takes no special talent or skill and absolutely no hard-to-find ingredients or equipment. The result is always gorgeous and, especially if you use this recipe, always delicious. Our version highlights our personal passion for mocha.

MAKES 16 SERVINGS

Cake

⅓	cup plus 4 teaspoons unsweetened cocoa powder
6	tablespoons cake flour
2	tablespoons cornstarch
½	teaspoon baking powder
¼	teaspoon baking soda
⅛	teaspoon salt
5	eggs, separated
1½	teaspoons vanilla extract
¾	cup sugar

Soaking Syrup

¼	cup granulated sugar
1	tablespoon Kahlúa or other coffee-flavored liqueur

Mocha Butter Icing

4	ounces unsweetened chocolate
1½	teaspoons instant coffee powder
2	tablespoons Kahlúa or other coffee-flavored liqueur
1	teaspoon vanilla extract
½	cup (1 stick) unsalted butter, softened
2	cups sifted confectioners' sugar
⅛	teaspoon salt
4 to 6	tablespoons heavy cream

Coffee Cream Filling

1	cup heavy cream, chilled
1	tablespoon instant coffee powder
¼	cup confectioners' sugar

Decoration

Unsweetened cocoa powder
Confectioners' sugar
Meringue Mushrooms (recipe follows)
Holly or other sprigs of winter greenery

1. To make the cake, preheat oven to 350° F. Butter a 10- by 15-inch jelly roll pan, then line with waxed paper or parchment paper and butter the paper. Dust the paper with 2 teaspoons of the cocoa, shaking off excess.

2. Sift together ⅓ cup cocoa, the cake flour, cornstarch, baking powder, baking soda, and salt. Set aside.

3. In a large mixing bowl, beat the 5 egg yolks with the vanilla and ¼ cup of the sugar until very thick and light and the mixture falls back in ribbons when beater is lifted, about 5 minutes. In a separate bowl, with clean beaters, beat the egg whites to soft peaks, then gradually beat in the remaining ½ cup sugar until stiff and glossy, but not dry.

4. Stir about one-quarter of the whites into the yolk mixture to lighten it, then sift about one-third of the flour mixture over the yolks and fold in gently. Then fold in about one-third of the remaining whites. Repeat to use all the flour mixture and all the whites. Fold in gently but thoroughly. Batter should be well blended, but take care not to overmix and thus deflate—a few streaks of white are fine.

5. Turn batter into the prepared jelly roll pan using a spatula to smooth it evenly. Bake in the center of the oven for 12 to 15 minutes until cake has risen and begins to pull away from the sides of the pan, and a toothpick comes out clean when inserted in center.

6. While cake is baking, sift remaining 2 teaspoons cocoa onto a large tea towel. As soon as cake is done, invert the pan onto the prepared tea towel. Carefully peel wax paper off cake, then roll the cake and the tea towel up starting from a long side. Let the cake cool on a rack. (Can be made a day ahead: Wrap in foil and refrigerate overnight or freeze up to 2 weeks.)

7. To make the soaking syrup, combine the granulated sugar and ¼ cup water in a small saucepan. Bring to a boil over medium heat, stirring constantly to dissolve sugar. Boil 1 minute. Remove from heat and stir in Kahlúa. Let cool before using. (Can be made 3 days ahead and refrigerated.)

8. To make the icing, melt the chocolate over low heat or in a microwave oven. Let cool slightly. Dissolve the coffee powder in the Kahlúa and vanilla extract. Set aside. In a medium mixing bowl, beat the butter until light, about 3 minutes. Beat in ½ cup of the confectioners' sugar and the salt, then beat in the chocolate and the coffee liquid until smooth. Beat in the remaining sugar and 4 tablespoons of the cream, adding additional cream by teaspoons until a fluffy spreading consistency is achieved. (Icing may be made a day ahead and refrigerated or frozen for 2 weeks. Remove from refrigerator at least 30 minutes before using, then beat again briefly if too stiff to spread easily.)

9. To make the coffee filling, stir the cream and coffee powder together in a mixing bowl. Whip just to soft peaks, then gradually whip in the confectioners' sugar until stiff peaks form. Chill until you are ready to use it, up to 2 hours.

10. To assemble, unroll cake and brush liberally with soaking syrup. Spread cake with the coffee cream filling to within ½ inch of the edges. Carefully reroll cake (without the towel) and place, seam side down, on a serving platter or a board. Ice the cake (including the ends) with the mocha butter icing, reserving about ⅓ cup for touch-ups. Refrigerate cake for at least 30 minutes or up to 2 hours to firm up icing.

11. Use a serrated knife to cut approximately 1½-inch-thick diagonal slices off each end. Affix the cut sides of these 2 diagonal slices to the sides of the log to resemble knots, using the reserved icing to secure them. Using the tines of a fork, score wavy lines down the length of the cake to resemble bark on a log. Refrigerate at least 4 hours before serving. (Can be assembled a day ahead and refrigerated, loosely covered with foil, or can be frozen up to 2 weeks; wrap the cake in foil after it has frozen for about 1 hour.)

12. Up to 30 minutes before serving, decorate the cake. Sift some cocoa onto the tray or board you have chosen to hold the cake to resemble dirt, then lightly sift confectioners' sugar over part of the cake and the tray to resemble snow. Garnish the tray and cake with greenery and meringue mushrooms. (Holly and its berries are not edible.)

Meringue Mushrooms

These dainty little morsels are a "natural" garnish to the bûche de Noël, but they are also quite fetching when heaped into a small napkin-lined basket to be given as a hostess gift. They are very easy to make, even for pastry bag novices. Like all meringues, they are most successful when made on a dry day.

MAKES ABOUT 20

2	egg whites, at room temperature
⅛	teaspoon cream of tartar
½	cup granulated sugar
2½	ounces semisweet chocolate
	Unsweetened cocoa powder

1.   Preheat oven to 200° F. Line a large baking sheet with parchment paper, affixing the paper to the sheet with dabs of butter at the corners. Lightly dust the paper with flour.

2.   In a mixing bowl, beat the egg whites and cream of tartar to soft peaks. Beat in the sugar, about 2 tablespoons at a time, until mixture is stiff and glossy and feels smooth to the touch.

3.   Spoon the meringue into a large pastry bag fitted with a ½- to ¾-inch plain tip. Use about half of the meringue to pipe out about 20 mounds ranging in size from about ½ to 1 inch in diameter. Use a damp finger to smooth the tops to resemble mushroom caps of various sizes. Pipe remaining meringue into about 20 upright "stems," each ranging from 1 to 1½ inches in height.

4.   Bake the meringues for 1 hour and 45 minutes, then turn off oven and let meringues cool in oven for 30 minutes. Carefully remove from paper to a wire rack.

5.   To assemble the mushrooms, melt the chocolate over low heat or in a microwave. Use the tip of a small, sharp knife to carve out a small hole in the bottom of each mushroom cap. (The stem will fit into this.) Spread or brush the bottoms of the caps with chocolate, then insert the pointed end of the stem into the hole in the cap. Carefully set the assembled mushrooms, upside down, on a rack and let stand at least 1 hour or until chocolate is set. (Store mushrooms tightly covered, at room temperature, for up to 3 days.)

6.   Just before serving, lightly sift cocoa over the tops of the mushrooms.

Laurel's Winter Berry Trifle

This spectacular trifle of Laurel's is a real tour de force, though very easy to put together. It looks very Christmassy, cloaked in red and white and crowned with a holly wreath decoration.

MAKES ABOUT 24 DESSERT PARTY SERVINGS; ABOUT 16 STANDARD SERVINGS

Vanilla–Almond Custard Cream

3	cups half-and-half
6	egg yolks
⅔	cup granulated sugar
1	tablespoon flour
1	tablespoon cornstarch
2	teaspoons vanilla extract
¼	teaspoon almond extract
1	cup heavy cream

Trifle and Assembly

1	1-pound commercial or homemade pound cake
½	cup Grand Marnier or other orange liqueur
1	16-ounce can jellied cranberry sauce
½	cup orange juice
2	teaspoons grated orange zest
2½	cups fresh raspberries or one 12-ounce package frozen unsweetened raspberries, partially thawed (reserve about 4 berries for holly decoration)
1	cup heavy cream
½	cup sliced almonds, lightly toasted
	Mint sprigs or other nontoxic smallish green leaves, to make holly decoration

About 8 small cranberries, for holly berries

1. To make the custard cream, heat the half-and-half in a heavy nonreactive saucepan until small bubbles form around the edges. Whisk together the egg yolks, sugar, flour, and cornstarch. Slowly whisk hot half-and-half into yolk mixture, return to the saucepan, and cook over medium heat, whisking almost constantly, until custard thickens and large bubbles begin to form just beneath the surface, about 5 minutes. Whisk in vanilla and almond extracts. Transfer to a bowl and whisk for a couple of minutes to release steam. Place a sheet of plastic wrap directly on surface of custard to prevent a skin from forming, and refrigerate for 1 hour, or until cold.

2. Whip cream to firm peaks. Fold into chilled custard and refrigerate until ready to use. (Can be made 1 day ahead.)

3. Use a 3½- to 4-quart glass bowl for the trifle. Cut pound cake into ½-inch slices; then cut each slice in half. Layer one-third of the cake slices, flat sides down, in the bottom of the bowl. Brush with about one-third of the Grand Marnier.

4. In a saucepan set over medium heat, whisk the cranberry sauce with the orange juice and zest until jelly reaches a pourable consistency. Spoon about one-third of the jelly over the cake, spreading evenly.

5. Spoon about one-third of the custard cream over the jelly, spreading to make an even layer with a spatula.

6. Scatter about one-third of the raspberries over the custard, trying to make sure that they are visible around the perimeter of the bowl.

7. Repeat layers 2 more times beginning again with cake brushed with liqueur, until you finish with a layer of cream topped with raspberries, reserving about 4 for the decoration. Refrigerate for at least 4 hours or up to 12 hours.

8. Whip the cream to firm peaks. Pipe through a pastry bag fitted with a star tip, covering top of trifle with rosettes. (Or spread cream on in an even layer.)

9. Sprinkle toasted almonds over the cream in a 2-inch circle around the outer edge of bowl to simulate a wreath. Refrigerate until ready to serve. (Can be made 2 hours ahead.)

10. Shortly before serving, use the mint leaves, cranberries, and reserved raspberries to create a holly branch decoration.

11. To serve, spoon out small portions.

Gingerbread Persons

We like this recipe because it's gingery, and the finished cookie, because it is made with butter, is not as rock-hard as are some.

MAKES ABOUT 4 DOZEN

Gingerbread Cookie Dough

4	tablespoons (½ stick) unsalted butter
⅓	cup granulated sugar
¼	cup molasses
1	egg
1¾	cups all-purpose flour
¼	teaspoon baking soda
¼	teaspoon salt
1¾	teaspoons powdered ginger
½	teaspoon cinnamon
½	teaspoon nutmeg
¼	teaspoon ground cloves
	Raisins (optional)

Royal Icing (see Note)

2	egg whites
¼	teaspoon cream of tartar
2½	cups confectioners' sugar

1. In the workbowl of a food processor, or in a mixer, combine the butter, sugar, molasses, and egg. Process until well mixed. (Mixture will look curdled.) Add the flour, baking soda, and salt, then the spices, stirring slightly to begin to distribute them. (If using mixer, stir dry ingredients together before adding.) Use long pulses to process until dough begins to clump together. Turn out onto plastic wrap, flatten into a disk, and wrap well. Refrigerate for at least 3 hours or for up to 3 days. (Dough may be frozen for 1 month.)

2. Preheat oven to 350° F. Working with half the dough at a time, roll out on a lightly floured surface to a thickness of ¼ inch. With gingerbread person (or other shapes) cutters, cut out cookies. Place 1 inch apart on lightly greased baking sheets. Use raisins for eyes and/or buttons, or mark features with a sharp skewer. Reroll scraps and cut more cookies.

3. Bake in preheated oven, reversing sheets halfway through the baking time, for about 12 minutes, until cookies are firm and brown on the bottoms. Cool on racks and decorate with royal icing if desired.

4. To make royal icing, beat the egg whites and cream of tartar with an electric mixer until frothy. Gradually add the confectioners' sugar. Beat for 4 to 6 minutes until stiff, glossy peaks form. (Can be made a day ahead and stored, tightly covered, in the refrigerator. If icing separates, beat again briefly.)

5. To decorate, spoon icing into a pastry bag fitted with a small plain tip, or make a cone out of parchment paper. Pipe out details on cookies, giving the people additional facial features. Let dry for 1 hour before storing (covered for 3 days or frozen for 2 weeks).

Note: If you are concerned about the small but real chance of salmonella contamination from uncooked egg whites, you can make the royal icing from meringue powder, following package directions. It is available by mail from Maid of Scandinavia (call 800-328-6722) or Wilton Enterprises (708-963-7100). The powder can be stored for many months.

Sugar-crusted Christmas Cutouts

This is our favorite cutout cookie recipe since the dough handles and rolls so easily and the flavor is simply delicious. We make them all year long in various appropriate shapes from Valentine hearts to July Fourth flags. Because the quantity of dough is too large to be made in a standard size food processor, we give directions here for making it in an electric mixer. However, if you have a large-capacity food processor, it will work fine.

MAKES ABOUT 5 DOZEN

4	cups all-purpose flour
1	teaspoon baking powder
½	teaspoon baking soda
½	teaspoon salt
¾	teaspoon grated nutmeg
1	cup (2 sticks) unsalted butter, softened
1½	cups granulated sugar
1	egg
½	cup sour cream
2	teaspoons vanilla extract
	Colored sugar or plain granulated sugar

1. In a mixing bowl, stir or whisk together the flour, baking powder, baking soda, salt, and nutmeg. Set aside.

2. Cream the butter with the sugar until light and fluffy. Beat in the egg, then the sour cream and vanilla. At low speed, beat in the flour mixture just until mixed, stopping to scrape down bowl as necessary. Wrap the dough in plastic, flatten into a dish, and chill at least 2 hours or up to 2 days. (Dough can be frozen for 1 month.)

3. Preheat oven to 350° F. Lightly grease large baking sheets.

4. Divide the dough into 4 parts and work with 1 part at a time, keeping remainder refrigerated. On a lightly floured surface, roll dough to a thickness between ⅛ and ¼ inch and cut with decorative cutters about 2 inches in diameter. Place cookies about 1 inch apart on prepared baking sheets. Sprinkle with colored or plain sugar as desired.

5. Bake in the center of the oven for 8 to 10 minutes, until edges are golden and cookies are very lightly colored. Remove to racks to cool. Store tightly covered up to 4 days or freeze up to 1 month.

Toni's Citrus Bars

Although we've always loved the idea of lemon bars, the sweetness of most recipes had put us off. Toni, who is one of the best bakers we know, uses a reduced amount of sugar in these, and she's added orange and lime zest for extra interest. They're really delicious!

MAKES 24 TO 36 SQUARES

Pastry Layer

1	cup all-purpose flour
2	tablespoons confectioners' sugar
¼	teaspoon salt
⅛	teaspoon mace
6	tablespoons (¾ stick) unsalted butter

Citrus Topping

2	eggs
⅔	cup granulated sugar
2	tablespoons all-purpose flour
½	teaspoon baking powder
1	tablespoon grated lemon zest
1	tablespoon grated orange zest
½	teaspoon grated lime zest
2	tablespoons lemon juice

1. Preheat the oven to 350° F. Grease an 8- or 9-inch square baking pan.

2. In the work bowl of a food processor, combine the flour, confectioners' sugar, salt, and mace. Pulse to combine. Cut the butter into several pieces and distribute it over flour mixture. Process until mixture is crumbly. Pour into prepared pan and, using the palm of your hand, flatten and press to make a smooth, even layer. Bake in preheated oven for 17 to 20 minutes, until crust is pale golden.

3. Meanwhile, to make the filling, whisk together the eggs, sugar, flour, baking powder, citrus zests, and juice. Pour over warm prebaked crust, smoothing with a spatula to make an even layer. Return to the oven and bake for 22 to 25 minutes, until topping is pale golden and just set.

4. Cool on a rack and cut into 24 to 36 squares. (Store, wrapped, in the refrigerator for up to 3 days, or wrap in a single layer and freeze for up to 2 weeks.)

Note: An 8-inch pan will take the longer baking times.

Bonnie's Lemon Lebkuchen

These delightfully spicy old-fashioned German honey cookies are a wonderful addition to any Christmas cookie selection. Bonnie makes them with grated lemon zest (instead of the more traditional citron), and glazes the cookies with a lemon wash. As they age, lebkuchen mellow and their flavor deepens.

MAKES ABOUT 40 COOKIES

Cookies
½	cup honey
½	cup dark brown sugar
1	egg
1½	teaspoons grated lemon zest
1¾	cups all-purpose flour
1	teaspoon ground cinnamon
1	teaspoon grated nutmeg
1	teaspoon ground allspice
½	teaspoon ground cloves
¼	teaspoon salt
¼	teaspoon baking soda
¼	teaspoon freshly ground black pepper

Lemon Glaze
¼	cup confectioners' sugar
1	tablespoon lemon juice

1. In the work bowl of a food processor (or in a mixer), combine the honey, brown sugar, egg, and lemon zest. Process until well mixed.

2. Add the flour, then the spices, salt, baking soda, and pepper, stirring slightly to distribute. Use long pulses to process until dough begins to clump together. (If using a mixer, stir the dry ingredients together before adding.) Dough will be soft and sticky. Turn out onto a sheet of plastic wrap and shape into a 6-inch square. Wrap well, place wrapped dough on a baking sheet or pie plate, and refrigerate for at least 6 hours or for up to 3 days. (May be frozen for 1 month.)

3. To make glaze, combine the sugar and lemon juice in a small bowl. Whisk until sugar is dissolved.

4. Preheat the oven to 350° F. Working with half the dough, and keeping remainder refrigerated, roll out on a floured board to ¼-inch thickness. Use a pastry wheel or a knife to trim edges and cut into rectangles approximately 2½ by 1½ inches. Transfer to greased baking sheets, spacing about 1 inch apart.

5. Bake in preheated oven for 10 to 12 minutes, until cookies are firm and edges are barely colored. Transfer to a rack. While they are still very warm, brush cookies with the glaze. Let glaze set at room temperature for about 30 minutes.

6. Lebkuchen can be eaten right away, but they are better if stored at room temperature in an airtight container for several days before serving. Cookies will harden and their flavor will intensify. (Can be frozen for 2 weeks.)

Nana's Sicilian Fig Cookies

Melanie's earliest memories of Christmas cookies are these gaily decorated, fig-filled dough slices. Variations on this classic Sicilian treat occasionally appear in Italian cookbooks, but this is the "authentic" version directly from Nana! They taste even better the day after baking—a rarity for cookies.

MAKES ABOUT 4 DOZEN

Dough

2½	cups all-purpose flour
⅓	cup granulated sugar
¾	teaspoon baking powder
½	teaspoon salt
½	cup (8 tablespoons) chilled vegetable shortening
2	eggs
¼	cup milk

Filling

2	cups (about 12 ounces) Calimyrna figs, stems removed
½	cup raisins
⅓	cup slivered almonds
¼	cup granulated sugar
¼	teaspoon ground cinnamon
1	teaspoon grated lemon zest
	Pinch freshly ground black pepper
¼	cup orange juice

Icing

1½	cups confectioners' sugar
2 to 3	tablespoons milk
¼	teaspoon vanilla extract
	Colored sprinkles

1. In a food processor or by hand, mix together the flour, sugar, baking powder, and salt. Distribute shortening over flour and pulse or cut in until mixture resembles fine crumbs. Whisk the eggs with the milk, then pour through the feed tube with the motor running, or stir in by hand. Mix just until dough begins to clump together. Place dough on a large sheet of plastic wrap, flatten to about a 6-inch square, then wrap and refrigerate at least 30 minutes or up to 2 days, or freeze up to 2 weeks.

2. To make the filling, place figs, raisins, almonds, sugar, cinnamon, zest, and pepper in work bowl of a food processor. Process until fruits and nuts are very finely chopped. With motor running, add orange juice through feed tube and process only until blended. Filling will be moist and sticky. (Can be used immediately or refrigerated up to 2 days. Return to room temperature before using.)

3. Preheat oven to 350° F. Lightly grease 2 large baking sheets.

4. Divide dough in 4 parts and work with 1 at a time, keeping remainder refrigerated. Divide filling into 4 parts. On a lightly floured surface, roll dough to a 4- by 14-inch rectangle. (Don't worry if edges are ragged.) Use your hands to distribute one-fourth of the filling in a 1-inch strip down center of dough. Use a spatula to help roll the long sides of dough over the center to enclose filling. Moisten your fingers to press down seam. Use a sharp knife to cut filled dough roll into 1-inch diagonal slices. Place slices,

inverted so seam side is down, about 1 inch apart on baking sheets. Repeat with remaining dough and filling. Bake 18 to 20 minutes, until bottoms are pale golden and dough is very lightly colored. Dough should not brown. Cool on racks.

5. To make icing, whisk confectioners' sugar with 2 tablespoons milk and the vanilla to make a thick drizzling consistency. If necessary, add milk by ½ teaspoonsful.

6. Drizzle tops of cookies liberally with icing, then quickly cover with colored sprinkles before icing sets. (This is easiest to do if cookies are placed very close together on wax paper.) Let icing set at least 1 hour. Store tightly covered up to 5 days. (Cookies can be frozen up to 2 weeks.)

Judy's Chocolate-dipped Pistachio Wafers

Brooke's friend Judy makes these every Christmas for the annual book group meeting at her house. This cookie has everything: a rich buttery dough spangled with colorful chopped pistachios, a dark chocolate glaze, and pistachio-dipped edges that add a final touch of elegance.

MAKES 4 DOZEN COOKIES

Pistachio Wafers

6	tablespoons (¾ stick) unsalted butter
⅔	cup granulated sugar
1	egg yolk
½	teaspoon vanilla extract
1	cup all-purpose flour
½	teaspoon baking powder
½	cup finely chopped pistachios

Chocolate Glaze

4	ounces semisweet chocolate
2	teaspoons vegetable oil
¼	cup finely chopped pistachios (optional)

1. In a food processor or electric mixer, cream together the butter and sugar. Add egg yolk and vanilla and mix until smooth. Add the flour and baking powder, stirring baking powder in slightly to begin to distribute it, and pulse or beat until flour is incorporated. Stir nuts in by hand. Turn out onto 2 sheets of plastic wrap and form into two 6-inch logs. Wrap well and refrigerate for at least 2 hours or for up to 3 days. (Dough can be frozen for 1 month.)

2. Preheat oven to 350° F. Using a sharp knife, cut chilled dough into rounds ¼ inch thick. Arrange 1 inch apart on ungreased baking sheets, reshaping into rounds if edges aren't symmetrical. Bake in preheated oven for 10 to 12 minutes, until edges are lightly browned and cookies are pale golden. Cool on a rack.

3. To make glaze, melt chocolate with oil in a double boiler or a microwave and stir until smooth. Dip one half of each cookie into glaze. (If glaze is too thick to dip, paint it on with a small knife.) Roll glazed edges in the chopped pistachios if desired. Place on racks and let stand for 2 hours or until glaze has set. (Store covered for 2 days at room temperature or freeze for 2 weeks.)

Brooke's Apple–Mincemeat Turnovers

Brooke's English heritage means that mincemeat and plum pudding were de rigueur during the winter holidays. Now, she likes to jazz up prepared mincemeat with chopped apple and an extra dose of brandy to make these dainty little turnovers with a pleasantly tangy cream cheese pastry.

MAKES 40 TO 45 CRESCENTS

Cream Cheese Pastry

2	cups all-purpose flour
¾	teaspoon salt
¼	teaspoon grated nutmeg
8	ounces cream cheese, softened
½	cup (1 stick) unsalted butter, softened

Brandied Apple Mincemeat

1½	cups prepared mincemeat
⅓	cup finely chopped peeled sweet apple, such as Golden Delicious
1	tablespoon brandy or Cognac
1	teaspoon lemon juice

Confectioners' sugar

1.   In a food processor or by hand, combine the flour, salt, and nutmeg. Pulse or stir to mix. Cut cream cheese and butter into pieces and distribute over flour. Process or work in shortening until dough begins to clump together. Turn out onto a sheet of plastic wrap, gather into a ball using the plastic as an aid, and flatten into a disk. Wrap well and refrigerate for at least 1 hour or for up to 3 days. (Dough may be frozen for 2 weeks.)

2.   To make the filling, combine the mincemeat, apple, and brandy in a small saucepan. Bring to the simmer and cook over medium heat for 3 or 4 minutes. Stir in lemon juice. Let cool before using. (Can be prepared several days ahead. Cover and refrigerate.)

3.   Preheat oven to 400° F. Working with half the dough at a time, keeping remainder refrigerated, roll pastry out on a lightly floured board to about ¹⁄₁₆-inch thickness. Using a 2½- to 3-inch cutter, cut out circles. Place a scant 1 teaspoon of filling in the center of each circle, brush edges of pastry lightly with cold water, fold over filling, and press edges with the tines of a fork to seal well. Arrange 1 inch apart on ungreased baking sheets and prick each turnover with a fork to release steam. Reroll scraps once.

4.   Bake in preheated oven for 13 to 16 minutes, until pastry is golden brown. Cool on a rack. (Store, covered, for up to 3 days, or freeze for 2 weeks.) Dust heavily with confectioners' sugar before serving.

Carol's Chocolate Almond Macaroon Bars

The bitter chocolate tempers the sweetness and adds an adult dimension to this delectable, rich, chewy bar.

MAKES ABOUT 5 DOZEN

Crust

1¾	cups all-purpose flour
½	cup packed light brown sugar
¾	cup (1½ sticks) unsalted butter
2½	ounces unsweetened chocolate, melted

Filling

1	cup flaked coconut
1	cup slivered almonds
1	cup granulated sugar
2	tablespoons all-purpose flour
1	teaspoon baking powder
¼	teaspoon salt
2	eggs
2	teaspoons vanilla extract
¼	teaspoon almond extract

Confectioners' sugar

1. Preheat oven to 350° F.

2. To make the crust, combine the flour, brown sugar, and butter in a food processor until mixture is well blended and resembles fine crumbs. Press dough firmly onto bottom of an ungreased 9- by 13-inch baking pan to make an even layer. Bake about 20 minutes, until edges are lightly browned and center is golden. Remove from oven and brush crust evenly with the melted chocolate. Let stand while making filling.

3. To make the filling, first toast the coconut and almonds separately in the 350° F. oven for 5 to 8 minutes, stirring often, until golden and fragrant. Watch carefully to prevent burning. Coconut will take less time than nuts. (Coconut and almonds can also be toasted in a microwave separately for about 5 minutes each; stir often.)

4. In a large mixing bowl, whisk together the sugar, flour, baking powder, and salt. Whisk in the eggs, vanilla, and almond extract until well blended. Whisk in the coconut and almonds.

5. Pour filling evenly over warm crust and bake for 18 to 20 minutes, until top is golden brown.

6. Let cool completely in pan. Use a sharp knife to cut into about 60 small bars. Store tightly covered (in baking pan is easiest) for up to 3 days. (Can be frozen up to 2 weeks.)

7. Shortly before serving, dust lightly with confectioners' sugar.

Marianne's Fruit-filled Thumbprints

These make a beautiful, jewellike presentation on a cookie tray. Marianne uses two kinds of preserves—a red one such as raspberry or strawberry and a golden one such as apricot or peach.

MAKES ABOUT 4 DOZEN

1	cup (2 sticks) unsalted butter
½	cup granulated sugar
	Pinch salt
2	eggs, separated
1	tablespoon grated orange zest
1½	teaspoons vanilla extract
2	teaspoons lemon juice
2½	cups all-purpose flour
1½	cups finely chopped walnuts or pecans
½	cup fruit preserves of choice

1. In a food processor or an electric mixer, cream butter with sugar and salt until light and fluffy. Beat in egg yolks, orange zest, vanilla, and lemon juice until smooth. Add flour and mix until just blended and smooth. Wrap in plastic wrap and refrigerate at least 1 hour or up to 2 days. (Can be frozen up to 2 weeks.)

2. Preheat oven to 350° F.

3. Pinch off pieces of dough and form into 1-inch balls. Dip each ball into unbeaten egg white, then roll in nuts to coat completely. Place 1½ inches apart on ungreased baking sheets. Use your thumb to make a depression in center of each cookie.

4. Bake cookies for 8 minutes. Remove from oven, re-form depression in center, and fill each with about ½ teaspoon fruit preserves. Return to oven and bake 6 to 8 minutes more, until cookies are lightly golden and set. Cool completely on racks. Store tightly covered up to 4 days or freeze up to 2 weeks.

Mary's Chocolate Macadamia Rum Balls

These scrumptious "cookies" are a breeze to make since they don't need baking. The macadamias, rum, and coffee give them an exotic edge and the touch of melted semisweet chocolate makes them just plain irresistible, especially when presented in little paper bonbon cups. Be sure to buy thin, real chocolate wafer cookies—they have been made for years by Nabisco.

MAKES ABOUT 5 DOZEN

1	9-ounce package chocolate wafer cookies
1	cup (4 ounces) macadamia nuts (see Note)
½	cup confectioners' sugar
½	teaspoon instant coffee granules
⅓	cup dark rum
3	tablespoons dark corn syrup
2	ounces semisweet chocolate, melted Confectioners' sugar or chopped macadamia nuts

1. In the work bowl of a food processor, pulverize the cookies to make about 2 cups fine crumbs. Place in a large mixing bowl. In the same food processor work bowl, finely chop the nuts with the confectioners' sugar, taking care not to overprocess and make the nuts oily. Add to the mixing bowl. Dissolve the coffee in the rum. Stir rum, corn syrup, and melted chocolate into crumb and nut mixture.

2. Pinch off pieces of dough and roll into ¾-inch balls. Roll each ball in confectioners' sugar or nuts. Place on wax paper and let stand about 15 minutes. Store tightly covered for up to 2 days or freeze up to 2 weeks. (If not serving within a few hours of making, reroll balls in confectioners' sugar 1 or 2 hours before serving to "freshen" the coating.)

Note: If nuts are salted, place in a strainer and rinse under cool water. Pat dry on paper toweling, then let stand at least 30 minutes to dry completely before chopping. Or toast lightly in a low-heat oven until dry.

New Year's Day Buffet

Lucky Foods to Start Off Right
FOR 12 TO 15

W E ' R E N O T R E A L sure when we first got involved with lucky foods. But being ever curious eaters, we always ask about the history of foods that are important to the culture of people we meet. For example, we have learned that many South Carolina natives would never begin a New Year without serving black-eyed peas and at least one cake or cracker or cookie studded with benne (sesame) seeds. Our German neighbors have special pretzels shipped in from Europe for their first-of-the-year celebration. We have also heard that some southern-bred people hold that their financial fortunes are in direct correlation to the amount of greens they consume on New Year's Day.

Now, we know that superstition has no place in an enlightened society. On the other hand, years of experience and countless resolutions have taught us that we can use all the help we can get.

Always ready to continue (or start) a worthy tradition, we thought it would be great fun to build a New Year's buffet menu around a good luck theme. Fortunately, our lucky ingredients happen to lend themselves quite nicely to some of our favorite recipes.

The menu just sort of evolved into a deep-South/Creole spread. A spicy jambalaya is the centerpiece, along with a colorful salad of black-eyed peas served on a bed of greens. Preceded by a couple of deliciously easy do-ahead hors d'oeuvres, and finished off with a soothingly creamy custard, chocolate "pretzels," and fortune cookies, the meal is just right for New Year's Day, but would also make a terrific brunch, lunch, or supper at any season.

It just might be true that these foods bring luck, but we both know that the real and lasting good fortune is in having our nearest and dearest with us to celebrate the New Year.

In Advance

THOUGH LUCK may be a key factor in the big picture of life, it isn't the basis for a successful party. Planning is. This party is an excellent example.

Because it has a definite theme, it's nice to prime the guests with a little advance information so that the lucky nuances are noticed. You might design an invitation illustrated with some of the lucky ingredients and good luck symbols.

You can start cooking for this party 2 weeks in advance (a pleasant thought for a holiday event). Make and freeze the benne seed coins, the mustard greens and bacon croustade, the double corn minimuffins, and the chocolate pretzels. Now is also a good time to scare up a fortune cookie source. Try your local Chinese restaurant.

The day before the party, partially cook the jambalaya, refrigerating the rice and meats separately. Make the salad dressing and slice the tangerines. Set up the bar and buffet table.

On the day of the party, make the custard, toss the salad, and thaw the stash in the freezer. An hour or so before serving the meal, finish the jambalaya.

Finally, plug in the coffee, and pick yourself a good fortune cookie!

If Time Is Short ...

☞ In lieu of the benne seed coins, offer a wedge of sharp Cheddar with sesame seed crackers.

☞ Substitute two 10-ounce tubes of refrigerated pizza dough for the homemade yeast dough in the croustade. Roll out to specified dimensions, then top and bake at 425° F. for 12 to 14 minutes.

☞ Call ahead to the fish market to request that they shell the crawfish or shrimp and to the butcher to ask him to bone the duck breasts.

☞ Buy corn muffins from a good bakery.

☞ Offer some store-bought chocolate cookies instead of making the chocolate pretzels.

Cranberry–Riesling Good Intentions

This very light, slightly tart and fruity spritzer is just the thing on New Year's Day. It is also lovely served from a punch bowl where the bright crimson color will add sparkle and festivity to the buffet table.

MAKES 12 TO 16 SERVINGS (13 CUPS)

2	12-ounce cans frozen cranberry juice, thawed
4	cups Riesling, chilled
6	cups club soda or seltzer, chilled
2	small lemons, thinly sliced

1. In a pitcher or other container, stir together the cranberry juice and the wine. (Can be mixed up to 6 hours ahead and chilled.)

2. When ready to serve, fill a large pitcher with ice cubes. Add cranberry juice mixture and club soda. Stir gently to mix. Serve in ice cube–filled glasses, each garnished with a lemon slice.

Benne Seed Coins

In South Carolina, where sesame seeds are called benne seeds, they have been savored since slave-trading days. Some sweet sesame seed confections are called good luck cookies, so we've added them to our menu as a savory cheese wafer and called them coins for even more luck.

MAKES ABOUT 100 WAFERS

½	cup sesame seeds
2	cups all-purpose flour
1	teaspoon baking powder
½	teaspoon salt
¼	teaspoon cayenne
10	tablespoons (1¼ sticks) unsalted butter, softened and cut into chunks
1½	cups (6 ounces) shredded sharp Cheddar cheese
7 or 8	tablespoons cold water

1.   In a small skillet set over medium heat, toast the sesame seeds for 1 to 2 minutes, stirring frequently, until lightly colored. Spread onto wax paper to cool.

2.   Combine the flour, baking powder, salt, and cayenne in the work bowl of the food processor. Pulse to blend. Add butter and cheese and pulse until mixture resembles coarse crumbs. Add water through feed tube, pulsing until dough begins to clump together. Turn out onto a sheet of plastic wrap and gather into a log shape about 1½ inches in diameter, rolling to make a smooth cylinder. Roll in sesame seeds until surface is covered. Place in freezer to chill for 30 minutes, or refrigerate for 2 hours. (Can be made 1 day ahead.) Reserve remaining sesame seeds.

3.   Preheat oven to 400° F. Cut dough into ⅛-inch slices. Dip one side of each wafer into remaining sesame seeds to cover and place, seeded sides up, on a lightly greased baking sheet. Bake for 8 to 11 minutes, until light golden. Cool on a rack. (Can be made 1 day ahead and stored in a covered container at cool room temperature. Or freeze up to 2 weeks.)

4.   Serve at room temperature, or reheat in a 350° F. oven for 5 minutes if desired.

Mustard Greens and Bacon Croustade

In certain parts of the American South, greens are believed to be good luck since they are the color of money. Though it is an excellent informal hors d'oeuvre, we also like to eat this croustade with scrambled eggs for a terrific family supper. If you can't find mustard greens, use collards, turnip, or dandelion greens, or even Swiss chard. They are almost interchangeable.

Incidentally, the garlic is pretty good luck too, especially if you have any evil spirits lurking about.

MAKES ABOUT 48 PIECES

Dough

3	cups all-purpose flour
1	package (2 teaspoons) rapid-rise or regular active dry yeast
1	teaspoon sugar
1	teaspoon salt
1	cup warm water (105° F. to 115° F.)
1	tablespoon olive oil

Filling

2	10-ounce packages mustard or other frozen chopped greens, or 2 pounds fresh young greens
½	pound bacon
1½	cups chopped onion
3	large cloves garlic, peeled and minced
1	cup heavy cream
¼	teaspoon freshly ground pepper
3	tablespoons grated Parmesan cheese Salt if needed
2	tablespoons yellow cornmeal

1.   To make the dough, mix the flour, yeast, sugar, and salt in a food processor. Combine water and oil and pour through feed tube with motor running. Process until a ball of dough forms, then continue to process about 45 seconds to "knead" dough. Place in an oiled mixing bowl and turn dough to oil top. Cover lightly and let rise until doubled (30 to 45 minutes with quick-rise yeast and about 1 hour for regular yeast).

2.   Meanwhile, make the filling. Cook the frozen greens according to package directions, then drain well and squeeze to press out moisture. Trim and cook fresh greens in boiling salted water for 5 to 10 minutes until just tender. Drain well, squeeze to press out moisture, then chop.

3.   In a large skillet, cook the bacon until golden brown and crisp. Remove, drain and crumble coarsely, and reserve. Pour off all but 4 tablespoons drippings in skillet. Add onion and sauté over medium-low heat for about 5 minutes, until softened. Add garlic and sauté 1 minute. Stir in greens, cream, pepper, and cheese. Taste and add salt if needed. Let mixture cool. (Can be made 1 day ahead and refrigerated. Return to room temperature to use.)

4.   Preheat oven to 500° F. Sprinkle two 10-by 15-inch jelly roll pans or baking sheets with the cornmeal.

5.   Punch dough down and divide in half. Roll or stretch each piece to a rough rectangle approximately 9 by 14 inches and place one on each cornmeal-dusted pans. Divide filling over each rectangle, spreading to within ¼ inch of the sides. Sprinkle each croustade with the reserved crumbled bacon.

6. Bake 12 to 14 minutes, alternating the position of the pans halfway through baking time, until edges are rich golden brown and crisp.

7. Use a large spatula to remove each croustade from its pan in a single piece. If serving immediately, place on a large wooden board, then use a pizza cutter to cut into about 24 pieces. (If planning to serve later, underbake the croustade by about 3 minutes, remove it from the baking sheet, and place on a rack to cool completely. Replace in the baking pan, cover with foil, and let stand at room temperature up to 4 hours or freeze up to 2 weeks. When ready to serve, reheat in a 400° F. oven for about 5 minutes, placing croustade directly on the oven rack.)

Red Bartlett Pear Wedges with Saga Blue Cheese

Though red Bartletts make a pretty presentation, other deliciously ripe pears of the season are also wonderful spread with the rich tanginess of Saga Blue cheese.

MAKES 12 TO 16 SERVINGS

1   12-ounce wedge Saga Blue or other spreadable blue-veined cheese
8   ripe red Bartlett or other pears

Place the cheese on a small board. Cut some of the pears into wedges and spread with cheese, then place additional pears in a basket set next to the cheese. Provide both a small knife for cutting and a spatula or butter knife for spreading the cheese.

Andouille, Crawfish, and Duck Jambalaya

This zesty, colorful Louisiana specialty works beautifully if assembled ahead, and is also eminently flexible. You could substitute shrimp for the crawfish, all chicken for the duck, and any spicy smoked sausage for the Cajun andouille.

MAKES 12 TO 15 SERVINGS

¼	cup vegetable oil
1½	pounds andouille or other spicy smoked sausage, cut into ¼-inch slices
2	boned and skinned duck breasts (about 10 ounces each), or 1½ pounds boneless chicken thighs, cut into 1½-inch pieces (see Note)
1	pound boned and skinned chicken breast, cut into 1½-inch pieces
1	teaspoon cayenne
3	large celery stalks, thinly sliced
2	large onions, peeled and coarsely chopped
3	large green peppers, cored, seeded and cut into ¾-inch dice
6	cloves garlic, peeled and minced
1	tablespoon dried thyme
3	cups long-grain rice
2	cups chicken broth
2	cups bottled clam juice
1	pound shelled crawfish tails or medium shrimp (see Note)
3	cups seeded, drained, and chopped canned plum tomatoes (from two 28-ounce cans)
1	bunch scallions, including green tops, thinly sliced
	Tabasco or other hot pepper sauce to taste

1. Heat 2 tablespoons oil in a large heavy skillet set over medium heat. Add sausage and sauté until nicely browned, about 8 minutes. With a slotted spoon, transfer meat to a bowl, leaving drippings in the pan.

2. Sprinkle duck and chicken with cayenne. Sauté in sausage drippings over medium-high heat until browned and cooked through, about 5 minutes. Transfer to bowl with the sausage.

3. Add remaining 2 tablespoons oil to drippings in the skillet and sauté the celery, onion, and peppers over medium heat until vegetables are somewhat softened, about 5 minutes. Add garlic and thyme and cook for 1 minute. Add rice and stir until coated with oil. Divide rice mixture between two 9- by 13-inch (or similar-size) baking dishes. Cover with foil. (Can be prepared 1 day ahead. Refrigerate rice and meats separately. Remove from refrigerator about 1 hour before continuing.)

4. Preheat oven to 350° F. In a large saucepan, bring the chicken broth, clam juice, and 2 cups water to a simmer. Divide between baking dishes of rice, stirring gently. Cover with foil. Bake 35 minutes.

5. Remove from oven and stir rice. Divide the crawfish or shrimp between the dishes, pushing it into the rice slightly. Arrange sausage, duck, and chicken over rice and scatter chopped tomatoes over top. (If rice has absorbed most of liquid, add up to ½ cup broth or water to each dish.) Cover and continue to bake until rice is tender and meats and fish are cooked, about 15 minutes.

6. Stir to distribute ingredients. Serve jambalaya directly from baking dishes or

transfer to a deep platter. Sprinkle with scallions before serving. Season with Tabasco or offer the bottle so that guests can season their own to taste.

Notes: If you can't find boned duck breasts, ask your butcher to bone out a breast from a whole duck. The price will be about the same. Crawfish can be used in either their raw or cooked state, depending on how they are available in your area. One pound of crawfish in the shell yields about 4 ounces of meat.

Lucky Black-eyed Pea and Pepper Salad on Mâche

Though neither born nor bred in the South, we nonetheless take very seriously the admonition that black-eyed peas must be eaten on New Year's Day to ensure good luck during the coming year. Since we couldn't work hoppin' John (black-eyed peas and rice) into this menu, we serve this colorful salad. You get extra luck if you present the salad on a bed of greens.

MAKES 12 TO 15 SERVINGS

Mustard–Honey Vinaigrette

¼	cup balsamic vinegar
2	teaspoons honey
2	teaspoons Dijon mustard
1½	teaspoons salt
½	teaspoon freshly ground black pepper
½	teaspoon Tabasco
2	cloves garlic, peeled and minced
¾	cup vegetable oil

Salad

2	10-ounce packages frozen black-eyed peas, cooked just until tender and drained, *or* two 14- to 16-ounce cans black-eyed peas, drained
1½	cups thinly sliced celery
2	red bell peppers, cored, seeded, and cut in rough ½-inch dice
1	yellow bell pepper, cored, seeded, and cut in rough ½-inch dice
⅔	cup chopped red onion
⅔	cup chopped parsley
5 to 6	cups mâche, arugula, or other tender, bitter greens

1. To make the dressing, whisk together the vinegar, honey, mustard, salt, pepper, Tabasco, and garlic. Whisk in the oil. (Can be made 1 day ahead.)

2. To make the salad, combine the peas, celery, peppers, red onion, and ½ cup of the parsley in a bowl. (Can be combined several hours ahead.) Add the dressing and toss gently. Refrigerate for at least 1 hour or up to 4.

3. To serve, arrange greens on a rimmed platter or in a shallow bowl to make a bed. Spoon salad over greens and sprinkle with the remaining parsley.

Double Corn Minimuffins

If you don't have minimuffin pans in your baking cupboard, now is a good time to buy a few. They are inexpensive and turn out the cutest little muffins you ever saw. In addition, these two-bite goodies are the perfect size for buffet service. Most standard muffin recipes (as well as cupcakes) can be baked in minipans. Cut the baking time in half and then start checking for doneness.

This recipe is an old family favorite and the canned creamed corn is an integral part of its success.

MAKES 48 MINIMUFFINS

2	cups all-purpose flour
2	cups yellow cornmeal
4	tablespoons dark brown sugar
2	tablespoons baking powder
1	teaspoon baking soda
1	teaspoon salt
2	8½-ounce cans creamed corn
1	cup buttermilk
2	eggs
½	cup vegetable oil

1.   Preheat the oven to 425° F. Grease 48 minimuffin cups.

2.   In a large mixing bowl, stir or sift together the flour, cornmeal, brown sugar, baking powder, baking soda, and salt. In another bowl, whisk together the corn, buttermilk, eggs, and oil. Form a well in the dry ingredients and pour the buttermilk mixture into the well. Stir just until all ingredients are moistened.

3.   Spoon batter into prepared muffin cups, filling each about three-quarters full. Bake in the center of the oven for about 10 minutes, until golden brown. Serve warm. (Can be baked up to 2 weeks ahead and frozen. Rewarm, wrapped in foil, in a 300° F. oven for about 5 minutes, or reheat gently in a microwave.)

Note: The batter will also make 24 standard-size muffins (bake for about 15 minutes) or two 9-inch-square pans of cornbread (bake 22 to 25 minutes).

Vanilla Nutmeg Chantilly Custard

Soothing, creamy, and not overly rich, this vanilla-scented custard is the perfect finish after a spicy main course such as jambalaya—and the perfect beginning to a new year.

MAKES 12 TO 15 SERVINGS

6	cups half-and-half or light cream
1	vanilla bean, split in half lengthwise (see Note)
9	whole eggs
5	egg yolks
1¼	cups sugar
½	teaspoon salt
½	teaspoon grated nutmeg

1. Preheat the oven to 325° F. In a large saucepan, heat the half-and-half with the vanilla bean over medium-low heat until small bubbles appear around the edges.

2. In a large bowl, whisk together the eggs, yolks, sugar, and salt. Gradually whisk in the hot half-and-half. With the point of a small sharp knife, scrape soft center out of the vanilla bean and add seeds to custard, discarding the pod. Pour custard through a sieve into one 9- by 13-inch or two 8- by 8-inch baking dishes. Place baking dish in a larger pan and half fill larger pan with hot water. Sprinkle custard with nutmeg.

3. Bake in center of the preheated oven for 25 to 35 minutes, until a knife inserted about 2 inches from the center comes out clean and custard is softly set but still shivers when moved. Remove baking dish from water bath and cool on a rack. Serve warm, at room temperature, or cool. (Can be made 6 hours ahead. Cover and refrigerate.)

Note: If you don't have a vanilla bean, use 4 teaspoons vanilla extract, adding it to the eggs with the sugar.

Sliced Tangerines in Curaçao

We like the impact of a single fruit here, but you can certainly vary this compote by adding slices of red-skinned apples, oranges, or kiwi.

MAKES 12 TO 15 SERVINGS

6 to 8	seedless tangerines
3 to 4	tablespoons Curaçao or other orange liqueur
	Mint sprigs, if available

1. Peel tangerines and cut into thin crosswise slices. If slices are large, cut rounds in half. (Can be done a day ahead.)

2. About an hour before ready to serve, toss fruit gently with liqueur. Present in a glass bowl, garnished with mint if desired.

Chocolate Pretzels

*Legend holds that a French monk first twisted the pretzel
into its traditional shape about A.D. 610 to imitate the folded arms of someone in prayer.
Over the centuries, the pretzel has come to be known as good luck and far be it
for us to dispute the theory, though we have stretched the concept a bit with this recipe.
These deep, dark, rich, nutty chocolate cookie "pretzels" sprinkled with coarse sugar "salt"
are so delicious that, for chocoholics, they may be the ultimate in good luck!*

MAKES 3 DOZEN COOKIES

1	cup pecan pieces
1½	cups all-purpose flour
1	cup (2 sticks) unsalted butter, cut in 16 pieces
⅔	cup granulated sugar
½	teaspoon salt
2	teaspoons vanilla extract
½	cup unsweetened cocoa powder
	Additional flour and cocoa
¼	cup turbinado sugar (see Note)

1.   In a food processor, very finely chop the pecans with ½ cup of the flour. Set aside.
2.   In the same work bowl, process the butter with the sugar, salt, and vanilla for 30 to 45 seconds, scraping work bowl once or twice, until smooth and creamy. Add nut mixture, remaining flour, and ½ cup cocoa. Process just until dough begins to clump. Scrape dough into a bowl or wrap in plastic and chill at least 1 hour, or freeze for 30 minutes, until firm enough to handle. (Dough may be made a day ahead and refrigerated or frozen up to 2 weeks. Thaw in refrigerator.)
3.   Preheat oven to 325° F. Have ready 2 large ungreased baking sheets. Mix together equal amounts flour and cocoa (about 3 tablespoons each) and sprinkle some of the mixture over a work surface.
4.   Divide dough into 36 pieces. Dust your hands with some of the flour/cocoa mixture and roll each piece on the work surface to form a rope about 8 inches long. Loop each end of the rope over the center to form the traditional pretzel shape. Arrange on the baking sheets, leaving about 1½ inches between cookies.
5.   Bake, 1 sheet at a time, in the center of the oven, for 18 to 20 minutes until cookies feel firm. Let cool about 3 minutes on the baking sheet, then use a spatula to carefully remove cookies to a rack to cool. (Cookies are fragile when hot, but will firm up nicely as they cool.)
6.   Place turbinado sugar in a shallow dish. While cookies are still slightly warm, dip tops into the sugar to resemble salt crystals. Let cool completely, then store up to 3 days in a tightly covered container. (Cookies can be frozen up to 2 weeks)

Note: Turbinado sugar (sometimes called sugar-in-the-raw) contains a bit of molasses, and the coarse crystals have a pale gold color. It is available in many supermarkets or natural food stores. If you cannot find it, use granulated sugar.

SUPER BOWL PARTY

Our Best Defense
FOR 12 TO 15

Quarter Keg (NO RECIPE)

∼

∼

∼

∼

Coffee (NO RECIPE)

MELANIE CLEARLY remembers watching the first Super Bowl on television. She prophesied to her football-fanatic husband that this silly media-hyped event would never catch on.

Now, after its silver anniversary, we realize that this extravaganza is more than a month-long extension of the football season. It is a reason to party in a month that otherwise would have as its peak the planning of a Groundhog Day event.

Super Bowl party timing etiquette has become somewhat of a standard, with snacks set out near the television sets at the beginning of the first quarter. Make the nibbles mostly self-serve, such as our savory pâté, a big basket of garlicky clam toasts, and a warming pot of sharp Cheddar fondue with assorted vegetable dippers. The main course, our friend "Big" Jim's picadillo, is served from an informal buffet table during the conveniently hour-long halftime. The Super Sundae bar is glitzy enough to accommodate a victory celebration while plenty soothing as sweet relief for the soreness of losing—sort of an insurance policy that the day will end happily no matter who wins on the field.

In Advance

WE PLAN A Super Bowl party menu to allow us plenty of time to watch the game while still giving the guests a super dinner.

When the playoffs begin, you can make the hot fudge and the butterscotch sauces, for they will keep in the refrigerator for 3 weeks (as long as no one know they're there).

The chicken liver pâté can be made 3 or 4 days in advance, and you can make the homemade ice cream a couple of days ahead. The pork picadillo and the cheese fondue will also keep for about 2 days.

A day before the party, make the orange-buttermilk salad dressing. Assemble the rice, but don't add the liquid yet. This is also a good time to set up your buffet and bar. Ask around to make sure someone in the group knows how to tap a keg.

On the day of the party, prepare the salad ingredients and the vegetables for the fondue. The pineapple dessert sauce will hold for several hours, but add the berries at the end. Make the biscuits. Then, only the garlic and clam toasts need real last-minute attention.

If Time Is Short ...

☞   Use purchased hors d'oeuvres such as nuts, cheeses, prepared pâté, and crackers, setting them out along with some fresh vegetables and dip.

☞   Use refrigerated biscuit dough (packaged in tubes and found in the dairy case) and bake just before serving.

☞   Buy premium-quality vanilla ice cream.

☞   Use good toppings in a jar, but don't skip the fresh fruit for the sundae bar. And don't buy canned whipped topping!

Cheddar and Ale Fondue with Vegetable Spears

Traditional cheese fondue uses Swiss cheese and white wine with cubes of French bread for dipping. We think that this zesty Cheddar and ale variation with vegetable dippers is every bit as worthy as the classic idea that inspired it. In addition, the fondue is far more stable as a make-ahead. Use any combination of vegetables that appeals to you.

MAKES 12 TO 15 SERVINGS

6	tablespoons (¾ stick) unsalted butter
½	cup all-purpose flour
2	teaspoons dry mustard
2⅔	cups milk
3	cups (two 12-ounce cans) flat ale or beer
8	cups (2 pounds) grated Cheddar cheese
1	teaspoon Worcestershire sauce
½	teaspoon cayenne
	Vegetables for dipping such as blanched broccoli spears and carrot sticks, boiled redskin potato slices, cooked Brussels sprouts, and/or bell pepper strips

1.   In a large, heavy saucepan, melt the butter. Stir in the flour and cook over medium heat for 2 minutes, stirring constantly. Stir in the mustard and cook 1 minute. Gradually whisk in the milk and ale, raise the heat to medium-high, and bring to a boil, stirring constantly. Reduce heat to medium-low and simmer, stirring, for 2 minutes. Remove pan from heat and add the grated cheese in 6 portions, whisking until each portion is melted before adding another. Season with Worcestershire and cayenne. (Can be made a day ahead and reheated very gently over very low heat.)

2.   To serve, transfer warm fondue to a fondue pot or keep warm in a small chafing dish set over very low flame. Arrange vegetables around pot.

Garlic and Clam Toasts

This is just as addictive as the famous white clam pizza, but a whole lot easier to make. Use fresh chopped clams from the fishmonger if you can get them. Otherwise, use the best-quality canned clams.

MAKES 12 TO 15 SERVINGS

4	cloves garlic, peeled and minced
½	teaspoon red pepper flakes
½	cup olive oil
2	8-ounce loaves Italian or French bread or one 16-ounce baguette
2	6½-ounce cans minced clams, drained, or 1 cup drained, freshly chopped clams
1	teaspoon dried basil
1	teaspoon dried oregano
6	tablespoons chopped parsley

1. Preheat the broiler. Steep the garlic and red pepper flakes in the oil for at least 10 minutes or up to several hours.

2. Cut the bread into ½-inch-thick diagonal slices. Place in single layers on 2 large baking sheets and broil about 4 inches from the heat source for about 30 seconds, until lightly toasted. Remove from broiler and turn bread so that untoasted side is up. (Can be done several hours ahead.)

3. Brush untoasted sides of bread with flavored oil, making sure to brush each with some of the garlic and pepper flakes. Sprinkle evenly with clams, then with basil, oregano, and finally parsley.

4. Broil 30 to 45 seconds, until lightly toasted and golden around the edges. Arrange on large platters to serve.

Peppercorn and Apple Pâté

The pleasant bite of green peppercorns and the sweetness of sautéed apple add interest to this rich, smooth chicken liver pâté. It keeps beautifully for several days in the refrigerator.

MAKES ABOUT 2½ CUPS

1	pound chicken livers
⅓	cup milk
¾	cup (1½ sticks) unsalted butter, softened
1	cup chopped onion
1	Granny Smith apple, peeled and chopped (about 1 cup)
¼	cup Cognac or brandy
2	teaspoons coarsely chopped green peppercorns
¾	teaspoon salt
¼	teaspoon mace
⅛	teaspoon ground cloves

Flat leaf parsley and about 2 teaspoons chopped green peppercorns for garnish
Cream crackers
Apple slices

1.   Trim livers of any tough membranes and yellow fat. Place in a bowl, cover with the milk, and soak for at least 3 hours or for as long as 12 hours in the refrigerator.

2.   Heat 2 tablespoons butter in a skillet. Add onion and apple and sauté over medium-low heat, stirring occasionally, for about 8 minutes, until softened and lightly browned. Spoon into a food processor. Do not wash the skillet.

3.   Pour off and discard chicken liver soaking liquid and dry livers on paper towels. Heat 2 more tablespoons butter in the skillet. Sauté chicken livers over medium-high heat for about 5 minutes, or until browned and firm but still pale pink inside. Spoon into food processor.

4.   Add Cognac to the still-warm skillet and stir to dissolve browned pan juices. Add liquid to food processor.

5.   Cut remaining 8 tablespoons (1 stick) softened butter into several pieces. Begin processing liver mixture, adding butter 1 piece at a time through the feed tube until mixture is a smooth purée. This will take approximately 2 minutes. Add green peppercorns, salt, mace, and cloves and pulse just to mix.

6.   Pack purée, which will still be quite loose at this point, into a crock. Cover well and refrigerate for at least 4 hours to allow flavors to mellow and blend. (Can be made 4 days ahead.)

7.   Remove from refrigerator 1 hour before serving. For garnish, press sprigs of parsley into surface of pâté and sprinkle with chopped green peppercorns. Serve spread on crackers or on slices of apple.

Big Jim's Pork Picadillo

The wonderfully complex hot/sweet/spicy overtone of this Cuban-inspired ground meat stew belies the simplicity of preparation of the dish. We like it even better the next day, when the flavors have had a chance to blend.

MAKES 12 TO 15 SERVINGS

4	pounds lean ground pork
2	large onions, peeled and chopped
2	tablespoons chili powder
2	teaspoons salt
2	teaspoons oregano
1	teaspoon ground cinnamon
½	teaspoon ground cloves
½	teaspoon cayenne
1	cup raisins
2	1-pound cans tomatoes in juice
1	large Golden Delicious apple, peeled and coarsely chopped
6	tablespoons cider vinegar
1	cup slivered almonds

1. Lightly brown the pork and onions in a large, heavy saucepan over medium heat, stirring often for about 5 minutes, until pork is cooked through and onion is softened. Drain off excess fat. Stir in chili powder, salt, oregano, cinnamon, cloves, and cayenne and cook, stirring for 1 minute. Stir in the raisins, tomatoes, apple, and vinegar, breaking up tomatoes with the side of a spoon.

2. Cover pan and simmer over low heat for 40 minutes. (Can be made 2 days ahead and reheated.) Just before serving, stir in the almonds.

Yellow Rice

Baking is our method of choice when cooking rice for a crowd. The addition of precious saffron adds a delicate flavor and gorgeous color. Less expensive turmeric gives the same golden hue and a different, though appealing, taste.

MAKES 12 TO 15 SERVINGS

6	tablespoons olive oil
2	cups chopped onion
3	cups raw long-grain rice
¾	teaspoon freshly ground pepper
½	teaspoon saffron or turmeric
6	cups chicken broth
	Salt as needed
6	tablespoons minced parsley

1. Preheat the oven to 350° F. Have ready a 9- by 13-inch or other shallow 3-quart baking dish.

2. Heat the oil in a heavy saucepan and sauté the onion over medium-low heat for about 5 minutes, until softened. Add rice, pepper, and saffron or turmeric. Stir about 15 seconds to coat rice grains with oil. (Can be made up to a day ahead and refrigerated. Return to room temperature before continuing.)

3. Spoon rice mixture into baking dish. Stir in broth. Cover tightly with foil and bake 45 to 55 minutes, until rice is tender and liquid has been absorbed. Season to taste with salt. (Can be held in turned-off oven for up to 30 minutes, or gently reheated in a microwave.)

4. Just before serving, add parsley and toss gently with a fork to mix and fluff rice.

Winter Spinach Salad Bowl—Orange Buttermilk Dressing

This salad looks beautiful on the buffet. Pour on the dressing and toss just before serving.

Orange Buttermilk Dressing

¼	cup orange juice
3	tablespoons white wine vinegar
1	tablespoon Dijon mustard
¼	cup mayonnaise
½	cup vegetable oil
½	cup buttermilk
2	teaspoons grated orange zest
½	teaspoon salt
½	teaspoon freshly ground black pepper

Spinach Salad Bowl

12 to 15	cups washed and dried spinach leaves, stems removed and torn into bite-sized pieces
2	heads endive
3	seedless oranges, peeled
1	cup pitted black olives
1½	cups thinly sliced peeled red onion

1. To make dressing, whisk together the orange juice, vinegar, mustard, and mayonnaise. Gradually whisk in the oil and the buttermilk. Stir in orange zest, salt, and pepper. (Can be made 1 day ahead.)

2. To assemble salad, heap spinach in a large, wide salad bowl. Trim endive and cut each head into quarters. Stand spears up around the outside of the bowl. Cut oranges into thin crosswise slices and cut each slice in half. Arrange overlapping around the outside edge of the bowl. Sprinkle olives over oranges and scatter onion slices over the top of the salad. (Can be assembled 3 hours ahead. Cover and refrigerate.)

3. Drizzle dressing over salad and toss just before serving.

Cornmeal and Cracked Pepper Biscuits

Our method of rolling and cutting ahead makes freshly baked biscuits easy to do for a crowd. Though they are best warm from the oven, they do reheat quite nicely. Don't omit the cornmeal, even though it seems to be a small amount, for its pleasant flavor and slightly coarse texture is a really nice addition.

MAKES 24 TO 30 BISCUITS

3½	cups all-purpose flour
¼	cup white or yellow cornmeal
2	tablespoons plus 2 teaspoons baking powder
2	tablespoons sugar
2	teaspoons cracked or very coarsely ground black pepper
1½	teaspoons salt
½	cup (8 tablespoons) solid vegetable shortening
½	cup (1 stick) chilled unsalted butter, cut in 8 pieces
1⅓	cups cold milk

1. Preheat oven to 450° F.
2. In a large mixing bowl (or large food processor), thoroughly combine the flour, cornmeal, baking powder, sugar, pepper, and salt. Rub (or process) in the shortening and butter until mixture resembles coarse meal. Pour in the milk all at once and stir (or process) just until dough clumps together.
3. Place dough on a lightly floured surface and knead 10 times. Pat or roll to ½-inch thickness and use a 2-inch biscuit cutter to make 24 to 30 biscuits, gathering and rerolling scraps as necessary. Place biscuits, 2 inches apart, on ungreased baking sheets. (Can prepare 2 hours ahead and refrigerate, covered with plastic wrap.) Bake in center of oven for 5 minutes, then lower oven temperature to 425° F. and bake an additional 7 to 10 minutes, until light golden brown and well risen.
4. Serve warm. (To reheat, wrap loosely in foil and heat for about 3 minutes in a 350° F. oven.)

Real Butterscotch Sauce

This takes about 10 minutes to make, and once you've tasted the real thing, you will never buy butterscotch sauce again.

MAKES ABOUT 2 CUPS

2	cups light brown sugar
⅔	cup heavy cream
½	cup (1 stick) unalted butter
¼	cup light corn syrup
2	teaspoons vanilla extract
½	teaspoon lemon juice

1. Combine the brown sugar, cream, butter, and corn syrup in a heavy saucepan. Slowly bring to a boil, stirring constantly to dissolve the sugar and melt the butter. Lower heat and simmer, stirring occasionally, for 4 minutes. Remove from heat, let cool about 3 minutes, then stir in the vanilla and lemon juice.

2. Serve warm ladled over ice cream. (Can be made 3 weeks ahead and refrigerated. Reheat gently in a saucepan or in a microwave oven.)

Rum-soused Pineapple and Raspberries

Add this to your sundae for a fresh tropical taste.

MAKES ABOUT 4 CUPS

1	fresh ripe pineapple
3	tablespoons granulated sugar
¼	cup dark rum
½	pint fresh raspberries

Peel and core the pineapple. Cut into slices and chop into rough ½-inch dice. Combine in a bowl with the sugar and rum. Cover and refrigerate for at least 1 hour or for up to 4 hours. Just before serving, add the raspberries and toss very gently.

Double Decadent Hot Fudge Sauce

The double decadence here is the touch of unsweetened chocolate that provides a sophisticated edge to our childhood fantasy of the gooiest, stickiest, and chocolatiest hot fudge sauce ever.

This sauce probably keeps more than 3 weeks, but we have never been able to keep people from eating it long enough to provide an accurate test.

MAKES ABOUT 2 CUPS

⅔ cup granulated sugar
½ cup unsweetened cocoa, preferably Dutch process
¾ cup heavy cream
½ cup light corn syrup
   Pinch salt
1 ounce unsweetened chocolate, chopped
5 tablespoons unsalted butter
2 teaspoons vanilla extract

1. Combine the sugar, cocoa, cream, corn syrup, and salt in a heavy saucepan. Bring slowly to a boil, stirring to dissolve the sugar. Lower heat and simmer, uncovered, for 5 minutes, stirring often. Remove from heat and add the chocolate and butter, stirring until melted and smooth. Stir in the vanilla.

2. Serve warm ladled over ice cream. (Can be made 3 weeks ahead and refrigerated. Reheat gently over very low heat, in the top of a double boiler, or in a microwave oven.)

Mid-winter Brunch

A Cure for the Doldrums
Buffet for 10 to 12

HAVE YOU EVER received an invitation right out of the blue, to a party given for just no reason whatsoever other than that it would be fun to get together? This brunch could, of course, be tied to an occasion—a birthday, a sports event, an out-of-town guest—but we think it's perhaps even more special if it's tied to nothing more than a wish to spend time with friends. A thoroughly American invention, brunch is intrinsically informal and inviting. In winter, it is also a surefire cure for the doldrums.

Start with the Bloody Marys. Ours are real zingers with fresh citrus juices and horseradish. Gravlax, a fabulous salmon classic, will make you an instant culinary star with its sophisticated taste and luxurious presentation. (In accepting your kudos, it's okay to leave out the part about the recipe being practically no work at all.)

Then move on to the pièce de résistance—choucroute garnie. With a literal translation of "garnished sauerkraut," this dish requires far more in the effort of finding good meats and sauerkraut than it does in the actual cooking. Coupled with and balanced by a big bowl of fresh watercress, this might just be the perfect cold-weather brunch main course.

Finally, linger over cups of steaming Vienna roast coffee, nibble on thin slices of golden caraway seed cake, and savor a colorful array of juicy exotic fruits.

As for decorating, even that is easy. Pots of multihued primroses and blooming winter bulbs will brighten even the dreariest winter day, as will upbeat and lively music. Of course, the key ingredient remains a guest list of friends who share a fondness for good times and good food.

If these instructions are faithfully followed, the cure for the doldrums will begin to take effect within minutes of the first doorbell chime. We guarantee it.

In Advance

REMEMBERING the old adage that the cure should not kill the patient, we believe that brunch preparations should be as easy and relaxed as the party itself. Almost everything can be made ahead and there are no heart-stopper recipes like soufflés or puffed anything

for that matter. This is simply prepared, simply good food.

A couple of weeks in advance you can make the cake (and the muffins, too, if you wish) and freeze them.

The gravlax must begin marinating at least 2 days ahead of serving in order to cure the salmon properly.

You can cook the choucroute the day before the party, as well as make the Virgin Mary base. Set the table and set up the bar.

On the morning of the brunch, slice the gravlax and prepare the platter. Cut up and arrange the fruit.

The only things to do at party time are to heat up the choucroute and plug in the coffee.

Now, that wasn't so bad, was it?

If Time Is Short ...

☛   Buy smoked salmon to serve instead of the gravlax.
☛   Purchase bran muffins from a bakery or offer a selection of bakery breads.
☛   Buy a pound cake or poppy seed cake from a bakery.

Mary's Bloody Marys

Melanie's sister Mary lives in Florida, loves to entertain at brunch, and makes a mean bloody Mary. Brightened with the tang of citrus, this pleasantly (but not overwhelmingly) spicy version is based on Mary's inspired recipe. We add the vodka as we mix each cocktail so that those who prefer can enjoy the Virgin Mary base on its own.

MAKES 12 SERVINGS

Virgin Mary Base

8	cups (2 quarts) tomato juice
⅓	cup lemon juice
⅓	cup lime juice
2 or 3	tablespoons prepared horseradish
4	teaspoons Worcestershire sauce
1	teaspoon Tabasco, or to taste

Bloody Mary Finish

1½	ounces vodka per cocktail
	Freshly ground black pepper
	Thin slices of lemon and lime for garnish
	Celery stalks with leaves for edible swizzle sticks
	Sprigs of fresh herbs for garnish, if desired

1. In a large pitcher, combine the tomato juice, citrus juices, horseradish, Worcestershire, and Tabasco. Stir well to combine. (Can be prepared a day ahead. Refrigerate.)

2. When ready to serve, stir base again to mix. Put ice cubes into an 10 to 12 ounce glass, add vodka, fill with ½ to ¾ cup tomato base, and stir. Sprinkle with fresh black pepper and garnish glass with citrus slices. Stand a celery stalk upright in each glass and garnish with fresh herbs if desired.

Homemade Gravlax on Pumpernickel

Though it takes a couple of days of marinating, this Swedish salt- and sugar-cured salmon is very simple to make and easy to serve. Be sure to use the very freshest salmon.

MAKES 12 TO 16 SERVINGS

Gravlax

1½ to 2 pounds salmon fillet (preferably center-cut), with skin left on one side
½   cup chopped fresh dill
3   tablespoons coarse salt
3   tablespoons sugar
1   tablespoon black or white peppercorns, crushed

Presentation and Garnish

1   package party pumpernickel, or a standard-size loaf of pumpernickel, slices quartered
Dill sprigs for garnish
Lemon slices for garnish
Softened unsalted butter

1.   Cut the salmon fillet in half lenthwise down the line of the backbone. Examine carefully for bones, removing any stubborn ones with tweezers.

2.   Place one piece of salmon, skin side down, in a glass baking dish just large enough to hold it. Sprinkle with the dill. In a small bowl, combine the salt, sugar, and crushed peppercorns and sprinkle over the salmon in the dish. Cover with the other half of the fillet, skin side up, to make a sort of sandwich.

3.   Cover dish with plastic wrap. Place a board or smaller dish over the plastic wrap and then use cans or a brick to weight the fish down.

4.   Refrigerate. Every 8 to 12 hours, turn the salmon and spoon juices back over the fish. Marinate for at least 48 hours or up to 4 days. The salt and sugar will cure and firm the fish.

5.   Scrape dill and peppercorns off salmon. Using a sharp knife and holding it almost parallel to the fish, cut thin diagonal slices, leaving the skin behind as you cut. Arrange on a platter with the pumpernickel and garnish with branches of dill and lemon slices. Accompany with a crock of butter. (Platter can be assembled 3 hours ahead. Drape with dampened paper towels, cover with plastic wrap, and refrigerate.)

6.   Provide a fork so that guests can assemble their own small open-faced sandwiches.

Note: Leftover unsliced gravlax can be refrigerated up to 3 days.

Simplified Choucroute Garnie

Though this is a simplified version, it loses none of the rich flavors of the Alsatian classic. The key, of course, is the quality of the sausages and smoked pork. A German butcher is a good place to start.

MAKES 10 TO 12 SERVINGS

2	large onions, peeled and chopped
2	large tart apples, peeled, cored, and sliced
½	cup vegetable oil
3	pounds sauerkraut, rinsed and drained
1½	teaspoons dried thyme
¾	teaspoon caraway seeds
10	crushed juniper berries or 3 tablespoons gin
2	bay leaves, broken in half
1½	cups white wine
12	thin smoked pork chops (4 to 5 ounces each)
2	pounds good-quality cooked German or Polish sausages such as bratwurst, weisswurst, and/or kielbasa
3	tablespoons chopped parsley

1. Preheat the oven to 325° F.

2. Sauté the onions and apples in the oil in a large skillet over medium-low heat, stirring often, for about 5 minutes, until onion is softened. Transfer the mixture to a large nonaluminum roasting pan or shallow casserole and stir in the sauerkraut, thyme, caraway seeds, juniper berries, bay leaves, and wine. Push the pork chops and sausage links into the sauerkraut.

3. Cover the pan tightly and bake for 45 to 60 minutes, until apple is soft and meats are thoroughly heated. Remove bay leaves. (Can be prepared a day ahead and refrigerated. If planning to cook ahead, underbake by about 15 minutes. Return to room temperature before reheating in a 325° F. oven for about 45 minutes or until hot.)

4. Serve directly from the roasting pan or spoon onto a large platter. Sprinkle with parsley.

Apricot–Walnut Bran Muffins

We love the combination of dried apricots and walnuts for this brunch, but other times we may use raisins, dried apples or figs, and hazelnuts or pecans. By the way, here's a useful cooking tip. In any recipe that calls for both oil and either molasses or honey, measure and pour the oil first, then place molasses and/or honey in the same unwashed measuring cup. It will pour out easily without sticking to the sides.

MAKES ABOUT 20 MUFFINS

2½	cups unprocessed bran
⅔	cup whole wheat flour
⅔	cup all-purpose flour
¼	cup dark brown sugar
2½	teaspoons baking soda
½	teaspoon salt
½	teaspoon cinnamon
½	teaspoon ginger
2	eggs
1¼	cups buttermilk
½	cup vegetable oil
⅓	cup honey
⅓	cup molasses
¾	cup chopped dried apricots
½	cup chopped walnuts

1. Preheat the oven to 400° F. Grease standard muffin tins or line with paper liners.

2. In a large mixing bowl, whisk together the bran, both flours, brown sugar, soda, salt, cinnamon, and ginger. (Can mix 1 day ahead. Store at room temperature.) In a separate bowl, whisk together the eggs, buttermilk, oil, honey, and molasses. (Can mix a few hours ahead.)

3. Add the liquid to the dry ingredients along with the apricots and nuts. Stir with a large spoon just until all ingredients are moistened. Do not overmix. Spoon into prepared muffin tins, filling each about three-quarters full.

4. Bake in the center of the oven for 15 to 18 minutes, until muffins are well risen, tops are richly browned, and a toothpick inserted in the center comes out clean. Turn out onto a rack.

5. Serve warm or at room temperature. (Although best freshly baked, these can be made up to 2 weeks ahead, cooled completely, and then frozen. Partially thaw, then place in a 300° F. oven for a few minutes to warm.)

Exotic Fruit Platter

The best tonic (short of a trip to Tahiti) that we know for the mid-winter doldrums is a platter of juicy, colorful, sweet fresh fruits. Luckily, the supersonic age has put a world of edible exotica as close as our supermarket. Choose whatever is most available and appealing to you—just keep in mind that color and texture are very important in any fruit plate.

SERVES 10 TO 12

4	blood oranges
3 or 4	kiwis
2	papayas
2	Asian pears
2	tablespoons granulated sugar, preferably superfine
2	teaspoons lemon juice
	Mint sprigs, if available

1. Use a sharp knife to peel away the skin and white pith from the blood oranges. Cut the red pulp crosswise into thin slices. Peel the kiwis and cut crosswise into thin slices. Peel the papayas, then cut in half lengthwise. Scoop out and discard all of the seeds. Slice the halves crosswise. Use a swivel peeler to peel the Asian pears, then core as you would an apple or pear. Cut the pears in half lengthwise, then cut into thin crosswise slices.

2. On a large serving platter, arrange the fruits in overlapping slices in the following order: oranges, pears, kiwi, papaya. Sprinkle with the sugar, then the lemon juice. (Can be arranged 3 hours in advance, covered, and refrigerated.) Just before serving, garnish platter with mint sprigs, if desired.

Brandied Caraway Seed Cake

This rich, buttery cake studded with crunchy, slightly salty seeds makes for an indescribably delicious result. And it's the perfect, not-too-sweet dessert for this brunch.

MAKES 12 SERVINGS

1	cup (2 sticks) unsalted butter, at room temperature
1	cup granulated sugar
⅓	cup light brown sugar
4	eggs, separated
¼	cup brandy or Cognac (see Note)
1	teaspoon vanilla extract
1½	cups all-purpose flour
¾	teaspoon baking powder
3	tablespoons caraway seeds
	Confectioners' sugar

1. Prepare an 8-inch tube pan (preferably springform) by buttering bottom and sides and lining bottom with parchment or wax paper. Preheat oven to 350° F.

2. With an electric mixer, cream together the butter and both sugars until mixture is light and fluffy. Add the egg yolks, brandy, and vanilla, and continue beating on high speed until light and smooth.

3. In a mixing bowl, sift together (or stir well with a wire whisk) the flour and baking powder. Stir in caraway seeds.

4. Add flour mixture to batter and combine on low speed or by hand just until no specks of flour remain. Do not overbeat.

5. In a clean bowl, beat the egg whites to firm peaks. Stir about one-third of the whites into the batter to lighten it; then fold remaining whites in gently but thoroughly until no streaks of egg white are visible. Batter will still be quite stiff.

6. Spoon into prepared pan, smooth top, and rap pan on the counter to settle batter. Bake on a middle rack of the preheated oven for 50 to 60 minutes, until cake has an even golden brown crust, pulls away from the sides of the pan, and a tester comes out clean.

7. Cool for 10 minutes, remove from pan, and cool completely on a wire rack. Wrap well in plastic wrap and refrigerate, or store in an airtight tin. (Cake is best if made at least 1 day ahead. Store in refrigerator for 2 or 3 days, or freeze.)

8. Bring to room temperature before serving. Sprinkle with powdered sugar, cut into thin slices, and arrange on a plate.

Note: The cake is also good made with Scotch, bourbon, or blended whiskey.

Valentine's Day

Love Potions à Deux
DINNER FOR TWO (EASILY DOUBLED FOR FOUR)

Passion Fruit Sours   80

~

Scallops and Salmon en Papillotes   80

~

Broiled Poussin on Radicchio with Balsamic Beurre Rouge   81
Lacy Potato and Turnip Galettes   82
Braised Peas, Prosciutto, and Bibb Lettuce with Chives   83
Small French Rolls (NO RECIPE)

~

Cherry Crème Brulées   84
Champagne (NO RECIPE)

~

Espresso (NO RECIPE)

~

Miniature Chocolates (NO RECIPE)

THERE IS A time and a place for everything. And we think that Valentine's Day is the time for a party for two and the place should be the intimate sanctuary of your own home. Love and food have been inextricably intertwined since Adam and Eve, so what better way to show you care than to prepare a dinner à deux, replete with all the loving attention to detail that can be more romantic than words?

Plan this "party" with at least as much care and thought as you do a bash for 30. Begin with the invitation, tucked, perhaps, into a shirt pocket or "mailed" underneath a pillow. Use your most beautiful linens and silver. You need only iron or polish two of everything, so the task is not difficult. Set a small table in front of the fireplace or light the room with candles. Whimsical Victorian paper cutout Cupids and place cards are an extra romantic touch. Chill the Champagne in a tableside ice bucket. And don't forget the music—perhaps a medley of personal favorites.

Dr. Ruth Westheimer assures us that "an

aphrodisiac is anything you think it is." So, with that in mind, we designed a menu that begins with passion fruit sours and goes on from there. Scallop and salmon papillotes, which look like butterflies or half hearts, are the perfect first course. We then move on to an artfully designed plate composed of half a broiled poussin (baby chicken) placed against a backdrop of magenta radicchio, lovely lacy potato and turnip cakes, and tiny peas accented with slivers of prosciutto. And for dessert, individual crème brulées with macerated sour cherries hidden in the bottom provide the sinfully rich finale.

Later there will be time for coffee and chocolates.

In Advance

THIS MENU, though elegant and romantic, is simplicity itself. It is also just as easy to prepare for a party of 4. Simply double the recipes.

The crème brulée custards can be baked a day ahead and refrigerated.

The papillotes can be assembled a few hours before baking and the butter sauce will hold for a couple of hours. You can prepare the poussin for broiling at this time, too. Put all the ingredients for the peas in a saucepan so they can be effortlessly cooked just before serving. The galette mixture can be grated and held for a couple of hours as well.

Now go take a long, hot, perfumy bath and put on your prettiest outfit.

The broiled poussins or game hens and the galettes can be cooked and served right away, but if you don't want to interrupt the conversation during dinner, you might want to hold them in a 200° F. oven while you enjoy the first course papillotes. Then all you will have to do is assemble the plates.

Sprinkle the crème brulées with sugar and run them under the broiler at dessert time.

If Time Is Short ...

☞ You can omit the passion fruit sours and start right in on the Champagne.

☞ Serve raw oysters, a renowned aphrodisiac, instead of the papillotes.

☞ Substitute individual heart-shaped cherry tarts from a bakery for the crème brulées.

Passion Fruit Sours

Passion fruit—flavored brandy, heady with the intense perfume of this tropical fruit, is lightened with lemon juice to make a wickedly potent cocktail.

For each drink

3	ounces (2 jiggers or a generous ⅓ cup) passion fruit—flavored liqueur or brandy, such as Alizé or La Grande Passion
2	tablespoons lemon juice
	Thin slices of lemon for garnish
	Maraschino cherries for garnish if desired

Use pretty 10- to 12-ounce stemmed glasses and fill with cracked ice or small ice cubes. Add passion fruit liqueur and lemon juice, stirring well to mix. Garnish each glass with a slice of lemon and a cherry if desired.

Scallops and Salmon en Papillotes

Because of their shape, these packets are called papillotes *(meaning "butterflies" in French), which is a romantic-sounding name in itself. And to take the Valentine theme further, these packets also happen to be heart-shaped.*

MAKES 2 SERVINGS

¼	pound salmon fillet, preferably skinless
2	ounces small bay scallops
1	tablespoon minced shallots
1	teaspoon chopped fresh tarragon, or ¼ teaspoon dried
1	tablespoon lime juice
	Salt and freshly ground black pepper
1	tablespoon olive oil
1	thin slice lime
2	sprigs fresh tarragon, if available

1. To make papillote packets, cut 2 pieces of parchment paper 14 inches long. Fold sheets in half the short way to make them 7 inches wide. Cut out two hearts so that when unfolded they measure approximately 13 inches wide and 11 inches long.

2. Cut the salmon across the grain into ½-inch-wide slices, leaving behind any dark flesh or skin. You should have about 8 strips. Lay salmon strips, overlapping them slightly, on half of each heart and divide scallops over each portion. Scatter with shallots and tarragon, drizzle with lime juice, and sprinkle lightly with salt and pepper. Drizzle with oil. Finally, place half of the slice of lime on each portion and top with a tarragon sprig.

3. Fold the other half of each heart over the fish. To seal packets, begin at the top of the heart and fold edges in ½ inch. Then make another fold overlapping with the first, to seal. Continue in this manner all the way around

the edge of the heart, twisting the bottom point to seal. (Packets can be made several hours ahead and refrigerated.)

4. Preheat the oven to 500° F.
5. Place packets on baking sheet and bake for 5 minutes. The papillotes will puff up from the steam trapped inside. Transfer to plates and serve immediately. To open, slit tops of packets with scissors or a knife to release steam and aromas.

Broiled Poussin on Radicchio with Balsamic Beurre Rouge

If you have a hard time finding these baby chickens (and you probably will), Cornish game hens work just as well and also taste terrific. In any case, have the butcher split them for you.

MAKES 2 SERVINGS

Balsamic Beurre Rouge

2	tablespoons red wine
1	tablespoon balsamic vinegar
1	teaspoon minced shallots
3	tablespoons chilled unsalted butter, cut in 9 pieces
½	teaspoon chopped fresh thyme, or ¼ teaspoon dried
	Salt and ground white pepper

Hens

1	1- to 1¼-pound poussin or Cornish game hen, split in half
½	teaspoon chopped fresh thyme, or ¼ teaspoon dried
1	tablespoon olive oil
	Salt and freshly ground black pepper
6	large leaves radicchio
	Fresh thyme sprigs, optional garnish

1. To make the butter sauce, simmer the wine, vinegar, and shallots in a small, nonreactive saucepan until reduced to 2 teaspoons. Remove pan from heat and whisk in the butter piece by piece, waiting until 1 piece is nearly incorporated before adding another. If the mixture cools too much to incorporate the butter, place pan over very low heat, but do not allow butter to melt completely. Stir in thyme and salt and pepper to taste. (Beurre rouge can be made 2 hours ahead and kept at room temperature. Reheat very gently in a small pan set over another pan of hot water.)

2. For the poussin, preheat the broiler. Use the palm of your hand to flatten the poussin to as even a thickness as possible. Use your fingers to loosen the skin from the breast meat portion. Spread the thyme between the meat and the skin. Brush all over with the oil and sprinkle with salt and pepper. Place the poussin halves, skin side up, on a rack in a broiling pan. Broil 6 to 7 inches from the heat source for 8 to 10 minutes, until rich golden brown. Turn, brush with the pan drippings,

[continued]

and broil about 8 minutes until juices run clear when the thighs are pierced with a knife tip. Turn and brush again, then broil about 1 minute more until skin is crisp. (Can be held in a 200° F. oven for about 30 minutes.)

3.   To serve, arrange the radicchio leaves as a bed on two serving plates. Set the poussin halves on the radicchio and spoon the butter sauce over. If desired, garnish with thyme sprigs.

Lacy Potato and Turnip Galettes

Idaho potatoes have the best consistency for these thin, crisp potato cakes. The turnip adds even more sophisticated flavor.

MAKES 2 SERVINGS

8	ounces (1 medium) Idaho russet potato
4	ounces (1 small) white turnip
¼	teaspoon salt
⅛	teaspoon freshly ground black pepper
	Pinch nutmeg
2	tablespoons vegetable oil

1.   Peel the potato and turnip, then coarsely grate either by hand or using the shredding disk of a food processor. Place the grated vegetables in several thicknesses of paper toweling or a tea towel, wrap up, and squeeze out as much liquid as possible. (Can be done 2 hours ahead.) Place vegetables in a bowl. Add the salt, pepper, and nutmeg, tossing to mix well.

2.   Heat the oil in a large skillet. Drop 4 mounds of the potato-turnip mixture into the skillet and use a spatula to flatten the mounds to an even thickness, and a size about 3 inches in diameter. Reduce heat to medium-low and cook the galettes for about 10 minutes, until undersides are golden brown. Turn carefully with a large spatula and cook for 7 to 9 minutes more, until crisp and brown and potatoes are cooked through. Though these are best served immediately, they can be held, uncovered, on a baking sheet in a 200° F. oven for about 30 minutes.

Braised Peas, Prosciutto, and Bibb Lettuce with Chives

The lettuce is used primarily to infuse the peas with flavor and moisture. After cooking, it can be discarded or chopped and added to the peas. We think the prosciutto adds an attractive look and delicious taste to this French classic.

MAKES 2 SERVINGS

1¼	cups tiny frozen green peas
1	tablespoon chicken broth or water
2	leaves Bibb lettuce
1	tablespoon finely slivered prosciutto (about 1 thin slice)
1	tablespoon snipped chives
	Salt and freshly ground black pepper

1. Place the frozen peas and broth in a saucepan. Lay the lettuce leaves over the top. Bring to a simmer, then cover and braise over medium-low heat for about 5 minutes, until the peas are tender.

2. Discard lettuce or chop and add to peas. Stir in prosciutto and chives. Taste and add salt and pepper as desired. Use a slotted spoon to serve.

Cherry Crème Brulées

If you have heart-shaped ramekins, this would be the time to use them.

MAKES 2 SERVINGS

2	tablespoons dried cherries, halved if large (see Note)
1	tablespoon kirsch or brandy
1	cup heavy cream
	Pinch salt
1	whole egg
2	egg yolks
1	tablespoon granulated sugar
½	teaspoon vanilla extract
2	tablespoons light brown sugar

1. In a small bowl, combine the cherries with the brandy. Set aside for at least 30 minutes or for up to 2 hours.

2. Preheat the oven to 300° F.

3. Drain cherries and divide them between two 8 to 10 ounce ramekins or custard cups.

4. In a nonreactive saucepan, heat the cream with the salt over medium heat until small bubbles appear around the edges. Whisk together the egg, yolks, and sugar. Slowly whisk the hot cream into the eggs, then return mixture to the saucepan and stir custard over low heat until it thickens enough to lightly coat the back of a spoon, about 5 minutes. Stir in the vanilla.

5. Strain custard into the prepared ramekins and set them in a shallow baking pan. Fill the pan with hot water to come halfway up the sides of the ramekins. Bake in the preheated oven for 20 to 25 minutes, depending upon the shape of the ramekins, until soft-set (set around the edges and still wobbly in the center).

6. Remove from water bath and cool to room temperature. Cover and refrigerate for at least 2 hours. (Can be made 1 day ahead.)

7. Preheat broiler. If you wish to make a heart-shaped design on the tops of the crème brulées, make a paper template by cutting a circle to fit the top of the ramekin. Cut a large heart out of the middle of the circle. Lay the template over the top of the custard and sieve brown sugar heavily into the heart-shaped space. Remove template. If you do not wish to make a heart, simply sieve brown sugar over the entire top of each custard.

8. Place crème brulées 2 or 3 inches from the broiler element and broil until brown sugar is caramelized and bubbly, about 1 minute. Keep oven door open and watch carefully to make sure sugar doesn't burn. It should be dark brown but not black.

9. Serve within about 15 minutes.

Note: Dried cherries are available at specialty food stores. If you can't get them, the crème brulées are just fine without them.

Spring

The Egg Hunt

Fiesta!

Bridal Shower

Way to Go, Matt!

THE EGG HUNT

A Fanciful Easter Brunch
BUFFET FOR 16

EASTER RANKS HIGH on our list of favorite holidays, for it remains relatively unspoiled by commercialism, doesn't take weeks to decorate for, and no one gets writer's cramp sending out Easter cards. But best of all, it comes at just the right time of year. Whether it falls in March or April, Easter spells the beginning of springtime.

Unlike Thanksgiving, when turkey is king, Easter offers a wealth of culinary traditions from Greek to Italian and Polish to Russian, as well as several from regional America. We love them all for their celebratory themes of renewal and gladness.

Since we think of it as a sunny holiday, one of our favorite ways to share Easter with family and friends is at midday buffet brunch, preceded by the traditional egg hunt in the backyard.

Early in the morning, a contingent of teenagers heads out on a highly secret mission to hide colored eggs, wrapped candy, and bright trinkets. Later, provided with grass-filled baskets, the young ones sprint off in search of Easter treasures while parents cheer (and drop broad hints) from the sidelines.

With appetites sparked by fresh air and the excitement of the hunt, everyone then comes in for frothy pink frappés and brunch.

In true American style, ham is the centerpiece meat. Of course, ham needs eggs, and a wonderfully easy baked frittata fits the bill quite nicely. Asparagus, another harbinger of spring, appears here as a lovely, simple composed salad with a lemony chive dressing. And the Greek Easter bread is a gorgeous circular braid, studded with colored eggs and glazed to a shiny baked finish. Every dish makes a spectacular buffet presentation, though none is difficult to make.

For the young guests, who are sometimes finicky (especially after early morning basket raids), it is prudent to set out an assortment of cereals in individual boxes.

The dessert table displays our personalized version of a favorite Sicilian celebration cheesecake, a heaped basket of the season's first strawberries, and the giant solid chocolate bunny whose ear serves as first prize in the egg hunt.

refrigerator. This is also a good time to order your ham.

The mustard sauce can be made 3 or 4 days in advance.

One to two days beforehand, make the cheesecake and refrigerate it, well wrapped. Dye the Easter eggs.

The day before the brunch, make the lemon-chive mayonnaise. You may also cook the potatoes and sauté the leeks for the frittata. Set the table.

On the morning of the party, send out a contingent to hide the eggs and candy. Blanch the asparagus for the salad. Take the bread out of the freezer and put the ham in the oven.

Then, make up the frappés and froth them up again in the processor or blender just before serving. And finally, arrange the asparagus salad, finish the frittata, and heap the berries in a basket.

In Advance

THIS SIMPLE but very special menu conforms to our theory that brunch should be a meal that is easy on the hostess. If guests are due to arrive in the late morning, it is essential that day-of-the party preparations be kept to a minimum.

About 2 weeks ahead you can make the Easter bread and freeze it, if you wish. Make the marmalade then, too, and keep it in the

If Time Is Short ...

☞ Serve fruit juices in lieu of the frappés.
☞ Use interesting prepared mustard sauces and marmalades if you don't have time to make your own.
☞ Buy a sweet yeast bread or some hot cross buns.
☞ Purchase a cheesecake from a good bakery.

Raspberry Yogurt Frappés

In New England, a frappé is first cousin to a milkshake, but usually lighter and frothier. Depending upon the size of your food processor or blender, this refreshing and tasty drink may need to be made in batches. Other fruits such as strawberries, peaches, nectarines, or bananas work equally well, with the sweetness adjusted according to the fruit and personal taste.

MAKES ABOUT 16 SERVINGS (11 TO 12 CUPS)

3	cups raspberries (fresh or frozen unsweetened, or lightly sweetened)
3	cups cold plain yogurt
5 to 6	tablespoons honey, depending upon sweetness of berries
2¼	cups cold milk
½	cup fresh whole raspberries and/or a few mint sprigs for garnish

1.   Purée the berries in a food processor or blender. Add the yogurt and honey and purée about 30 seconds, until smooth and thickened. With the motor running, add the milk and process for 30 to 40 seconds, until thick and frothy, much like a milkshake.

2.   Serve immediately, poured into stemmed glasses and garnished with a few whole berries or mint sprigs. (Mixture can be put together up to 4 hours ahead and refrigerated. Process again just before serving to regain the frothy texture.)

Baked Smoked Ham

The centerpiece of this brunch menu, a beautiful baked and glazed smoked ham, is as delicious as it is pretty. Buy your ham from a good local source or mail-order ahead from one of the specialty smokehouses around the country. If you are not buying a whole ham, you have a choice of butt or shank end. The butt is meatier, but many think the shank is more flavorful. Either way, buy from a quality source and you won't go wrong.

MAKES ABOUT 16 SERVINGS WITH SOME LEFTOVERS

1	8- to 10-pound bone-in, fully cooked smoked ham
½	cup dark brown sugar
½	cup orange juice or half juice and half white wine
½	teaspoon dry mustard
16 to 20	whole cloves
1	bunch watercress sprigs for garnish Orange slices studded with whole cloves for garnish

1. Preheat the oven to 350° F. Trim fat from ham to about ½ inch if this has not already been done. Place ham, fat side up, on a rack in a shallow baking pan. Bake about 1 hour.

2. In a small saucepan over low heat, stir together the brown sugar, orange juice, and mustard until the sugar dissolves. Remove baking pan from oven. Use a sharp knife to score the fat on the ham with crossing sets of diagonal lines to form diamonds, then brush the ham with the glaze. Stud scored diamonds with the whole cloves. Return to the oven and bake an additional 30 to 45 minutes, until a thermometer inserted in the thickest part of the ham registers about 140° F. to be sure that the ham is fully heated. (The general rule of thumb is 12 minutes per pound.)

3. Transfer ham to a carving board and let stand, covered with foil, for about 15 minutes before carving. Use a sharp knife to thinly carve about two-thirds of the ham, leaving remainder whole to serve as decoration. Arrange the ham slices, overlapping, around the whole portion on a serving platter. Garnish platter with watercress sprigs and orange slices studded with whole cloves.

Wild Thyme Honey–Mustard Sauce

Your family will keep requesting this wonderful sweet/sour sauce long after the party is over. It's great on sandwiches, and also as a dip for raw vegetables.

½	cup Colman's dry mustard (see Note)
⅔	cup white distilled vinegar
⅓	cup white wine
3	eggs
½	cup honey
½	teaspoon salt
1	tablespoon chopped fresh thyme, or 1 teaspoon dried

1. In a small mixing bowl, stir together the mustard, vinegar, and wine. Cover and let stand at room temperature for 4 hours, or for as long as overnight.

2. In the top of a double boiler or in a stainless-steel bowl set over simmering water, whisk together the eggs, honey, and salt. Whisk in the mustard mixture. Cook over barely simmering water, whisking every 5 minutes or so, for 35 to 45 minutes, until sauce is the consistency of a thinnish mayonnaise. Stir in the chopped thyme.

3. Cool to room temperature, whisking sauce occasionally as it cools. Transfer to a covered container and refrigerate. (Can be made 3 or 4 days ahead.)

Note: Colman's is a high-quality nationally available brand of dry mustard and will give consistent results. If you can't get it, a good-quality finely powdered brand of mustard should work fine.

Leek and Potato Frittata

This simple, savory frittata is well suited to a buffet, since it can be served either hot or at room temperature.

MAKES 16 ACCOMPANIMENT SERVINGS

1	pound waxy potatoes
¼	cup olive oil
4	cups thinly sliced leeks, including light green parts (5 to 6 medium leeks)
12	eggs
¾	teaspoon salt
½	teaspoon freshly ground black pepper
⅛	teaspoon nutmeg
½	cup (2 ounces) shredded Gruyère or Swiss cheese

1. Preheat the oven to 375° F. Generously butter a 9- by 13-inch or other 3-quart shallow baking dish.

2. Cook the unpeeled potatoes in boiling, salted water until just tender. Drain and cool, then peel and slice thinly. (Can prepare a day ahead and refrigerate.)

3. Heat the oil in a large skillet and sauté the leeks over medium-low heat, stirring often, for about 5 minutes, until softened but not colored. (Can prepare a day ahead and refrigerate.)

4. Whisk the eggs with the salt, pepper, and nutmeg until well blended but not frothy.

5. Spread the potatoes evenly over the bottom of the baking dish, then spread the leeks evenly over the potatoes. Pour in the egg mixture and sprinkle with the cheese.

6. Bake in the center of the oven for 25 to 30 minutes, until eggs are set and frittata is puffed and lightly browned.

7. Serve hot or at room temperature. (Frittata can be made several hours ahead.)

Asparagus with Lemon-Chive Mayonnaise

Asparagus has lots of visual appeal, especially in this attractive, make-ahead salad. The flavored mayonnaise is also delicious on broccoli or thickly sliced tomatoes.

MAKES 16 SERVINGS

Lemon-Chive Mayonnaise

1	cup good-quality commercial mayonnaise
2	teaspoons lemon juice
½	teaspoon grated lemon zest
¼	teaspoon freshly ground black pepper
2	tablespoons snipped chives
2 to 3	tablespoons milk

About 4	pounds thin asparagus (approximately 6 spears per person)
1	head Boston or other soft lettuce
2	teaspoons snipped chives
1	lemon, thinly sliced

1. To prepare the sauce, stir together the mayonnaise, lemon juice, zest, pepper, chives, and enough milk to make a thick pouring consistency. (Can make 1 day ahead. Cover and refrigerate.)

2. Trim the asparagus by bending and breaking off woody ends at their natural breaking point. Bring a large pan of salted water to a boil. Add the asparagus and cook about 2 minutes, until just crisp-tender. Remove with tongs to a strainer and refresh under cold water until asparagus is cool. Drain well, then use immediately or wrap in plastic and refrigerate up to 4 hours before using.

3. To assemble, line a platter with the lettuce leaves. Arrange the asparagus, tips outward, in an attractive, overlapping pattern on the lettuce. Pour or ladle the mayonnaise in ribbons over the center of the stalks, leaving the tips exposed. (Can be assembled about 1 hour ahead and refrigerated, uncovered or lightly covered.) Just before serving, sprinkle the mayonnaise with 2 teaspoons snipped chives and garnish the platter with lemon slices.

Alice Hasapis's Classic Greek Easter Bread

Actually, it is Alice's mother who usually makes the bread for Easter, but the baking of the fragrant braided ring subtly flavored with anise and embedded with colored Easter eggs is part of the wonderful tradition that Melanie's friend Alice shared with her. The large tsoureki, *as the bread is called in Greece, is most impressive, but it might be more practical to bake 2 braided loaves if your family is smaller. The unused one will freeze just fine, although you might want to omit the Easter egg decoration, which is not meant to be eaten anyway.*

MAKES 1 LARGE BRAIDED RING SERVING 16, OR
2 SMALLER BRAIDED LOAVES EACH SERVING 8

2	packages (2 teaspoons) active dry yeast (see Note)
⅓	cup warm water (105° F. to 115° F.)
1¼	teaspoons anise seeds
1	cup milk
½	cup (1 stick) unsalted butter, cut in pieces
⅔	cup granulated sugar
1¼	teaspoons salt
3	eggs
1	teaspoon grated orange zest
1	teaspoon grated lemon zest
1	teaspoon vanilla extract
5½ to 6	cups all-purpose flour
4	hard-cooked eggs, colored (see Note)
1	egg beaten with 2 teaspoons milk for glaze
1	teaspoon sesame seeds

1. Sprinkle the yeast over the warm water and set aside to proof for about 10 minutes, until bubbly.

2. Crush the anise seeds in a mortar with a pestle or by placing them in a small plastic bag and crushing with a flat mallet or a rolling pin. Combine anise seeds and milk in a saucepan and bring just to a simmer. Remove from heat and add the butter, sugar, and salt. Stir until butter is melted and mixture is lukewarm.

3. In a large bowl of an electric mixer with a dough hook, or by hand in a large mixing bowl, beat the eggs with the orange and lemon zests and the vanilla. Stir in the yeast and milk mixtures until well blended. Continue to beat while adding enough flour to make a moderately soft but manageable dough.

4. Knead with the dough hook for about 5 minutes, or by hand on a lightly floured surface for about 10 minutes, until smooth and elastic. Place in a large buttered bowl, turning the dough to butter the top. Cover lightly with a towel and let rise about 1½ hours, until doubled. (Dough can be made a day ahead and allowed to rise in the refrigerator for 12 to 16 hours.) Punch down.

5. To make the large ring, divide the dough into 3 parts and shape each piece on a lightly floured surface into a 30-inch rope. Lay the ropes side by side and braid them, pinching both ends. Transfer the braid to a large buttered baking sheet and form into a circle, pinching the 2 ends together firmly. (If making 2 smaller loaves, divide dough in half, then work with 1 portion at a time. Make three 20-inch strips and braid into a long loaf.

[c o n t i n u e d]

Do not form into a ring. Place 2 loaves on buttered baking sheet or sheets.) Press the colored eggs into the braids or loaves. Brush with about half of the egg wash. Cover lightly and let rise again for about 1 hour, until doubled.

6. Preheat the oven to 350° F. When the dough has risen, brush again with the egg wash and sprinkle with the sesame seeds. Bake in the center of the oven for 35 to 45 minutes (30 to 35 minutes for smaller loaves), until bread is rich golden brown, a skewer inserted comes out clean, and the bread sounds hollow when tapped. Transfer to a rack to cool. Serve on the day the bread is baked or wrap well and freeze up to 2 weeks.

Note: Fast-rising yeast can be used. Rising times will be cut in half. This type of yeast is not recommended for a refrigerator rise.

Traditionally the eggs are dyed red by soaking in beet juice. However, you can use any color Easter egg dye that you wish.

Rhubarb–Ginger Marmalade

Since rhubarb speaks of spring, we always like to include it somewhere in the Easter menu. It makes a delicious, easily made marmalade spiked with the sweet bite of crystallized ginger.

MAKES ABOUT 2 CUPS

4	cups thinly sliced rhubarb, fresh or frozen
2	cups granulated sugar (see Note)
1	tablespoon lemon juice
4	teaspoons finely chopped crystallized ginger

1. In a medium nonreactive saucepan combine the rhubarb, sugar, and lemon juice. Bring to a full rolling boil, reduce heat, and simmer uncovered over medium-low heat, stirring frequently, for about 15 minutes, or until thickened. Since marmalade thickens quite a bit as it cools, begin testing for doneness after about 10 minutes by spooning a small amount onto a plate and putting in the freezer for a couple of minutes. Marmalade should be thick but spreadable when cool.

2. Remove from heat and stir in the chopped ginger.

3. Store in a covered container in the refrigerator. (Can be made 3 weeks ahead.)

Note: Rhubarb varies in sweetness. The red part of the stalk is sweeter than the green. If yours has a lot of green, increase sugar somewhat.

Candied Orange Ricotta Cheesecake

Sicilians love extravagant sweets for important celebrations, and no holiday in Italy is more important than Easter. There are as many variations on the classic ricotta cheese "pie" theme as there are outspoken Sicilian cooks who make them. Melanie can personally attest to more than a few heated family discussions on the topic! Here is our version. Serve this rich cake in small slices.

MAKES ABOUT 16 SERVINGS

Crust

1	tablespoon unsalted butter, softened
⅓	cup crushed graham crackers (from 3 whole crackers)

Ricotta Cheesecake

½	cup golden raisins
¼	cup rum or orange juice
8	ounces cream cheese, softened
15 or 16	ounces ricotta cheese
¾	cup granulated sugar
¼	teaspoon salt
4	eggs, separated
2	teaspoons vanilla extract
⅓	cup candied orange peel or citron, chopped into ¼-inch chunks
1	teaspoon grated lemon zest
1	tablespoon lemon juice
¼	cup all-purpose flour

1. Coat the inside of a 9-inch springform pan with the softened butter. Sprinkle with the graham cracker crumbs, tilting pan so crumbs adhere about halfway up sides and spreading any excess evenly over the bottom. Wrap bottom of pan with a single sheet of heavy-duty foil, bringing it all the way up the sides. (This is to prevent cake batter from leaking.) Refrigerate pan until ready to fill. Preheat oven to 325° F.

2. In a small saucepan, combine the raisins and rum or juice. Heat gently for 2 minutes, cover, and let stand at room temperature while mixing the cake.

3. In a large mixing bowl, combine the cream cheese, ricotta, sugar, and salt. Beat with an electric mixer at high speed until cheeses are smooth. Beat in egg yolks and vanilla. Add candied orange peel or citron, grated lemon zest, and lemon juice, beating until well blended. Add flour and beat at medium just until blended. Stir in raisins and their soaking liquid.

4. In a clean bowl, beat the egg whites until firm but not dry. Fold whites into batter and transfer to prepared pan, smoothing top. Place cake pan in a larger baking pan and fill with hot water to come halfway up the sides of the cake pan.

5. Bake in the center of the preheated oven for 50 to 55 minutes, until top is pale gold and a knife inserted 3 inches from the edge comes out clean. Center should still be slightly wiggly. Turn oven off and cool in the oven for 45 minutes. Remove pan from water bath and cool on a rack at room temperature until tepid. Wrap well and refrigerate. (Can be made 2 days ahead.)

6. To serve, run a knife around the cake and lift off springform sides. It's easiest to leave cake on the springform base. To cut, use a sharp knife, wiping it clean for each new cut.

Fiesta!

A Meatless Mexican Supper
For 8

ONE OF THE THINGS we like best about Mexican and American Southwest food is its reliance on lots and lots of fresh vegetables and fruits. Tortillas, cheese, beans, rice, and chiles are the staples of most Mexican meals. Meat, if it shows up at all, often plays a support role and, to our minds, could easily be omitted.

So, in this party, that is exactly what we do. In addition to featuring dishes that we really love to eat and to serve, the menu's meatless aspect is particularly appealing to many of our friends these days.

Our fiesta , which is a party that really can be planned in any season, can be enjoyed as a sit-down supper or just as easily as an informal indoor or outdoor buffet. In either case, use the brightest linens and china that you have. Go for fresh painted daisies or other colorful flowers, and put them in terra cotta pots or interesting, off-beat jars. Beg, borrow, or buy a couple of sombreros and some mariachi music tapes. Get a piñata (lots of party shops can order them) and make it the decorative focal point.

However you plan to serve the supper, allow plenty of premeal time and space for the basket or bowl of addictively crisp tortilla chips and the colorful trio of salsas. Tall glasses of light, white, fruity sangria set the tone for this contemporary party. The lasagne, with its extra cheese filling and spicy tomato and pepper sauce, is sure to be an instant hit with absolutely everyone, and the two colorful salads round out the main course quite nicely. The sweet-tart, spiked lime mousse and the dark chocolate brownies offer a dessert choice, but we bet that everyone will have some of each.

Because much of the food is designed for make-ahead preparation and simple serving, even the cook will agree that this is a true fiesta!

In Advance

THIS SIMPLE MENU looks bountiful and bright, but is amazingly easy to prepare.

Begin about a week ahead by making, then freezing, both the margarita mousse and the brownies.

Two or three days ahead, mix up the base for the sangria and make the dressing for the salads. Buy the avocados so they have time to ripen.

The day before the party, assemble the lasagne and fry the tortilla chips if you plan to do them yourself.

On the morning of the party, make the two salsas and the guacamole base (adding the avocados an hour or two before serving). Put together the bean salad. In the afternoon, slice the oranges and onions for that salad.

Shortly before the party, finish the sangria and heat the lasagne. If desired, also warm the tortilla chips for a few minutes in the oven while the lasagne is baking.

If Time Is Short ...

☞ Buy good-quality tortilla chips instead of frying your own. Purchased chips are better if they're crisped in a hot oven for a few minutes before serving.

☞ You could substitute a tropical fruit compote for the margarita mousse.

White Sangria

Light, refreshing, and very fruity, this sangria is a perfect cocktail for almost any informal party, but is especially nice as a counterpoint to the spicy foods in this menu. Be sure to allow at least 1 tall glassful per person, but make up lots of extra base since it keeps well and people just love it. If you want to make it a nonalcoholic fruit punch, omit the brandy and wine, replacing them with more orange juice and seltzer.

MAKES ABOUT 2 QUARTS

1	cup orange juice
¼	cup lemon juice
2	tablespoons peach brandy
2	tablespoons sugar, superfine or granulated
4	cups white wine
2	cups sparkling water or seltzer
1	small orange, thinly sliced
1	small lemon, thinly sliced
1	small lime, thinly sliced

1. Combine the orange juice, lemon juice, peach brandy, and sugar. Refrigerate this base at least 2 hours or up to 2 days.

2. Shortly before serving, pour the juice mixture into a large pitcher or punch bowl. Stir in the wine and sparkling water. Add fruit slices and stir gently.

3. Serve over ice in tall glasses.

Pico de Gallo Salsa

Jicama makes a wonderful addition to our version of this light and fresh salsa. Great as a dip for tortilla chips, salsa is also terrific as a condiment with grilled steaks, seafood, chicken, or chops. Though all ingredients can be chopped in a food processor, we like the texture of hand preparation here.

MAKES ABOUT 3 CUPS

2	tablespoons vegetable oil
1½	tablespoons lemon juice
½	teaspoon salt
1	pound peeled, seeded, and finely diced plum tomatoes, to make about 2 cups
1	small red bell pepper, cored, seeded, and chopped, to make about ¾ cup
½	cup finely diced peeled jicama
½	cup chopped onion
2	tablespoons chopped fresh cilantro

1 to 2	fresh or canned jalapeño peppers, minced
1	clove garlic, peeled and minced Cilantro sprigs for garnish (optional)

1.   In a mixing bowl, whisk together the oil, lemon juice, and salt. Stir in the remaining ingredients except cilantro sprigs. Refrigerate at least 1 hour or up to 6 hours before using.

2.   Serve from a decorative bowl garnished with cilantro sprigs if desired.

Tomatillo Salsa

Fresh tomatillos are worth seeking out for their wonderful, lemony flavor. If you can't find them, use canned tomatillos, following the directions at the end of the recipe.

MAKES ABOUT 2 CUPS

1	pound tomatillos (see Note)
⅔	cup minced onion
2	cloves garlic, peeled and minced
1 to 2	fresh or canned jalapeño peppers, minced
½	teaspoon salt
6	tablespoons chopped cilantro
2	tablespoons water, if needed

1.   Remove the papery brown husks from the tomatillos. Place in a saucepan with water to cover, bring to a simmer, and cook for about 5 minutes, until just tender. Drain and refresh under cold running water to stop the cooking.

2.   Finely chop the tomatillos and combine in a bowl with the onion, garlic, jalapeño, salt, and cilantro. (Can be made several hours ahead.)

3.   Stir salsa just before serving. If it has thickened too much, stir in some water.

Note: Two 10-ounce cans of cooked tomatillos can be substituted. Simply drain and chop by hand; do not cook.

Cilantro Guacamole

A good guacamole is one that retains some texture, which is the reason we suggest making this by hand rather than in a food processor.

MAKES ABOUT 2 CUPS

1	plum tomato, seeded and finely chopped
1	fresh or pickled jalapeño, minced
2	tablespoons minced scallions, white and pale green parts only
2	tablespoons chopped cilantro
1½	tablespoons lime juice
2	large ripe avocados
½	teaspoon salt
⅛	teaspoon freshly ground black pepper
	Tabasco to taste
	Sprigs of cilantro or thin slices of lime for garnish

1. Combine the chopped tomato, jalapeño, scallion, and cilantro in a bowl. Stir in the lime juice. (Can be made 8 hours ahead. Cover and refrigerate.)

2. Peel the avocados, cut into chunks, and coarsely mash in a large bowl, using a potato masher or a large fork. (The avocado should not be completely smooth.) Stir in the tomato base and add salt and pepper. Taste for seasoning and add several drops of Tabasco if you like your guacamole spicier. (Can be made 3 hours ahead. Bury an avocado pit in the guacamole and squeeze a little additional lime juice over it to help prevent it from turning brown.)

3. Serve guacamole with the tortilla chips.

Fresh Tortilla Chips

If you have a source for really good tortilla chips, by all means purchase them. But for an incomparable homemade treat, fry these up fresh yourself!

MAKES 8 SERVINGS

1	10-ounce package corn tortillas
	Vegetable oil
	Salt

1. Use scissors to cut each tortilla in 6 or 8 wedges.

2. Heat about ¼ inch oil in a large skillet. Fry the tortilla pieces in batches, taking care not to crowd the pan, over medium-high heat for 30 to 45 seconds. Turn with a slotted spoon or tongs and fry about 30 seconds on the other side until crisp and lightly browned around the edges.

3. Drain on paper toweling and sprinkle with salt. Serve warm or at room temperature. (Can be made a day ahead and stored, tightly covered at room temperature.) If desired, warm the chips before serving by heating in the oven for a few minutes at 350° F.

Corn, Black Bean, and Red Pepper Salad

This goes beautifully with the lasagne, but can also stand alone as a delicious vegetarian main course.

MAKES 8 SIDE-COURSE SERVINGS

Balsamic-Honey Vinaigrette

3	tablespoons balsamic vinegar
2	teaspoons honey
1½	teaspoons Dijon mustard
1	clove garlic, peeled and minced
½	teaspoon salt
¼	teaspoon red pepper flakes
¼	teaspoon freshly ground black pepper
¼	cup olive oil
3	tablespoons vegetable oil

Salad and Garnishes

2	cups cooked black beans, prepared from dried beans, or one 1-pound can, rinsed and drained
2	cups corn kernels, fresh or thawed frozen
1	cup thinly sliced celery
1	cup red pepper strips, 1 inch long, ¼ inch wide
½	cup thinly sliced scallions, including green tops
3	tablespoons chopped cilantro
1	small bunch arugula

1. To make the dressing, combine the vinegar, honey, mustard, garlic, salt, and both peppers in a small bowl or covered container. Whisk until honey is dissolved. Gradually whisk in the oils. (Can be made 2 or 3 days ahead.)

2. In a large bowl, combine the beans, corn, celery, and red pepper. Pour most of the dressing over, tossing gently to combine. Taste for seasoning and refrigerate for at least 1 hour. (Can be made 8 hours ahead.)

3. When ready to serve, add the scallions and cilantro and toss again gently. Arrange arugula leaves on a rimmed platter and spoon salad into the center. Sprinkle with additional cilantro or scallions if desired.

Queso Fresco "Lasagne"

Happily, pasta is no longer limited to Italian cooking. With the increased availability of pasta sheets, imaginative cooks are using them for all sorts of wonderful dishes. If you have guests with varying degrees of heat tolerance, sprinkle only half of the lasagne with the chopped jalapeños, if you wish.

MAKES 6 TO 8 SERVINGS

1	pound fresh pasta sheets, or 12 strips (about 12 ounces) dry lasagne noodles

Sauce

2	tablespoons oil
2	medium onions, peeled and coarsely chopped
2	medium green bell peppers or Italian frying peppers, cored, seeded, and coarsely chopped
2	large cloves garlic, peeled and minced
2	tablespoons chili powder
1	teaspoon ground cumin
1	teaspoon dried oregano
2	16-ounce cans plum tomatoes in juice
	Salt to taste

Filling

3	cups (24 ounces) ricotta cheese
1	egg, lightly beaten
⅓	cup chopped cilantro
¼	cup chopped parsley
	Pinch cayenne
8	ounces shredded Monterey Jack cheese
6	ounces shredded Cheddar cheese
1 or 2	fresh or canned jalapeño peppers, minced (optional)

1. If using very fresh pasta, it does not need to be cooked before assembling the lasagne. Cook dried pasta in a large pot of boiling, salted water until al dente. Drain well, rinse under cold water, then reserve pasta.

2. To make the sauce, heat the oil and cook the onions, peppers, and garlic over medium-low heat, stirring often, for about 5 minutes until vegetables begin to soften. Add the chili powder and cook, stirring, for 1 minute. Stir in the cumin and oregano, then the tomatoes with their juices. Bring to a simmer, breaking up the tomatoes with the side of a spoon. Simmer over low heat, uncovered, for about 15 minutes. Taste and season with salt if needed.

3. To make the filling, stir together the ricotta, egg, cilantro, parsley, and cayenne.

4. To assemble the lasagne, use an attractive 3- or 4-quart baking dish (not aluminum), such as a 10- by 14-inch lasagne pan or a 9- by 13-inch casserole, though it is not necessary that it be rectangular. Spread a thin layer of sauce on the bottom of the dish, then make a layer using one-third of the pasta, then a layer of one-half of the ricotta filling. Combine the Monterey jack and Cheddar cheeses and sprinkle one-third over the ricotta. Spoon on one-third of the remaining sauce. Make another layer with half of the remaining pasta, all of the remaining ricotta filling, half of the remaining shredded cheeses, and half of the remaining sauce. Top with the remaining pasta and sauce. Reserve remaining shredded cheeses. (Can assemble a day ahead. Cover with plastic wrap and refrigerate. Return to room temperature to bake.)

5. When ready to bake, preheat oven to 350° F. Bake, covered, for 40 minutes. Uncover, sprinkle with remaining shredded cheeses and the optional jalapeños, then bake 10 minutes more, until cheese is melted and bubbly. Let the lasagne stand about 10 minutes to firm up before cutting into squares.

Sliced Oranges on Romaine with Toasted Cumin Vinaigrette

This vinaigrette is also nice as a dressing for spinach salad. The walnut oil adds an interesting dimension, as does toasting the cumin seeds.

MAKES 8 SERVINGS

Toasted Cumin Vinaigrette

3	tablespoons red wine vinegar
1	tablespoon orange juice
1	clove garlic, peeled and minced
½	teaspoon Dijon mustard
½	teaspoon toasted cumin seeds (see Note)
¼	teaspoon salt
6	tablespoons vegetable oil
2	tablespoons walnut oil, or additional vegetable oil

Salad

3	medium seedless oranges
1	red onion, thinly sliced
1	head romaine lettuce
	Coarsely ground fresh black pepper

1. To make the vinaigrette, whisk together the vinegar, juice, garlic, mustard, cumin seeds, and salt. Whisk in the oils until well blended. (Can be made 2 days ahead. Whisk to reblend before using.)

2. Peel the oranges and cut away all white pith. Slice oranges about ¼ inch thick and onions quite thinly. Line a large platter with lettuce, then make an alternating and overlapping layer of orange and onion slices. Sprinkle with pepper. (Can be made 1 hour ahead. Cover and refrigerate.)

3. Shortly before serving, drizzle salad with vinaigrette.

Note: Cumin seeds can be toasted in a small skillet over medium heat for 4 or 5 minutes, stirring occasionally. Grind with a mortar and pestle.

Margarita Mousse

This cool lime dessert, reminiscent of the famous drink, is the perfect finale to a spicy meal. Both the cooked meringue and the gelatin helps it to stand up to advance preparation. Be sure to zest the limes before you squeeze them for juice.

MAKES 8 SERVINGS

1	package unflavored gelatin
⅔	cup fresh lime juice
4	eggs, separated
1¼	cups sugar
	Pinch salt
¼	cup grated lime zest (green part only)
2	tablespoons tequila
2	tablespoons Cointreau
1	cup heavy cream, chilled
1	tablespoon lime zest curls (see Note)

1. Soften the gelatin for at least 5 minutes in 3 tablespoons of the lime juice.

2. In a heavy saucepan, whisk together the egg yolks, ¾ cup of the sugar, and the salt. Whisk in the remaining lime juice and the ¼ cup grated zest. Cook over medium-low heat, stirring constantly, until the mixture thickens enough to coat the back of a spoon and nearly comes to the boil. Remove from heat and whisk in the softened gelatin, the tequila, and the Cointreau. Pour into a large mixing bowl and chill, stirring often, until mixture just mounds when dropped from a spoon, about 30 minutes.

3. In a small saucepan, stir together 2 tablespoons water and the remaining ½ cup sugar. Place the egg whites in a large bowl of an electric mixer and begin beating at medium-low speed. At the same time, start cooking the sugar and water over medium heat, stirring constantly until sugar is dissolved. Raise heat

to high and bring to a boil. Check egg whites, which should now be at soft peaks. With mixer at high speed, slowly drizzle the hot syrup down the side of the bowl (not near the beaters where it will splatter). When syrup has been incorporated, continue beating for 1 or 2 minutes, until meringue is cooled. Then, with mixer on low speed, pour chilled lime mixture into meringue and mix only a few seconds, until blended.

4. Whip the cream to soft peaks and fold it into the lime mixture.

5. Spoon into a decorative 1½- to 2-quart serving bowl or into individual goblets. Chill, covered with plastic wrap, for at least 4 hours or up to 36 hours. (Mousse may be made a week ahead and frozen. Thaw overnight in the refrigerator.)

6. Shortly before serving, sprinkle with the lime zest curls. Serve spooned onto dessert plates, or in goblets.

Notes: The goal of our cooked meringue method is to have the sugar syrup come to a full boil at about the same time that the egg whites reach soft peaks. You may need to remove the syrup from the heat for a minute or 2, then return to a boil, or you may need to stop beating the whites for a minute or so while the syrup reaches a boil. We do not use a candy thermometer and are not sticky about an exact temperature, so this is not really a classic Italian meringue, but rather a loose variation that we find produces a very stable, creamy smooth dessert.

To make lime zest curls, use a citrus zester to peel long strips of only the green part of the lime. Or, use a swivel peeler to cut long strips, then cut the strips lengthwise into very thin slivers. (The zest may be cut up to 4 hours ahead of serving. Wrap in plastic and store in the refrigerator.)

Spiced Chocolate Pecan Brownies

Mexican chocolate is fragrant with vanilla and just a hint of cinnamon, and these fudgy pecan brownies reflect those flavors. They also cut easily and freeze beautifully.

MAKES 20 TO 24 PIECES

½	cup (1 stick) unsalted butter
2	ounces unsweetened chocolate
2	eggs
1	cup sugar
1	teaspoon vanilla extract
½	cup all-purpose flour
¼	teaspoon cinnamon
¼	teaspoon salt
⅛	teaspoon freshly ground black pepper
½	cup chopped pecans

1. Melt the butter and chocolate together in a saucepan set over low heat or in a glass bowl in the microwave. Set aside to cool for about 5 minutes.

2. Preheat the oven to 350° F. Butter or coat lightly with vegetable spray an 8- or 9-inch square baking pan.

3. In a large mixing bowl, whisk together the eggs and the sugar. Add the vanilla. Gradually whisk in the melted and cooled chocolate mixture.

4. In a small bowl, stir together the flour, cinnamon, salt, and pepper. Stir the flour mixture into the chocolate mixture. Stir in the pecans.

5. Pour batter into the prepared pan and bake in the center of the preheated oven for 25 to 30 minutes, until a cake tester inserted two-thirds of the way in from the edge of the pan comes out clean. The center should still be slightly sticky, as the brownies will continue to cook a little after they come out of the oven.

6. Cool on a wire rack for 15 minutes. Cut into 20 or 24 pieces. Cool completely before storing or serving. (Can be made 1 day ahead or frozen for a week or two.)

BRIDAL SHOWER

A Tea Party
FOR 20

HOSTING A PARTY for the daughter of my oldest and dearest friend was an honor and a delight. Jennie positively glowed at this, her first shower. Altogether fetching in an old-fashioned lacy pink dress, she was demure but radiated an unabashed enthusiasm that set the tone for the whole party.

The guest list ranged in age from an amazingly mature four-year-old to the fiancé's octogenarian grandmother. As everyone arrived, fancy packages of all sizes and shapes were stacked on a ribbon-bedecked table.

After a glass of light and fruity blush wine punch and a nibbling of spiced pecans, we moved into the dining room for tea. The afternoon sun streamed onto the white-linen-covered table and a cut crystal bowl of peach tulips. The sides of the table were devoted to pretty trays of tea sandwiches. Stacks of small china plates, napkins, and forks were at one end, and at the opposite end stood my own mother's silver tea service, complete with sugar cubes, clove-studded lemon slices, and brewed Ceylon tea. Guests filled their plates, then retired to the living room for wedding talk. The second dining room visit was to the dessert table, with its splendid array of miniature lemon tartlets, chocolate cookie hearts, and the towering coconut layer cake. Fortified with another cup of tea and a plate of sweets, we returned to the living room for the real fun of the party.

Later, while gathering up the remains of ribbons and wrapping papers, pictures of bridal showers past and years gone by crept into my memories. I poured myself another cup of tea, cut a slim slice of cake, and sat down to enjoy a nostalgic tear, and another few of joy for Jennie and her future.

In Advance

WHETHER YOU DO THIS as a bridal tea, a baby shower, or a christening, there is a fair amount of last-minute work to executing a proper tea party. We strongly recommend enlisting the aid of a close friend or two who would no doubt be honored to assist in such lovely tasks.

Up to 2 weeks ahead, make and freeze the mocha wafers, the cake layers, the lemon curd filling, and the unbaked tartlet shells.

The pecans and the candied violets will keep for several days.

The day before the party, bake the tartlet shells, make the lobster-tarragon filling, the chive butter, and the chutney butter for the tea sandwiches.

On the morning of the tea, bake the scones. Fill and frost the cake. Make the base for the punch. Then begin making the sandwiches. To help keep them from drying out, cover with a layer of slightly damp paper towels before wrapping the platters with plastic wrap. Shortly before the guests are due to arrive, fill the tartlets with lemon curd and split and fill the scones.

Now, all that's left is to brew the tea and welcome the guests.

If Time Is Short ...

☛ Offer salted mixed nuts instead of the spiced pecans.

☛ Serve glasses of sparkling blanc de noir instead of making the punch, especially if your party is smaller.

☛ Prepare tiny jam sandwiches on thinly sliced oatmeal bread in lieu of the oat scones.

☛ Buy good-quality lemon curd in a jar at a specialty food shop.

☛ Order the cake, some tartlets, and delicate chocolate cookies from a bakery.

☛ Buy candied violets from a gourmet shop. Candied rose petals are also available.

Blush Wine Punch

Cassis, a French liqueur made from black currant juice, adds a pleasant bittersweetness to this pretty pink punch. It looks lovely ladled from a large punch bowl, but if you don't have one, serve the punch from a big glass pitcher, using ice cubes instead of a block of ice.

MAKES ABOUT 4½ QUARTS

2	1½-liter bottles good-quality blush wine
1¼	cups crème de cassis
½	cup lemon juice
1	quart club soda
	Mint sprigs

1. Combine the wine, cassis, and lemon juice in a large (approximately 8-quart) punch bowl. (Can be done early in the day.)
2. Shortly before serving, add a large block of ice to the punch. Add club soda and stir gently to mix. Garnish with sprigs of mint.
3. Ladle out into small punch cups, adding a mint sprig to each one.

Spiced Pecans

This is a wonderful mid-afternoon nibbler! For the best flavor, buy nuts from a vendor who does a high volume in sales. They will be much fresher.

MAKES 4 CUPS

¼	cup vegetable oil
2	tablespoons sugar
1½	teaspoons ground cinnamon
1	teaspoon ground nutmeg
½	teaspoon ground allspice
¼	teaspoon ground cloves
4	cups (1 pound) pecan halves

1. Preheat the oven to 325° F.
2. Place the oil in a large mixing bowl and stir in the sugar, cinnamon, nutmeg, allspice, and cloves. Add the pecans and toss to coat well.
3. Spread pecans on 2 baking sheets and bake about 15 minutes, stirring 2 or 3 times and alternating the position of the baking sheets once, until nuts are fragrant and toasted. Watch carefully to prevent burning.
4. Cool and store up to a week in a tightly covered container.

Radish Blossom and Chive Butter Sandwiches

The thinly sliced radish "blossoms" with their chive "stems" are a very pretty, easy-to-make tea sandwich decoration. In addition, they taste terrific.

MAKES 48 TEA SANDWICHES

Chive Butter

¾ cup (1½ sticks) unsalted butter, softened
2 tablespoons snipped chives
1 tablespoon minced parsley
½ teaspoon Dijon mustard
¼ teaspoon salt

Radish Blossoms and Assembly

12 thin slices firm white bread
16 small radishes, very thinly sliced
16 fresh chive blades
    Parsley sprigs
    Whole radishes with stems and leaves, or whole radish flowers, for garnish (see Note)

1. To make the chive butter, blend together all ingredients. Use immediately or refrigerate up to 1 day. Return to room temperature before spreading.

2. To assemble the sandwiches, trim the crusts from the bread, then spread each slice with about 1 tablespoon chive butter. Cut each slice into 4 squares. Overlap two radish slices on each sandwich to form the "blossom." Use 1-inch lengths of chives as "stems" and attach "leaves" of parsley. (Can assemble up to 2 hours ahead. Arrange on a platter, cover with dampened paper toweling and plastic wrap, then refrigerate.)

3. Garnish with whole radishes or radish flowers.

Note: Whole radish flowers can be made with an inexpensive gadget available at most specialty cookware stores. They can also be cut by hand by making 4 outside downward slices on a whole radish, taking care not to cut all the way through. Soak the cut radishes in iced water for at least 1 hour, and they will fan out and "bloom."

Tarragon–Lobster Salad Tea Sandwiches

This is most elegant with lobster and makes very good use of an expensive treat. But the sandwiches can also be made with lump crabmeat. Use long, thin baguettes of French bread for the nicest presentation.

2	cups finely chopped cooked lobster meat (see Note)
½	cup finely chopped celery
½	cup mayonnaise
2	teaspoons lemon juice
1½	teaspoons chopped fresh tarragon, or ½ teaspoon dried
¼	teaspoon freshly ground black pepper
2	slim French bread baguettes, about 8 ounces each
	Fresh tarragon sprigs for garnish (optional)

1. In a mixing bowl, gently but thoroughly stir together the lobster, celery, mayonnaise, lemon juice, tarragon, and pepper. (Can be made a day ahead and refrigerated.)
2. Cut about 40 slices of bread, each about ¼ inch thick. Spoon about 1 tablespoon lobster salad on each bread slice. If desired, garnish each open-faced sandwich with a fresh tarragon leaf. (Though these are best served soon after assembling, they can be finished about 1 hour ahead. Arrange on a platter, cover with plastic wrap, and refrigerate.)
3. Arrange on a platter and garnish with additional tarragon sprigs, if desired.

Note: A live lobster weighing about 1 to 1¼ pounds will yield about 6 ounces or 1 cup cooked meat. You will need 2 lobsters for this recipe. Either cook the lobster yourself in a large pot of boiling, salted water for about 15 minutes or, better yet, call ahead and ask the fishmonger to cook it for you. Most are very obliging.

Smoked Chicken, Watercress, and Chutney Tea Sandwiches

Boneless smoked chicken breasts are available in many good delicatessens and they are quite easy to slice. If you can't find them, substitute smoked turkey.

MAKES 32 TEA SANDWICHES

½	cup (1 stick) unsalted butter, softened
¼	cup chopped chutney, such as Major Grey's
1½	teaspoons lemon juice
16	very thin slices whole wheat bread
8	ounces smoked chicken breast, sliced moderately thin
1 to 2	bunches watercress

1. In a small bowl, thoroughly mix together the butter, chutney, and lemon juice. (Can make a day ahead and refrigerate. Return to room temperature before using.)

2. Trim the crusts from the bread. Spread each slice with about 2 teaspoons chutney butter, then lay a slice of chicken over half of the slices, cutting the chicken to fit neatly. Cover with the remaining bread slices, then cut the sandwiches diagonally into quarters. Insert the stem of a sprig of watercress inside each sandwich, allowing the sprig to stick out decoratively. (Can assemble up to 2 hours ahead. Arrange on a platter, cover with lightly dampened toweling, then wrap in plastic and refrigerate.)

3. When ready to serve, garnish platter lavishly with additional watercress sprigs.

Irish Oat Scones with Damson Plum Jam

Rolled oats lend a sweet, nutty flavor, pleasantly chewy texture, and a beautiful pale buff color in this scone recipe. The secret to making feather-light scones is to work the dough as little as possible.

MAKES ABOUT 50 SCONES

2	cups all-purpose flour
1	cup quick rolled oats (see Note)
1	tablespoon baking powder
2	teaspoons sugar
¾	teaspoon salt
6	tablespoons (¾ stick) chilled unsalted butter
2	eggs
¾	cup milk
	Butter
	Damson plum jam, or other jam of choice

1. Preheat the oven to 400° F.

2. In a bowl, combine the flour, oats, baking powder, sugar, and salt. Stir well to combine. Cut the butter into about 10 pieces and work into the flour with your fingertips until the mixture resembles coarse meal.

3. In a small bowl, whisk together the eggs and milk. Add to the dry ingredients and mix just until the dough begins to come together. Turn out onto a floured board and knead a few turns until a smooth dough forms. Roll or pat out to a thickness of ½ inch. Use a 1½-inch cutter to cut out scones, placing them ¾ inch apart on an ungreased baking sheet. Reroll and cut scraps.

4. Bake in the preheated oven for 12 to 15 minutes, until scones are a speckled light golden brown. (Can be made several hours ahead. Reheat in a 400° F. oven for 5 minutes before serving.)

5. To serve, split scones, spread with butter and jam, and replace tops. Arrange on a platter or in a napkin-lined basket.

Note: Use quick or 1-minute rolled oats in this recipe. Do not use regular old-fashioned rolled oats or instant oatmeal.

Lemon Tartlets in Walnut Pastry

Lemon curd is versatile and easy to make. This tart/sweet rich lemon custard is an elegant tartlet filling and just as good spread on morning toast. The crisp, slightly bitter walnut pastry is a particularly nice foil for the sweet filling. Tiny, 2-bite tartlet molds are available in most specialty stores.

MAKES 28 TO 32 TARTLETS

Lemon Curd Filling

3	eggs
3	egg yolks
1¼	cups sugar
1	tablespoon grated lemon zest
½	cup lemon juice
⅛	teaspoon salt
¼	cup (½ stick) unsalted butter, cut into 6 pieces

Walnut Pastry

⅓	cup walnut pieces
1½	cups all-purpose flour, divided
½	teaspoon salt
½	cup (1 stick) cold unsalted butter, cut into 12 pieces
¼	cup ice water, approximately

Garnish

Candied Fresh Violets (recipe follows)

1.   To make the filling, whisk the whole eggs, yolks, and sugar together in a heavy, non-reactive saucepan until thick and lemon-colored. Whisk in the lemon zest, juice, and salt. Add the butter. Cook over medium-low heat, stirring constantly with a wooden spoon, until steam rises from the custard and it is close to the boiling point, 6 to 8 minutes. It will be very smooth and thick. Force through a strainer into a bowl. Cover and refrigerate at least 2 hours until cold, or up to 3 days. (Curd can be frozen up to 2 weeks.)

2.   To make the pastry, place the walnuts and ¼ cup of the flour in work bowl of a food processor and pulse until nuts are finely ground but not pasty. Remove and set aside. Without washing work bowl, add remaining 1¼ cups flour and salt, then pulse to combine. Distribute butter over flour and pulse until mixture resembles small peas. Pulse in ground nuts just until blended. With motor running, add water through feed tube and pulse just until dough begins to clump together. If it seems too dry, add additional water by teaspoons. Gather pastry into ball, flatten into a disk, wrap in plastic, and freeze about 20 minutes to firm it up. (Dough can also be refrigerated at least 45 minutes or up to 2 days before rolling, or can be frozen up to 2 weeks.)

3.   Working with half of the pastry at a time, roll out on a lightly floured surface to approximately 1/16 inch thick. Cut out pieces to fit the shapes of small, 1½- to 2-inch tartlet molds. Ease dough into molds, press against sides, then trim flush with top. Prick 2 or 3 times with a fork, then place shells on a baking sheet and set in the freezer for 30 minutes or up to 2 weeks.

4.   Preheat the oven to 450° F. degrees. Bake
[c o n t i n u e d]

tartlet shells, directly from the freezer, for 10 to 12 minutes, until lightly browned around the edges and light golden in the center. Using a pot holder to protect your hands, invert tartlets and remove pastry from pans. Cool completely on a rack. (Can be made a day ahead. Store covered at room temperature.)

5. To assemble, spoon about 1 tablespoon lemon curd into each tartlet shell. Garnish each with a single candied violet. Serve immediately or refrigerate, lightly covered, up to 3 hours.

Candied Fresh Violets

Of course, you can buy candied violets, but it is fun to make them yourself. Instead of the usual brushing with egg white and then dipping in sugar, we have devised a far easier method. It also works for tiny pansies.

MAKES ABOUT 40 CANDIED VIOLETS

1   cup granulated sugar
⅓   cup water
About 40 fresh, unsprayed violets or tiny pansies

1. Bring the sugar and water to a rolling boil over medium heat, stirring constantly to dissolve sugar. Cover pan and cook 30 seconds, then uncover and boil for 1 minute. Remove from heat, pour into a heatproof bowl, and let cool until tepid.

2. Place a metal rack over a sheet of wax paper to catch drips. Cut the violets so that there is a 1-inch length of stem. Holding by the stem, gently submerge the violet flower in the syrup. Remove and allow excess to drip back into pan. Set flowers on the rack and let dry for at least 12 hours, turning by the stem a couple of times to promote even drying and keep blossoms from sticking to the rack. When dry, the violets will still be slightly sticky, but prettily glazed. (Can be made several days ahead and stored, uncovered, at cool dry room temperature.)

3. You will have extra sugar syrup, which can be stored indefinitely in a tightly covered container, then rewarmed and used again. If crystals form, bring back a boil to dissolve them, then cool and proceed as directed.

Coconut Raspberry Shower Cake

This elegant cake, frosted with whipped cream and crowned with a shower of snowy white shredded coconut, looks glorious—and tastes wonderful. Inside is a triple-layer coconut-enriched yellow butter cake filled with raspberry jam. At this time of year, we like to decorate desserts with edible fresh flowers.

MAKES 16 TO 20 SERVINGS

Cake

1	cup flaked or shredded sweetened coconut
1¼	cups milk
3	cups cake flour
1	tablespoon baking powder
½	teaspoon salt
1	cup (2 sticks) unsalted butter, softened
2	cups sugar
4	eggs, separated
1	teaspoon vanilla extract
½	teaspoon almond extract

Coconut-Almond Cream

2	cups chilled heavy cream
½	cup confectioners' sugar
½	teaspoon almond extract
1	cup flaked or shredded sweetened coconut

Filling

⅔	cup all-fruit (no sugar added) raspberry preserves
	Edible unsprayed spring flowers such as pansies for decoration

1. To make the cake, heat the coconut and milk to a simmer in a saucepan. Remove from heat and let steep for at least 30 minutes. Strain into a bowl, pressing on coconut to extract all liquid. Measure out and reserve 1 cup coconut milk, adding more milk if necessary. Discard the coconut.

2. Preheat the oven to 350° F. and butter three 9-inch cake pans. Line bottoms of pans with parchment or wax paper. Sift together the flour, baking powder, and salt. Set aside.

3. With an electric mixer, cream the butter with the sugar until fluffy. Beat in the egg yolks, 1 at a time. Beat in the vanilla and almond extracts. Add the milk and dry ingredients alternately, in thirds, mixing the batter only until just blended.

4. In a clean bowl with clean beaters, beat the egg whites to firm but not dry peaks. Stir about one-third of the whites into the batter to lighten it; then fold batter and whites together. Batter will be quite thick. Divide evenly among the 3 pans, smoothing to even.

5. Bake in the preheated oven for 25 to 28 minutes, until the layers test done in the center. Cool in the pans on a rack for 10 minutes, then turn cakes out onto racks to cool completely. (Can be made 2 weeks ahead and frozen. Thaw in wrappings before proceeding.)

6. To make the coconut-almond cream, whip the cream to soft peaks. Beat in the sugar and almond extract and continue beating to stiff peaks. Use within about an hour.

[c o n t i n u e d]

7. To assemble cake, trim layers by cutting off any domes with a serrated knife to make them as flat and even as possible. Spread half of the filling on each of 2 layers and stack the cake. Spread top and sides with the coconut-almond cream, making a smooth, even layer, and sprinkle coconut over sides and top. Refrigerate uncovered until serving time. (Can be frosted 6 hours ahead. Remove from refrigerator about 1 hour before serving.) Decorate with fresh flowers if desired.

8. To serve, cut with a long serrated knife.

Mocha Wafers

Though heart-shaped cookies are especially pretty for a bridal tea, this dark chocolate dough is equally delicious as circles, squares, or even reindeers.

MAKES ABOUT 4 DOZEN

1½	ounces unsweetened chocolate
½	teaspoon instant coffee or espresso powder
1	teaspoon Kahlúa or water
6	tablespoons (¾ stick) unsalted butter
¼	cup light brown sugar
⅓	cup granulated sugar
1	egg
1	teaspoon vanilla extract
1	cup all-purpose flour
½	teaspoon baking powder
¼	teaspoon baking soda
	Pinch salt

1. Melt the chocolate in a microwave oven or in a small pan set over hot water. Cool to lukewarm. Dissolve the coffee in the Kahlúa.

2. In a food processor or an electric mixer, cream the butter with both sugars until smooth. Add egg, vanilla, dissolved coffee, and melted chocolate. Process or beat until blended. Add the flour, baking powder, soda, and salt. (If making in a mixer, whisk or sift these dry ingredients together first.) Process or beat until smooth and a stiff dough forms. Gather into a ball, flatten into a disk, wrap in plastic, and freeze about 30 minutes to firm up. (Dough can also be refrigerated for at least 2 hours or up to 2 days, or frozen up to 2 weeks.)

3. When ready to bake, preheat oven to 375° F. Lightly flour a work surface and a rolling pin. Working with half of the dough at a time, roll ⅛ inch thick. Cut with 2-inch heart-shaped cookie cutter or other shapes of your choice. Chill and reroll scraps once. Place cookies about 1 inch apart on ungreased baking sheets. Bake in the center of the oven for 7 to 9 minutes, until gentle pressure of a fingertip leaves no mark on the surface. Transfer to racks to cool completely. Store tightly covered up to 3 days. (Cookies can be frozen up to 2 weeks.)

WAY TO GO, MATT!

A Graduation Buffet
FOR 25

Carmen Miranda Fruit Punch   130

~

Shrimp with Spicy Red Sauce   131
Mrs. Robinson's Minipizzas   132
Crudité Assortment with Roasted Garlic Sauce   133

~

Texas-style Brisket   134
All-American Barbecue Sauce   135
Calico Coleslaw   136
Tomatoes and Sweet Onions with Gorgonzola Vinaigrette   137
Kaiser Rolls (NO RECIPE)

~

Carrot Cake with Lemon Cream Cheese Frosting   138
A Bowl of Cherries (NO RECIPE)

ETWEEN US, we've had five children graduate from high school in the past few years, so by now we consider ourselves quite the experts in commencement festivities. To celebrate these occasions, we always throw a party, each one designed to fit the personality of the graduate.

Matt wanted a big barbecue. Fortunately, the weather was perfect, for we had strung a giant congratulatory banner and tied bunches of helium baloons all over the backyard. Matt's school colors provided the decorating scheme carried out in tablecloths, plates, napkins, and even the flowers.

For a party like this, start with a fruit punch, colorful minipizzas, spicy shrimps, and vegetable munchies with a mellow garlic dipping sauce. Barbecued brisket sends out an irresistible aroma that invariably brings them to the table at the first call. Young and old love the combination of smoky meat and spicy sauce on big, soft rolls. Bowls of coleslaw and a platter of sliced tomatoes and sweet onions are the natural accompaniments to this main course.

For Matt's party, we naturally honored his request for his favorite homemade carrot cake, and added our proud, heartfelt, handwritten message: "Way to go, Matt!"

For all of our favorite graduates, we can't resist the edible metaphor of a giant bowl of sweet cherries. On this big day, life is just that!

In Advance

GRADUATION DAY (or the day of any big party for that matter) is busy enough without having to worry about much last-minute cooking, so we planned this menu to be as deliciously trouble-free as possible.

A couple of weeks before the party the cake can be baked, frosted, decorated, and then frozen. You can make the barbecue sauce and the spice mixture for the brisket then, too.

Two days ahead, make the punch base, the spicy red sauce for the shrimp, the roasted garlic dip, and the Gorgonzola dressing.

The day before the party, cook and slice the brisket. Make the coleslaw, cook the shrimp, and cook the bacon for the pizzas. You can prepare the vegetables for the crudités

late in the day if you wrap them in damp paper towels or seal in plastic bags with a couple of ice cubes added.

On the day of the party, assemble the pita pizzas, split the rolls, and slice the fruit for the punch. Slice the tomatoes and onions for the salad.

Shortly before the party, reheat the brisket and the sauce. Assemble the hors d'oeuvre platters, and finish the punch.

Way to go, mom and dad!

If Time Is Short ...

☛ Omit the punch and offer a pitcher of fresh fruit juice and a plate of cut-up tropical fruits along with an assortment of soft drinks.

☛ Call ahead and ask your fishmonger to shell and devein the shrimp, or buy good-quality frozen ready-to-cook shrimp.

☛ Some specialty food shops sell excellent ready-made fresh cocktail and barbecue sauces.

☛ Order the cake from someone who has a reputation for both expert baking and talented decorating.

Carmen Miranda Fruit Punch

Tea lends an intriguing flavor to this light, fruity punch, which is garnished with all the wonderful, colorful tropical fruits that you might find decorating Carmen Miranda's famous hat. It yields about 40 small cups, so you'll need to offer other soft drinks, too, or double the recipe.

MAKES 5 QUARTS

Fruit and Tea Base
6	tea bags
6	cups boiling water
1	cup sugar
½	cup lemon juice
½	cup grenadine syrup

Punch Assembly and Garnish
2	quarts 7-Up
1	quart club soda
	A selection of some of the following: sliced strawberries, citrus fruits, kiwi, guava, star fruit, bananas, pineapple, or maraschino cherries

1.   To make the base, tie the tea bags together, pour boiling water over them, and let steep in a nonreactive saucepan or large bowl for 5 minutes. Remove tea bags, add sugar, and stir until it dissolves completely. Cool to room temperature and stir in the lemon juice and grenadine. (Can be made 2 days ahead. Cover and refrigerate.)

2.   When ready to make the punch, pour base into a large glass pitcher or punch bowl. Add ice and pour in the sodas. Float fruit in the punch.

3.   Pour or ladle into small punch cups to serve.

Shrimp with Spicy Red Sauce

For this occasion, buy as many shrimp as you can afford!

MAKES ABOUT 25 SERVINGS

Spicy Red Sauce
2	cups chili sauce
¼	cup grated fresh horseradish, or drained prepared horseradish
3	tablespoons minced parsley
2	tablespoons minced shallots
2	teaspoons lemon juice
¾	teaspoon Tabasco, or to taste

Shrimp:
1	tablespoon salt
4	peppercorns
3	slices lemon
50 to 75	medium or large shrimp (2½ to 3 pounds)
	Parsley sprigs and lemon wedges for garnish

1. To make the sauce, combine all the ingredients in a bowl. Cover and refrigerate for at least 2 hours to develop flavors. (Can be made 2 days ahead. Remove from refrigerator 1 hour before serving.)

2. Bring a large pot of water to the boil. Add salt, peppercorns, lemon slices, and the shrimp. Cook for about 3 minutes, or until shrimp turn pink. Drain into a colander and run under cold water to stop the cooking. Peel and devein the shrimp, leaving the tails on if possible. Transfer to a bowl, cover, and refrigerate. (Can be prepared a day ahead.)

3. Heap the shrimp on a rimmed platter and place a bowl of the cocktail sauce alongside. Garnish with parsley and lemon wedges.

Mrs. Robinson's Minipizzas

Split pita breads make a terrific pizza base, and Mrs. Robinson's topping combination of bacon, cheese, and tomato is sure to please everyone.

MAKES ABOUT 80 WEDGES

1	pound thin-sliced bacon
8	6- or 7-inch pita breads
5 or 6	plum tomatoes, very thinly sliced
1	red onion, peeled, thinly sliced into rings, and separated
1½	cups grated sharp Cheddar cheese
1½	cups grated Monterey Jack cheese
⅓	cup slivered fresh basil
½	teaspoon dried red pepper flakes
¼	cup olive oil

1.   Cook the bacon in a skillet over medium-low heat until crisp. Drain on paper towels and chop into approximately ¾-inch pieces. (Can be done a day ahead. Refrigerate.)

2.   Split the pitas by using a serrated knife to cut all the way around the perimeter of each bread. Arrange, cut sides up, on baking sheets and toast under broiler for 1 or 2 minutes until just barely colored.

3.   Divide tomatoes and onion slices among the rounds and sprinkle with the chopped bacon.

4.   In a small bowl, combine the cheeses, basil, and pepper flakes. Divide mixture among the rounds. (Can be prepared several hours ahead. Cover and refrigerate.)

5.   Preheat the broiler. Drizzle pizzas with the olive oil, place about 5 inches from the heat source, and broil for 1 or 2 minutes, until cheese is bubbly and edges are browned.

6.   Cut each round into 4 or 6 wedges, arrange on a napkin-lined platter, and pass.

Crudité Assortment with Roasted Garlic Sauce

Slow-roasting a whole head of garlic tames its bite and melts the cloves into a sweet, mellow purée. Use a toaster oven for the roasting if you have one.

MAKES 25 HORS D'OEUVRE SERVINGS

Roasted Garlic Dip

1	whole head garlic
2	teaspoons olive oil
1½	cups commercial mayonnaise
1½	cups sour cream
1	tablespoon coarse-grain mustard
¾	teaspoon freshly ground black pepper
½	teaspoon salt
¼	cup minced parsley
1	tablespoon chopped fresh thyme

Crudité Assortment

Red, green, and yellow peppers, cut in strips
Celery sticks
Cucumber slices
Radishes
Fennel sticks
Carrot sticks
Jicama sticks

1. Cut the top quarter off the head of garlic. Place on a sheet of foil, drizzle with the oil, and wrap in the foil, crimping edges to seal. Place on a baking sheet and roast in a 250° F. oven for 2 hours, until garlic cloves are golden brown and very soft. When cool enough to handle, squeeze garlic out of skin and mash to a purée with a fork.

2. In a bowl, combine the mayonnaise, sour cream, mustard, pepper, and salt. Add the garlic purée and whisk until well blended. Stir in the parsley and thyme. (Dip can be made 2 days ahead.)

3. When ready to serve, arrange vegetables of your choice on a large platter and place a bowl of the dip in the center. (Can be assembled several hours ahead. Cover vegetables with damp paper towels, then wrap in plastic wrap and refrigerate.)

Texas-style Brisket

Beef brisket is one of the tastiest cuts of meat around. The trick to it is lengthy cooking until it becomes "falling-apart" fork tender. If you have a smoker or a covered barbecue grill, you can cook the meat outdoors, but our oven method requires far less watching, and the brief grilling at the end imparts a richly charred coating and smoky flavor. Either way, the brisket and the tangy sauce can be completely prepared ahead. For outdoor cooking instructions, see the note at the end of the recipe.

MAKES 24 TO 30 SERVINGS

Spice Mixture

¼	cup chili powder
2	tablespoons salt
2	tablespoons paprika
4	teaspoons garlic powder
4	teaspoons freshly ground black pepper
2	teaspoons cayenne
2	teaspoons white pepper
1	teaspoon ground cumin
2	whole briskets, about 8 pounds each
1	recipe All-American Barbecue Sauce (page 135)
30 to 40	kaiser rolls, split

1. Combine the chili powder, salt, paprika, garlic powder, three peppers, and the cumin. (Can be done several weeks ahead. Store tightly covered at room temperature.)

2. Rub the spice mixture liberally onto all sides of the briskets so that they are completely coated. Let stand 1 or 2 hours at room temperature, or refrigerate up to 24 hours, but bring back to room temperature before cooking.

3. To prepare indoors, preheat oven to 325° F. Wrap meat in heavy-duty aluminum foil and place in a shallow pan on a rack over about ¼ inch of water. Bake for 5 to 6 hours, until meat is very tender, adding water to the pan as necessary.

4. Build a medium barbecue fire. Unwrap meat and grill 10 to 15 minutes per side until charred on the outside.

5. Let meat stand for about 15 minutes, then slice thinly across the grain. (Can be prepared to this point a day ahead. Put meat slices, all juices, and about ½ cup water in a large baking pan. Coat with about 1 cup barbecue sauce. Cover with foil and refrigerate. To reheat, return to room temperature. Bake, covered, in a 300° F. oven for about 1 hour, until hot. Add small amounts of water or sauce if meat seems to be getting dry.)

6. Shortly before serving, heat the barbecue sauce just to a simmer. Transfer the meat to a platter and put the rolls in a basket alongside. Guests make their own sandwiches by piling the meat and a spoonful of sauce into the rolls.

Note: To cook on a smoker, follow manufacturer's directions for brisket. To cook on a covered grill, build an indirect charcoal fire and soak several handfuls of mesquite or hickory chips in water for at least 15 minutes. Place a shallow pan of water under the grill grids where the meat will be placed. Let the fire die back so that it is not fiery hot. Toss some of the wood chips onto the fire. Place the meat above the water pan. Cover the grill and smoke the meat for 3 hours, adding coals and wet chips as needed to maintain a temperature of approximately 190 to 220° F. After 3 hours, wrap the meat in heavy-duty aluminum foil and continue to smoke for an additional 3 to 4 hours until the meat is very tender.

All-American Barbecue Sauce

This wonderful barbecue sauce keeps well in the refrigerator. We like to have it on hand all summer for chicken, burgers, and pork chops, as well as brisket.

MAKES ABOUT 7 CUPS, ENOUGH FOR 24 TO 30 SERVINGS

6	tablespoons vegetable oil
2	large onions, peeled and finely chopped
4	cloves garlic, peeled and minced
4	teaspoons dry mustard
2	teaspoons paprika
½	teaspoon cayenne
2	cups ketchup
2	cups chili sauce
½	cup molasses
6	tablespoons Worcestershire sauce
¼	cup cider vinegar
¼	cup lemon juice
2	bay leaves, broken in half
1½	cups (12 ounces) beer
2	tablespoons bourbon whiskey

1. Heat the oil in a large nonaluminum saucepan. Add the onions and garlic and sauté over medium-low heat for about 5 minutes until the onion is softened. Stir in the mustard, paprika, and cayenne and cook 1 minute. Add the remaining ingredients and stir to blend well. Simmer gently, uncovered, stirring often, for 20 to 25 minutes.

2. Use the sauce immediately or let cool, then cover and refrigerate for up to 2 weeks before using.

Calico Coleslaw

This is our favorite creamy coleslaw recipe and is, we think, a perfect accompaniment for barbecued ribs or chicken as well as brisket.

MAKES ABOUT 12 CUPS, OR ABOUT 25 SERVINGS

Creamy Dressing

1½	cups mayonnaise
½	cup sour cream
2	tablespoons red wine vinegar
¼	cup grated onion
2	tablespoons sugar
1½	tablespoons Dijon mustard
2	teaspoons salt
½	teaspoon freshly ground black pepper

Vegetables

2½	pounds green cabbage (about 1 large head)
½	pound red cabbage (about ½ small head)
1	large carrot
	Outer leaves of red and green cabbage for garnish

1. To make the dressing, whisk all ingredients together. (Can be made 1 day ahead. If planning to use immediately, whisk in bowl in which coleslaw will be made.)

2. Thinly slice the green and red cabbage and grate the carrot

3. Toss the vegetables with the dressing. Cover and refrigerate at least 2 hours or up to 12 hours.

4. Serve from a decorative bowl lined with red and green cabbage leaves, if desired.

Tomatoes and Sweet Onions with Gorgonzola Vinaigrette

Use mild, sweet onions such as Vidalias for this salad. If none are available, red onion is a fine substitute.

MAKES 25 SERVINGS

Gorgonzola Vinaigrette
- ½   cup white wine vinegar
- 1   cup olive oil
- 1   cup crumbled Gorgonzola
- ¼   cup minced parsley
- ¾   teaspoon coarsely ground black pepper

Tomato and Sweet Onion Salad
- 8   cups torn romaine leaves
- 6   large meaty tomatoes, 8 to 10 ounces each
- 2   large sweet onions, peeled and sliced
  Flat-leaf parsley sprigs

1. To make the dressing, whisk all the ingredients together in a bowl. (Can be made 2 days ahead. Cover and refrigerate.)
2. For the salad, spread the lettuce out onto 1 very large platter or 2 smaller platters. Slice the tomatoes and arrange in overlapping rows over the lettuce. Separate the onion into rings and arrange over the tomatoes. (Can be made several hours ahead. Cover and refrigerate.)
3. Just before serving, drizzle with the Gorgonzola dressing and garnish platter with sprigs of parsley.

Way to Go, Matt!

137

Carrot Cake with Lemon Cream Cheese Frosting

You're never too old to eat your carrots and this is a delicious way to obey mom. If you wish to make a smaller dessert, simply halve all the ingredients and bake in one 9- by 13-inch pan.

MAKES 24 TO 30 SERVINGS

Cake

4	cups all-purpose flour
1	tablespoon baking powder
1	tablespoon baking soda
1	tablespoon cinnamon
1	teaspoon salt
1	teaspoon ground nutmeg
1	teaspoon ground ginger
2¼	cups granulated sugar
1	cup light brown sugar
8	eggs
1	tablespoon vanilla extract
1	tablespoon grated orange zest
1½	teaspoons grated lemon zest
2	tablespoons orange juice
2	tablespoons lemon juice
1	cup (2 sticks) unsalted butter, melted and cooled
1	cup vegetable oil
5	cups (about 1½ pounds) grated carrots
2	cups chopped walnuts
¾	cup currants, optional

Lemon Cream Cheese Frosting

19	ounces cream cheese, softened
1⅛	cups (2 sticks plus 2 tablespoons) unsalted butter, softened
1	tablespoon grated lemon zest
1	tablespoon lemon juice
1	tablespoon vanilla extract
9	cups confectioners' sugar

Decoration

1	cup chopped walnuts
	Purchased decorator icing, optional
	Purchased marzipan carrots, optional

1.   To make the cake, preheat the oven to 350° F. Butter two 9- by 13-inch baking pans. Line bottoms with parchment or wax paper.

2.   Sift together the flour, baking powder, baking soda, cinnamon, salt, nutmeg, and ginger. In a large bowl of an electric mixer, beat together both sugars and the eggs for 3 to 4 minutes, until fluffy and nearly doubled in volume. Beat in the vanilla, orange and lemon zests, and orange and lemon juices. Beat in the butter and oil. Add the flour mixture and beat just until blended and smooth. (If your mixer bowl is quite full, you may need to transfer to a larger bowl at this point.) By hand, stir in the carrots, nuts, and currants.

3.   Divide the batter between the 2 pans, spreading evenly. Bake for 40 to 50 minutes, until cake begins to pull away from sides of pans and a toothpick inserted in the center comes out clean. (If you are baking both cakes in the same oven, reverse positions on racks after 35 minutes.) Cool in pans on racks for 10 minutes. Run a knife around the edge of the pans to loosen the cakes, then invert to remove from pans. Carefully peel off parchment paper and invert again so cakes are right side up. Cool completely. (Can be made 3 weeks ahead, wrapped, and frozen.)

4.   To make the frosting, beat the cream cheese and butter together until fluffy. Beat in the zest, lemon juice, and vanilla, then gradually beat in confectioners' sugar until smooth and spreadable.

5. To assemble, place cakes side by side, touching, on a large board. Frost top and sides so that they become 1 sheet cake. Press chopped nuts onto sides of cake. Top of cake can be decorated with names or other designs using decorator icing and/or marzipan carrots. If cake is not to be decorated, save some of the nuts to sprinkle on top. (Cake can be assembled and frosted a day ahead and refrigerated, or up to 2 weeks ahead and frozen. To freeze frosted cakes successfully, place, unwrapped, in the freezer for about 2 hours until frosting is very firm, stick toothpicks in the cake to protect frosting, then wrap in foil.)

SUMMER

Happy Fortieth Anniversary

Ravinia Picnic

Mediterranean Grill

Summer Whites

Ice Cream Social

The Family Reunion

HAPPY FORTIETH ANNIVERSARY

A Summertime Jubilee
BUFFET FOR 30 TO 35

ALWAYS READY for an excuse to have a party, even Brooke was a bit in awe of this event. Her parents' fortieth anniversary, 4 children spread out from Maine to Alaska, and 9 grandchildren—definitely something to celebrate!

The party would be at Brooke's house, so she was the person to send out the invitations, rent the plates and glassware, and plan grocery lists. Martha, her nearest sister, drove down a few days ahead and plunged into the actual food preparation, while Valerie and Kirby came from the West Coast in time to set up the tables, do some last-minute cooking, and buy the Champagne.

The day came, the weather was glorious, and the party began outdoors with a lovely pastel wine punch cooled with a fabulous rose-filled ice block. Platters of delectable finger-sized hors d'oeuvres were passed by the older kids while a little of the big band sound drifted in the background.

The buffet table, indoors, was laden with cold foods as eclectic as the gathering. A platter of delicate stuffed chicken breast slices and shallow bowls of brightly hued salads highlighted the herbs from Brooke's garden.

After giving a lot of thought to having a bakery make the cake, Brooke decided to undertake this project as a creative labor of love, and the result, in its handmade simplicity, was even more spectacular than she had hoped. A glass bowl filled with strawberry mousse added an old-fashioned yet light contemporary touch to the dessert table.

Though planned for an important anniversary party, the easy-to-prepare and do-ahead qualities of this menu make it equally appealing for a wedding supper, a graduation gala, or anytime a summer celebration is in order.

In Advance

EVEN THOUGH this menu is lengthy, it is doable without help. Nearly every dish can be made in advance, and since all the food except the crab cakes is served cold or at room temperature, there is virtually nothing in the way of last-minute cooking.

As soon as you finalize the menu and guest list, take stock of your china, linen, glassware, and silver, and then rent or borrow whatever you need to supplement it. Also well in advance, tidy up the garden (if you're planning to use a yard) and plant a few pretty flowers.

Two weeks before the party, make and freeze the filled and frosted cake layers and the dinner rolls. Shop for all the nonperishable food and paper goods, and order the wine and liquor.

A week beforehand, make the strawberry meringue mousse, the crab cakes, and the ice block for the punch, adding them to your freezer stash. Make the green tapenade and keep it in the refrigerator. Order the boned chicken breasts.

Two days ahead, cook the beef for the salad, make the basil ricotta filling for the chicken breasts, and make the salad dressings and the tarragon mayonnaise.

The day before the party, assemble and decorate the cake, and since it takes up a good deal of room, you might want to beg space in a neighbor's refrigerator. You can also stuff the chicken breasts and make the couscous salad. The beef can be sliced and the snow peas blanched for the Thai beef salad.

Now, on the big day, all you really have to do is assemble the beef salad, slice the tomatoes and the melon, and cook the chicken breasts. Thaw the frozen items. The cake needs only the final decoration of fresh flowers. At the last minute, you have only to heat the crab cakes.

If Time Is Short ...

☞ Instead of roasting or grilling the fillet for the Thai beef salad, buy good-quality rare roast beef from a take-out shop.

☞ Buy the dinner rolls from a good bakery.

☞ Order the cake from a bakery, or hire a talented friend to create one for you.

☞ Omit the rose ice block from the punch and add ice cubes at the last minute. Garnish with rose petals or a rose blossom.

☞ Substitute a big bowl of sliced, lightly sweetened strawberries for the strawberry meringue mousse.

Rose Petal Wine Punch

This sophisticated wine punch, lightly scented with both rosewater and the raspberry essence of framboise, makes a spectacular presentation in a crystal punch bowl with an easy-to-make but stunningly beautiful rose-filled block of ice floating in the center.

MAKES ABOUT 35 SERVINGS

For the ice block

3   unsprayed, partially opened full-size roses (pink, yellow, or peach color) with 6-inch stems, rinsed

For the punch

16   cups dry white wine, chilled
1   cup framboise
2   teaspoons rosewater (see Note)

Small unsprayed rose petals and leaves, rinsed and dried, for garnish

1.   To make the ice block, rinse out a half-gallon cardboard milk or juice carton. Cut off the top and trim sides to about 7 inches. Place roses in carton. Fill to within 1 inch of the top with boiled and cooled or distilled water. Freeze at least 24 hours or until solid. (Can be made a couple of weeks ahead.)

2.   To make the punch, combine the wine, framboise, and rosewater in a large punch bowl. Remove the cardboard from the ice block and float the cube in the center of the punch. Sprinkle small rose petals and leaves on top of the punch, if desired.

Note: Rosewater is available at specialty food stores, some grocery stores, and at well-stocked pharmacies. Airtight, it will keep nearly forever. Commonly used in Middle Eastern cooking, it can be added very sparingly to plain cake batters or custards for an elusive, exotic flavor.

Melon with Cracked Black Pepper

Guests can use their fingers to pick up a wedge, or, if you prefer, the melon can be cut in cubes and skewered with toothpicks.

MAKES 1 LARGE PLATTER

1 honeydew melon, ripe but firm
1 cantaloupe, ripe but firm
  Coarse salt
  Cracked black pepper

1. Halve and seed melons, remove rinds, and cut into slim wedges. Arrange overlapping on a large flat platter. (Can be prepared 2 hours ahead. Wrap and refrigerate.)
2. Just before serving, sprinkle lightly with salt and generously with cracked or coarsely ground black pepper.

Tiny Crab Cakes with Tarragon Mayonnaise

Lump crabmeat from Chesapeake Bay is unbeatable for flavor, but we also like these authentically seasoned crab cakes with other good-quality crab.

MAKES ABOUT 50 HORS D'OEUVRES

Tarragon Mayonnaise
¾ cup mayonnaise
2 tablespoons chopped fresh tarragon leaves, or 2 teaspoons dried tarragon
1 teaspoon lemon juice

Crab Cakes
2 eggs
2½ cups fresh white bread crumbs
⅓ cup minced scallions, white and green parts
2 tablespoons mayonnaise
2 teaspoons lemon juice
1 teaspoon Worcestershire sauce
½ teaspoon Old Bay Seasoning or other Maryland seafood seasoning mix
¾ teaspoon dry mustard

¼ teaspoon cayenne
12 to 16 ounces Maryland lump crabmeat, picked over, or two 6½-ounce cans crabmeat, drained and picked over
¼ cup vegetable oil

Fresh tarragon springs, optional garnish

1. To make the tarragon mayonnaise, mix together all ingredients. Refrigerate at least 4 hours or up to 3 days.
2. To make the crab cakes, in a large mixing bowl beat the eggs, then add 1½ cups of the bread crumbs, the scallions, mayonnaise, lemon juice, Worcestershire sauce, Old Bay Seasoning, mustard, and cayenne. Blend well.

[c o n t i n u e d]

Add the crabmeat and mix carefully with your hands, taking care not to break up the crab too much.

3. Form into about 50 tiny patties, using a scant tablespoon for each patty. Place remaining 1 cup crumbs on a plate and lightly dip each side of the patties in the crumbs. (Can be made 1 day ahead and refrigerated.)

4. Heat half the oil in a large skillet. Sauté as many crab cakes as will comfortably fit in the skillet over medium heat for about 2 minutes per side until rich golden brown and crisp.

Place in a single layer on a foil-lined baking sheet. Repeat to sauté remaining crab cakes, adding more oil as needed. (Can be made 1 day ahead and refrigerated or frozen for 1 week.)

5. If crab cakes are made ahead, remove from refrigerator or freezer and let stand 30 minutes, then heat in a 350° F. oven for about 5 minutes until hot and crisp. Place on a platter and dab about ¼ teaspoon tarragon mayonnaise atop each. Garnish with fresh tarragon sprigs, if available.

Green Tapenade on Toasts

Tapenade, traditionally made with black olives, is a delightfully potent Provençal spread. We have left out the usual capers, as we find this lovely green version has plenty of flavor without them.

MAKES ¾ CUP, FOR ABOUT 50 HORS D'OEUVRES

1	4-ounce jar pitted green olives
½	cup parsley sprigs, preferably flat leaf
1	large clove garlic, peeled
2	anchovy fillets
1	teaspoon lemon juice
½	teaspoon freshly ground black pepper
¼	cup olive oil
50	small (1½-inch) unsalted melba rounds
	Leaves of flat-leaf parsley

1. Place olives in a strainer. Rinse well under cold water and drain.

2. Combine the olives, parsley, garlic, anchovies, lemon juice, and pepper in a food processor. Pulse to coarsely purée. With the motor running, pour the oil through the feed tube until a thick paste is formed. (Can be made 1 week ahead.)

3. Spread about ¾ teaspoon of tapenade on each melba toast. Arrange on a tray and decorate each round with a single parsley leaf. (Assemble no more than 1 hour before serving.) Alternatively, put out a bowl of tapenade and surround with melba toasts.

Chicken Breasts Stuffed with Basil Ricotta

This ricotta-stuffed chicken is perfect for any summer buffet. It can be made ahead, it's simple to assemble, looks beautiful on the table, and *tastes delicious!*

MAKES 35 BUFFET SERVINGS OR 12 REGULAR MAIN COURSE SERVINGS

1⅓	cups ricotta cheese
½	cup grated Parmesan cheese
⅓	cup minced scallions, including green tops
⅓	cup slivered fresh basil
⅓	cup chopped parsley
1	teaspoon salt
½	teaspoon freshly ground black pepper
½	teaspoon grated nutmeg
12	chicken breast halves (about 6 ounces each), boneless but with skin intact
3	tablespoons olive oil
	Additional salt and pepper
	Fresh basil sprigs for garnish

1. In a mixing bowl, combine the ricotta, Parmesan, scallions, basil, parsley, salt, pepper, and nutmeg. Mix thoroughly with a wooden spoon. (Can prepare 2 days ahead.)

2. Loosen the skin from 1 side of each chicken breast and insert about 1½ table-spoons of filling under the skin. Smooth skin around the filling and the meat, tucking the 2 ends under to form a rounded dome shape. Place side by side, close together, in an oiled 9- by 13-inch baking dish, drizzle with the olive oil, and sprinkle lightly with salt and pepper. (Can be prepared 1 day ahead. Cover and refrigerate.)

3. Preheat oven to 350° F. Uncover chicken and bake in the center of the oven for 35 to 40 minutes, until skin is lightly browned and juices run clear when pierced with a sharp knife. Baste once during the cooking time with pan juices. Cool for at least 15 minutes before slicing. (Can be baked 2 hours ahead. Hold at cool room temperature.)

4. Serve warm or at room temperature. Cut each breast crosswise into 3 slices and fan out on a serving platter. Garnish lavishly with basil.

Thai Beef and Snow Pea Salad

Strips of rosy rare beef and bright vegetables tossed with a pungent sesame-ginger dressing makes a beautiful presentation on the buffet. Although a whole tenderloin may sound extravagant, there is absolutely no waste with this fork-tender boneless cut. Any leftover dressing is good on a vegetable salad.

MAKES 35 BUFFET SERVINGS

Sesame-Ginger Dressing

1⅓	cups red wine vinegar
6	tablespoons soy sauce
1½	cups peanut or vegetable oil
1½	cups sesame oil
2	tablespoons minced fresh ginger
6	cloves garlic, peeled and minced
1¼	teaspoons dried red pepper flakes
1½	teaspoons freshly ground black pepper

Beef Salad

1	5- to 6-pound whole beef tenderloin, approximately 4 inches in diameter
6	tablespoons olive oil
	Salt and freshly ground black pepper
2	pounds snow peas, strings removed
⅔	cup sesame seeds
6	red bell peppers, cored, seeded, and thinly sliced
1	pound fresh mushrooms, sliced
1	head romaine lettuce

1. To make the dressing, thoroughly combine all ingredients in a large jar or plastic container. (Can be made 2 days ahead.)

2. To cook the meat, preheat the oven to 450° F. Rub the fillet with ¼ cup of the olive oil and sprinkle with salt and pepper. Place on a rack in a shallow pan and roast for 15 minutes. Drizzle with remaining 2 tablespoons of oil and continue roasting for about 20 minutes, or until the meat registers 120° (rare) on an instant-read meat thermometer. Remove to a platter and cool to room temperature. Or, grill the oiled meat over moderately hot coals for about 25 minutes, or until a meat thermometer registers rare. (Meat can be cooked 2 days ahead. Wrap and refrigerate.)

3. Cut the meat into ¼-inch slices, then stack the slices and cut into strips about ½ inch wide. Add any accumulated juices to the dressing. (Can be done 1 day ahead. Wrap and refrigerate.)

4. Bring a large pot of water to the boil. Blanch the snow peas for about 30 seconds, until they turn a bright green. Drain in a colander, refresh under cold running water, wrap in paper towels, and refrigerate until ready to use. (Can be prepared 1 day ahead.)

5. Toast the sesame seeds by stirring them in a skillet set over medium heat for 2 or 3 minutes, until golden and fragrant. (Can be prepared 1 day ahead.)

6. Combine beef, snow peas, red pepper strips, and sliced mushrooms in a large bowl. Drizzle with just enough dressing to coat, and toss gently. Sprinkle with about two-thirds of the sesame seeds and toss again. (Can be prepared 2 or 3 hours ahead.)

7. To serve, heap salad on a bed of romaine on a large platter. Drizzle with a little more dressing and sprinkle with remaining sesame seeds.

Couscous Garden Salad

Couscous is the tiny Moroccan semolina pasta that simply soaks in hot water to soften. If you can't get it, pastina or rice would make an excellent substitution. In this colorful salad the vegetables are cut into a small dice in keeping with the scale of the couscous and the salad is dressed with a green parsley and mint-scented vinaigrette.

MAKES 35 BUFFET SERVINGS

Mint-Parsley Vinaigrette

2	cups mint sprigs
1⅓	cups parsley sprigs
5	cloves garlic, peeled
6	tablespoons lemon juice
½	cup white wine vinegar
2	teaspoons salt
2	teaspoons freshly ground black pepper
2½	cups olive oil

Salad

2	teaspoons salt
5	cups instant couscous
3	cups chopped red onion
3	cups finely diced celery
3	cups finely diced carrots
3	cups finely diced zucchini
2½	cups sliced black olives
	Mint sprigs for garnish

1. To make the dressing, combine the mint, parsley, garlic, lemon juice, vinegar, salt, and pepper in a food processor. Pulse to blend. With motor running, slowly pour oil through the feed tube. (Can be made 1 day ahead.)

2. Bring 8½ cups water to the boil in a large saucepan. Add the salt and the couscous. Remove from heat and let stand for 6 minutes. Transfer to a bowl, fluffing couscous with a fork. Stir in chopped vegetables.

3. Pour dressing over couscous, stirring gently to blend. Refrigerate for at least 1 hour. (Can be made 8 hours ahead.)

4. To serve, transfer to a decorative bowl and garnish with mint sprigs.

Tomatoes with Oil, Vinegar, and Chives

5   pounds ripe tomatoes
¼   cup extra-virgin olive oil
2   tablespoons balsamic vinegar
      Salt and freshly ground pepper to taste
¼   cup snipped chives
      Chive flowers for garnish (optional)

1. Core tomatoes and cut into slices. Arrange fanned out on a large platter. (Can be sliced 2 to 3 hours ahead.)
2. When ready to serve, drizzle with the oil and vinegar, sprinkle with salt and pepper, and scatter chives over the tomatoes. Garnish with chive flowers if available.

Dinner Rolls

Use the recipe for Poppy Seed Pan Rolls, page 208, but omit the poppy seeds.

Strawberry Meringue Mousse

This mousse, one of our warm weather favorites, is especially light and airy with the pure essence of strawberry shining through. To ensure a stable meringue we use a variation on a cooked Italian—style meringue. Before beginning the recipe, check the note at the end for an explanation of this method.

MAKES ABOUT 35 BUFFET SERVINGS OR 12 TO 16 REGULAR SERVINGS

¼   cup orange juice
1   tablespoon lemon juice
2   envelopes unflavored gelatin
3   pints fresh strawberries
1⅓   cups granulated sugar
½   cup Grand Marnier or other orange liqueur
6   egg whites
1   cup heavy cream, chilled
      Mint sprigs for garnish

1. Combine orange and lemon juices in a small bowl. Sprinkle gelatin over and let soften for at least 5 minutes.
2. Set aside 8 of the prettiest berries, preferably ones with stems, for the decoration. Purée remaining berries in a food processor. You should have about 3 cups purée. Set aside 2 cups. Combine remaining 1 cup purée with ⅔ cup sugar in a saucepan. Cook over low heat, stirring often, until mixture just begins to simmer and sugar is dissolved. Remove from heat.

3. Scrape softened gelatin into the hot berry mixture and stir until dissolved. Stir in remaining 2 cups berry purée and the Grand Marnier. Pour into a large mixing bowl and refrigerate, stirring often, for 30 to 40 minutes, or until mixture mounds softly when dropped from a spoon.

4. In a small saucepan, stir together ¼ cup water and remaining ⅔ cup sugar. Place the egg whites in large bowl of an electric mixer and begin beating at medium-low speed. At the same time, start cooking the sugar and water over medium heat, stirring constantly until sugar is dissolved. Raise heat to high and bring to a boil. Check egg whites, which should now be at soft peaks. With mixer at high speed, slowly drizzle the hot syrup down the side of the mixing bowl (not near the beaters where it will splatter). When syrup has been incorporated, continue beating for 1 or 2 minutes, until meringue is cooled. Then, with mixer on low speed, pour strawberry mixture into meringue and mix only a few seconds until blended.

5. Whip the cream to soft peaks and fold it into the mousse.

6. Turn into a decorative 3-quart bowl and chill at least 4 hours or up to 36 hours before serving. (Can be frozen for up to 1 week and thawed for 24 hours in the refrigerator.)

7. Shortly before serving, decorate top of mousse with reserved berries and the mint sprigs.

Note: The goal of our cooked meringue method is to have the sugar syrup come to a full boil at about the same time that the egg whites reach soft peaks. You may need to remove the syrup from the heat for 1 or 2 minutes, then return to a boil, or you may need to stop beating the whites for a minute or so while the syrup reaches a boil. We do not use a candy thermometer and are not sticky about an exact temperature, so this is not really a classic Italian meringue, but rather a loose variation that we find produces a very stable, creamy smooth mousse.

Wedding Memory Cake

Lightly flavored with almond and frosted with a rich, satiny white chocolate butter icing, this wedding cake is both beautiful and delicious. The bonus is that it is far easier to make and assemble than you might believe. In fact, the entire decorated cake (minus the flowers) can be completed well ahead, and no special talent or cake-decorating experience is necessary! If you have a heavy-duty, large capacity (5-quart bowl) standing mixer, the cake and icing can be made in single batches. If you must use a portable mixer, you may need to divide the recipes in half and make two batches in succession. A few pieces of special equipment are needed for this cake. You can get cardboard cake rounds at baking supply stores, or you can make your own rounds by cutting circles from sturdy boxes and covering them with aluminum foil. A 12-inch round cake pan is necessary and can be found at most specialty cookware stores. The 8-inch pan we favor is a regular springform pan, since it can also be used for cheesecakes and the like.

MAKES 35 SERVINGS

Cake

1	cup (4 ounces) coarsely chopped or whole almonds with skins
4	cups all-purpose flour
2	teaspoons baking powder
1	teaspoon salt
1	pound unsalted butter, softened
3½	cups granulated sugar
12	eggs, separated
4	teaspoons vanilla extract
1	teaspoon almond extract

Filling

1½	cups apricot or peach spreadable fruit preserves (no sugar added)
2	teaspoons Amaretto or brandy
1½	cups raspberry spreadable fruit preserves (no sugar added)
2	teaspoons kirsch or brandy

Icing

30	ounces white chocolate chips or baking bars, chopped
1½	cups (3 sticks) unsalted butter, softened
12	ounces cream cheese, softened
1	tablespoon vanilla extract

¾	teaspoon almond extract
6	cups confectioners' sugar

Assembly and decoration

1	cardboard cake round 12 inches in diameter
1	cardboard cake round 8 inches in diameter
2	yards 1-inch-wide pastel ribbon
	Small fresh nontoxic flowers such as freesia, violets, rosebuds, baby's breath, or pansies

1. Preheat the oven to 325° F. Butter one 12-inch round cake pan and one 8-inch round cake pan, each at least 2 inches deep. Unless pans have removable bottoms, line the bottom of each with a round of parchment or wax paper.

2. Finely chop the almonds along with ½ cup of the flour in a food processor. Sift remaining 3½ cups flour with the baking powder and salt. Stir in chopped almond mixture.

3. In a large mixer, cream the butter with the sugar until light in color. Beat in the egg yolks,

beating for about 3 minutes, until light in color. Beat in the vanilla and almond extracts until blended. With mixer at low speed, beat in the flour mixture just until well blended. In a large, clean, dry mixer bowl with clean beaters, beat the egg whites just until they hold stiff peaks (do not overbeat). Stir about ¼ of the whites into the batter to lighten, then fold in remaining whites just until blended.

4. Divide the batter between the 2 pans, using about two-thirds for the large pan and about one-third for the smaller pan. Bake in the center of the oven (if you need to use two racks, stagger the pans to allow heat circulation, and reverse positions after 40 minutes of baking), until cakes are golden brown with tops that spring back lightly when touched and a cake tester inserted in the center comes out clean. This will take 55 to 60 minutes for the 8-inch cake and 65 to 70 minutes for the 12-inch cake.

5. Let the cakes cool in their pans on racks for 10 minutes. Then turn out of the pans, removing the parchment, and allow to cool completely. (Can be made 2 days ahead and refrigerated or 2 weeks ahead and frozen.)

6. To make the filling, stir together the apricot fruit spread and the Amaretto, then push through a strainer to remove solids. Repeat the procedure with the raspberry fruit spread and the kirsch to make the 2 fruit fillings. (Can be made 3 days ahead and refrigerated.)

7. To make the icing, melt the white chocolate in a microwave oven on lowest setting or in the top of a double boiler set over hot water. Watch carefully, stirring often, and remove the chocolate from the heat source when a few solid pieces remain. Stir until they melt and chocolate is smooth. Let cool until just lukewarm. In a large mixer bowl, beat the butter and cream cheese until light, then blend in the vanilla and almond extracts. Beat in the white chocolate until blended and smooth, then beat in the confectioners' sugar until smooth. If the frosting is too soft, refrigerate for about 30 minutes until spreadable. (Can be made 2 days ahead and refrigerated. Remove from refrigerator about 30 minutes before using to allow it to become spreadable.)

8. To assemble, use a serrated knife to cut each cake horizontally into 3 layers. (This is easiest to do if you mark the layers with toothpicks to use as a cutting guide.) Place the bottom 12-inch layer on the 12-inch cardboard round, using a dab of icing to anchor it. Spread with 1 cup apricot filling, leaving a ¼-inch border uncovered. Top with middle 12-inch layer and spread with 1 cup raspberry filling, leaving a ¼-inch border uncovered. Center top 12-inch layer over cake. Fill and assemble the 8-inch layers in the same manner, using the 8-inch cake round and remaining fruit fillings.

9. To frost, use a flat, slim metal spatula to cover the sides and top of the 12-inch cake with about 2¾ cups icing. Frost the 8-inch cake with about 1¾ cups icing. Refrigerate or freeze remaining icing to use as decoration. (There will be plenty of extra icing to use for decoration or to patch flaws. Any leftovers can be frozen for later use.) Refrigerate cakes for about 2 hours to firm up icing before continuing with decoration. (Iced cakes be frozen for up to 2 weeks at this point. When ready to decorate, remove from freezer and thaw at least 1 hour in refrigerator.)

[c o n t i n u e d]

10.   To assemble, place the 12-inch cake on a platter. Carefully set the 8-inch layer in the center of the larger layer.

11.   To decorate, cut a 40-inch-long piece of ribbon and wrap around bottom of the 12-inch cake, pressing in lightly so ribbon will adhere. Repeat on the 8-inch layer with a 27-inch-long piece of ribbon. If necessary, secure ribbon with straight pins. Spoon remaining icing into a pastry bag fitted with a small round or star tip. Pipe small balls or rosettes around the top edge of both cakes. Refrigerate at least 2 or up to 24 hours.

12.   Arrange the flowers to decorate the cake. Serve at cool room temperature. (May be decorated with flowers up to 4 hours ahead and refrigerated.)

13.   To slice, use spatulas to lift off top (8-inch) cake, then slice it. Bottom (12-inch) cake should be cut into squares for serving.

Ravinia Picnic

A Sophisticated Preconcert Picnic
For 8

Napa Valley Sparkling Chardonnay (NO RECIPE)

~

Curried Cashews   162
Cherry Tomatoes with Saga Blue Cheese Dip   162

~

Iced Cantaloupe Soup with Nasturtium Garnish   163
Chicken and Summer Vegetable Mosaic   164
Sauce Rouge   165
Sauce Verte   165
Basil and Scallion Baguettes   166

~

Apricot Almond Tart   167

~

Viennese Coffee (NO RECIPE)

THE RAVINIA FESTIVAL is a midwest tradition. Since this magnificent yet blissfully idyllic park opened its gates in 1904, Ravinia has hosted a summer-long festival of musical arts and theater. In the golden era of the 1920s, Ravinia became known as the summer opera capital of the world, and it continues to attract thousands of men and women who come each season to enjoy the renowned performances.

But that is only part of the Ravinia experience. The more than 36 acres of beautifully landscaped wooded and grassy areas form a spectacular backdrop for specimen flowers, lush foliage, and notable outdoor sculpture.

Over the years, it has become a delightful tradition to take a preconcert picnic to savor while enjoying the sunset of a summer evening at Ravinia. For some, the lovely setting becomes an Edwardian fantasy of white linen and organdy framed by deep green grass, of silver candelabra flickering against dimming twilight, and of fine crystal stemware tinkling in warm breezes.

Picnic hampers are filled with all manner of elegant edibles and, over the years, Ravinia has become as much a showcase for creative summer cuisine as it has for talented artistic performances.

Melanie was introduced to the Ravinia Festival as a guest during the first summer she and her husband lived in Chicago as young marrieds. Immediately enraptured, they became regular attendees and frequently hosted picnics for good friends who shared their love of both food and music.

This menu is one of her favorites and every time she serves it, now most often in a Connecticut meadow against a chorus of crickets, or in her own backyard on white-napped tables with the Chicago Symphony on tape, it continues to bring back memories of a special time in a special place.

In Advance

PART OF THE BEAUTY of hosting a picnic is that, of necessity, *everything* must be made and packed well before it is actually to be served. *And* the house doesn't have to be cleaned!

For an important picnic such as this one, carrying containers and coolers, as well as serving dishes, plates, glasses, utensils, coffee cups, soup bowls, and napkins should be very carefully inventoried. Think about illumination and pack candles or lanterns and matches. Iron a pretty tablecloth, and don't forget a corkscrew and a vase for flowers. Finally, take your packing checklist to the picnic so you won't forget to bring it all home.

Bake and freeze the baguettes up to 2 weeks before the occasion. Mix and roll out the pastry for the tart and freeze that.

About 3 days beforehand, make the curried cashews.

The day before the picnic, make the chicken mosaic. Then do the cheese dip and the 2 sauces.

Then, on the morning of the day of the picnic, bake the tart. Blanch and chill the vegetable garnish for the chicken mosaic. Make and chill the melon soup. Thaw the bread. Cut garden flowers (including the nasturtiums for the soup) and wrap stems in damp toweling.

A few hours before leaving, unmold and slice the chicken terrine. Pack all the food in containers, to transport in picnic hampers or coolers, and make a couple of thermoses of coffee.

If Time Is Short ...

☞ For the sauce rouge, use one 7-ounce jar of drained roasted red peppers.

☞ For the herbed baguettes, use two packages of refrigerated French bread dough. Follow our recipe directions for filling and baking.

☞ Use one disk of refrigerated pie crust from the dairy case for the tart.

Curried Cashews

A truly addictive nibbler! Another time, substitute almonds.

MAKES ABOUT 3 CUPS

1	pound salted cashews
¼	cup vegetable oil
2	teaspoons curry powder
	Salt

1. Preheat the oven to 300° F.
2. Toss the cashews with the oil and curry powder until thoroughly coated. Spread in an even layer on a baking sheet. Roast 20 to 25 minutes, stirring a couple of times. When done, they will give off a toasty aroma and be nicely browned. Taste and toss with a little salt if desired.
3. Cool and then store tightly covered for up to 3 days.

Cherry Tomatoes with Saga Blue Cheese Dip

This hors d'oeuvre is a perfect prelude to a light summer dinner. Depending upon your culinary color scheme, miniature yellow tomatoes can be substituted for or combined with the red cherry tomatoes. If you are a goat cheese fancier, try using a soft chèvre such as Bucheron in place of the Saga Blue cheese.

MAKES 8 SERVINGS

4	ounces Saga Blue or other soft blue cheese, softened
3	ounces cream cheese, softened
3	tablespoons milk
2	tablespoons minced shallots
2	tablespoons minced parsley
	Freshly ground black pepper
2	pints cherry tomatoes with stems

1. Thoroughly blend both cheeses, milk, shallots, minced parsley, and black pepper in a food processor or using an electric mixer. (Can be made up to 24 hours ahead, covered and refrigerated. Return to room temperature before using.)
2. Serve the tomatoes accompanied by the dip.

Iced Cantaloupe Soup with Nasturtium Garnish

The flavor of this lovely, light soup comes from the heady perfume of ripe cantaloupe. Yogurt adds body, and the edible nasturtium garnish gives a peppery dimension as well as an extra-summery fillip to the soup. If you wish, you may substitute another melon such as honeydew, Crenshaw, or Persian for the cantaloupe. Avoid watermelon, however, for it is (you guessed it) too watery.

MAKES 8 SERVINGS (ABOUT 9 CUPS SOUP)

8	cups chilled cubed cantaloupe
6	tablespoons honey
2	tablespoons lime juice
2	teaspoons grated lime zest
1	cup dry white wine
1½	cups plain yogurt
½	teaspoon freshly ground pepper
¼	teaspoon salt
	Nasturtium flowers for garnish

1. If you do not have a large food processor, you may need to make the soup in 2 batches. In a food processor, purée the melon with the honey, lime juice, and zest. Add the wine and process a few seconds to blend. Add the yogurt, pepper, and salt and process briefly to blend. Serve immediately or chill up to 4 hours.

2. If taking to a picnic, transport in a thermos, then serve in small bowls or cups. Garnish each serving with a nasturtium flower.

Chicken and Summer Vegetable Mosaic

When unmolded and sliced, this terrine, studded with jewellike diced vegetables, truly looks like a gorgeous mosaic. Served with its 2 sauces—a green and a red—it makes the perfect centerpiece for this elegant picnic. It's also great on a buffet, sliced and presented on a big platter.

MAKES 8 SERVINGS (ABOUT 16 SLICES)

Terrine

¾	cup diced carrots
1	cup (about 8 ounces) ½-inch lengths slender green beans
¾	cup yellow squash (outside ½ inch only), cut into small dice (see Note)
1½	pounds skinned and boned chicken breasts
1	egg
2	cups heavy cream, chilled
¼	cup minced shallots
1½	teaspoons salt
½	teaspoon grated nutmeg
¼	teaspoon cayenne
¼	teaspoon freshly ground black pepper
1	cup (a 6-ounce piece) smoked ham, diced

Garnish

24	slender green beans, blanched and chilled
6	carrots, peeled, cut into julienne, blanched, and chilled

1.   Preheat oven to 350° F. Butter a 5- by 9-inch loaf pan.

2.   Bring a large pot of water to the boil. Add salt, and the carrots, and cook at a rapid boil for 45 seconds. Add green beans and yellow squash and cook for 1 minute. Drain into a colander, run under cold water until vegetables are cold, and drain on paper towels.

3.   Make sure all tendons and gristle are removed from chicken, and cut into 2-inch chunks. Place in work bowl of a food processor and add egg. Begin processing, adding cream gradually through feed tube, to make a smooth purée. Transfer to a bowl and stir in shallots, salt, nutmeg, and peppers. Fold in the diced ham and the vegetables. Pack into prepared pan, lay a sheet of buttered parchment or wax paper over chicken mixture, and cover tightly with foil.

4.   Place in a large baking pan and pour in hot water to come halfway up the sides of the loaf pan. Bake in preheated oven for 1¼ to 1½ hours, or until an instant read themometer registers 140° F., the loaf is firm, and juices run clear.

5.   Cool at room temperature for 45 minutes. Drain off any liquid. Place another loaf pan on top of the chicken and fill with heavy cans to weight the terrine and make its texture denser and easier to slice. Refrigerate for at least 4 hours. (Can be made 2 days ahead.)

6.   To serve, drain off any accumulated liquid, unmold, and cut into ½-inch slices. Arrange overlapping on a platter. (Can do several hours in advance.) Salt and pepper the beans and julienned carrots and use to garnish the terrine. Serve with a spoonful each of the sauce verte and sauce rouge on the side.

Note: To prepare yellow squash, remove lengthwise strips of unpeeled squash about ½ inch thick. Discard core with seeds and cut strips into dice.

Sauce Rouge

Roasting the red peppers lends a subtle smoky taste to this beautiful sauce.

2   large (at least 8 ounces each) red bell
    peppers
1   large shallot, peeled
2   tablespoons tomato paste
1   tablespoon balsamic vinegar
    Pinch sugar
½   cup olive oil
½   teaspoon Tabasco

1. To roast the peppers, blacken on all sides on a grill or over a gas flame. Or cut in half, place on a piece of foil, and broil skin side up until blackened. Place in paper bag, fold over top to seal, and let stand for 10 minutes to steam off skins. Peel off the blackened skin and remove ribs and seeds.

2. Place peppers in the work bowl of a food processor with the shallot, tomato paste, vinegar, and sugar. Begin processing, adding the oil in a thin stream until purée is smooth. Season to taste with Tabasco. Store in covered container in refrigerator. (Can be made 1 day ahead.)

Sauce Verte

Fragrant green herbs and zippy mustard and capers lend color and a boost of flavor to commercial mayonnaise. This sauce also makes a wonderful dip for raw or blanched vegetables.

MAKES ABOUT 1½ CUPS

2   cups packed parsley sprigs
¼   cup tarragon sprigs, or 2 teaspoons
    dried
1   clove garlic, peeled
2   tablespoons lemon juice
2   teaspoons Dijon mustard
1   teaspoon drained capers
1   cup commercial mayonnaise

Place parsley, tarragon, garlic, lemon juice, mustard, and capers in food processor. Pulse to blend. Add mayonnaise and process for about 1 minute to purée well. Store in covered container in refrigerator. (Can be made 1 day ahead.)

Basil and Scallion Baguettes

Given the limitations of a home kitchen in Connecticut as opposed to a brick oven in Lyon, we think that this is the best American/French bread we have ever tasted. A tiny amount of cornmeal added to the dough more nearly approximates the texture of baguettes enjoyed in France. French bread pans produce the classic shape, but baking sheets can be used. Be sure to follow the baking method, for it is the secret to the wonderful crust. For this party, we turn the basic bread into an aromatic and attractive spiral. You can, of course, vary the herbs or omit the embellishments entirely.

MAKES 2 LOAVES

3	cups white bread flour
1	package (2 teaspoons) active dry yeast
3	tablespoons yellow cornmeal
1½	teaspoons salt
1¼	cups warm water (105° F. to 115° F.)
2	tablespoons olive oil
½	cup chopped fresh basil
½	cup chopped scallion, including green parts
1	egg white beaten with 2 teaspoons water for glaze

1.   In a food processor, mix together the flour, yeast, 1 tablespoon cornmeal, and salt. With the motor running, pour the water through the feed tube until a ball forms. Process about 45 seconds to "knead" the dough. Place dough in a lightly oiled bowl, turning to oil the top. Cover lightly and let rise 1 to 1½ hours in a warm place until doubled.

2.   Grease two French bread baguette pans or a large baking sheet. Sprinkle with remaining 2 tablespoons cornmeal, tapping out excess.

3.   Punch dough down and divide in half. On a lightly floured surface, roll each half to a rectangle approximately 8 by 14 inches. Brush each with half of the oil and sprinkle with half of the basil and the scallions. Pat gently into dough. Roll up from the long side and pinch the ends and the long seam gently to seal. Place, seam side down, in prepared pans or well apart on the baking sheet. Use a sharp knife or a razor blade to make diagonal slashes at 1-inch intervals. Cover lightly and let rise about 45 minutes, until nearly doubled.

4.   Meanwhile, preheat oven to 450° F. Place a shallow pan of hot water in the bottom or on the lowest shelf of the oven.

5.   Brush the risen dough gently with egg white glaze, taking care not to let any drip onto the pan. Bake in the center of the oven for 10 minutes. Brush again with glaze, rotate position of pan from front to back, and bake 8 to 10 minutes more, until loaves are firm and light golden. Use a small spatula to carefully loosen loaves from pans, invert directly onto oven rack and brush bottoms with glaze. Bake 8 to 10 minutes longer until loaves are deep golden brown and crusty on all sides.

6.   Cool bread on racks. Serve within 6 hours or wrap in foil and freeze up to 2 weeks. Thaw frozen loaves at room temperature.

Note: Quick-rise yeast reduces rising times by about half.

Apricot Almond Tart

This beautiful fruit tart is a natural to serve for dessert at a dressed-up picnic. Here we exploit the affinity of apricots and almonds. Sliced nuts are sprinkled over the bottom of the tart shell, and also lend their richness and crunch to the streusel topping.

MAKES 8 SERVINGS

Almond Pastry

1¼	cups all-purpose flour
2	teaspoons sugar
¼	teaspoon salt
½	cup (1 stick) unsalted butter, chilled and cut into small pieces
¼	cup sliced almonds

Apricot Filling and Streusel Topping

⅓	cup brown sugar
⅓	cup sliced almonds
3	tablespoons flour
1	tablespoon coarsely chopped candied ginger
3	tablespoons unsalted butter, chilled and cut into 6 pieces
1	pound (about 8 medium) fresh apricots
1	tablespoon brandy or apricot brandy

Brandied Chantilly Cream

½	cup heavy cream
1	tablespoon confectioners' sugar
2	teaspoons brandy or apricot brandy

1. To make the pastry, mix the flour, sugar, and salt in a food processor. Distribute the butter evenly over the flour mixture and process until butter is the size of small peas. With machine running, drizzle 3 or 4 tablespoons ice water through feed tube and process until dough begins to come together. Gather into a ball and flatten into a disk. Wrap in plastic and refrigerate for at least 30 minutes. (Can be made 2 days ahead.)

2. Roll dough out on a lightly floured surface to a 12-inch round. Transfer to a 10-inch tart pan with removable bottom. Press dough into sides of pan and trim edges. Prick with a fork and scatter almonds evenly over bottom of shell, pressing them in with your hand. Freeze for at least 30 minutes.

3. Position rack in lowest third of the oven and preheat to 425° F. Bake tart shell for 20 to 22 minutes, or until pastry is a light golden. If pastry puffs, press to flatten. Cool completely on rack. (Can be made 1 day ahead. Cover and store at room temperature.)

4. For the streusel topping combine sugar, almonds, flour, and ginger in a food processor. Process until nuts are finely chopped. Distribute butter over sugar mixture and process until mixture resembles coarse meal. (Can be made 2 days ahead. Refrigerate.)

5. Position rack in the center of the oven and preheat to 375° F. Pit and quarter the apricots and toss with brandy to coat. Arrange apricots cut sides up in the tart shell and sprinkle evenly with streusel topping. Bake in preheated oven for about 45 minutes, or until topping is a rich golden brown and fruit is tender. Cool on rack. (Can be made 8 hours ahead.)

6. In a chilled bowl, whip the cream to soft peaks. Add powdered sugar and brandy and beat until just blended. (Can be made 3 hours ahead. Refrigerate.) Serve a spoonful of cream with each slice of tart.

Mediterranean Grill

A Sophisticated Summer Supper
For 6

W E WOULD, of course, like to be able to relate to you a story of our summer spent on a sun-drenched Greek island, in a villa set in an olive grove on a hilltop overlooking the azure Medi-terranean. There would be a fragrant herb garden outside the kitchen door, and we would tell you of our daily trips to the local market for dewy fresh vegetables, lush ripe fruits, and rustic seeded breads. Good friends would join us in the evening to share an informal but special evening meal under the stars.

That summer remains a fantasy for the future, but given the increasing availability of excellent Mediterranean ingredients right here at home, this simple but sophisticated menu is the next best thing.

Our general rule of thumb for all easy summer dinner parties is that the preprandial snacks require absolutely no fussing. Fortunately, supermarkets have finally expanded beyond canned olives and packaged cheese and now offer an array of imported goodies just begging to be assembled into an inviting-looking platter. So we can easily start with a selection of olives, vegetables, and cured meats and fish that one would be likely to eat on a terrace overlooking the sea.

For the main course, we suggest a mustard-coated butterflied leg of lamb, marinated and grilled over fragrant rosemary branches. The accompanying colorful summer vegetables also make use of the grill, and the orzo, the rice-shaped pasta tossed with lemon and fresh mint, adds another summery note.

Set in a pool of orange-scented crème anglaise, fresh raspberries are the star of the dessert course. Add a plate of buttery almond wafers for a final flourish.

In Advance

THOUGH THIS MENU is designed to be quite simple—and could in fact easily be cooked all on one day—a good part of it lends itself to advance planning as well.

The roll of cookie dough can be made a couple of weeks ahead, frozen, and then sliced as needed for baking. The finished cookies also freeze well, or can be stored in a tightly covered tin for a couple of days.

A day ahead you can make the custard sauce. If you're planning to marinate the lamb overnight, make the marinade, coat the meat with it, and refrigerate.

On the afternoon of the party, slice the vegetables for grilling and make the garlic-lemon oil for the orzo.

An hour or so ahead, arrange the hors d'oeuvre platter. Time the fire so that the vegetables and meat are grilled at the last minute, and finally, cook the orzo and toss it with its seasonings.

If Time Is Short ...

☛ Instead of a custard sauce, the raspberries could be served with plain pouring cream.

☛ Bakery cookies could stand in for the almond wafers.

Hors d' Oeuvre Platter

You should select whatever is most appealing at your market.

A SELECTION OF THE FOLLOWING:

Caper-stuffed anchovies
Thinly sliced prosciutto
Niçoise or mixed cured black and green olives
Fennel, cut into strips
Marinated artichoke hearts
Cornichons

Dried Italian sausage
Cherry tomatoes
Tuna in olive oil
Herbed chèvre
Small radishes with stems
Water biscuits or other plain crackers

Arrange attractively on a large platter.

Mustard–Rosemary Grilled Lamb

A whole leg of lamb would be too much meat for 6, but you can ask your butcher or meat manager for half a leg, preferably from the shank end, boned and butterflied. If you have fresh rosemary, tossing a few branches on the fire adds its resinous fragrance to the smoke and permeates the meat.

MAKES 6 SERVINGS

Mustard-Rosemary Marinade

2	tablespoons Dijon mustard
2	cloves garlic, peeled and minced
2	teaspoons chopped fresh or dried rosemary
2	teaspoons red wine vinegar
1	teaspoon freshly ground black pepper
½	teaspoon cayenne pepper
¼	cup olive oil
1	3½-pound half leg of lamb, boned and butterflied (approximately 3 pounds boned weight)
3 or 4	branches rosemary

1.   Whisk together the mustard, garlic, rosemary, vinegar, black pepper, and cayenne pepper. Gradually whisk in the oil.

2.   Trim most of fat from top of lamb, leaving a very thin layer. Brush with marinade and refrigerate overnight, or let stand at cool room temperature for 1 to 4 hours.

3.   Build a charcoal fire or preheat a gas grill. Cook the meat over moderately hot coals and a few branches of rosemary until nicely charred on both sides but still pink within, about 15 to 20 minutes total. Remove to a carving board and let rest for a few minutes before cutting into thin crosswise slices. Serve with juices spooned over meat.

Lemon Mint Orzo Pilaf

Of course orzo tastes the same as any other pasta, but because it is typically Greek, it seems just right with this Mediterranean menu.

MAKES 6 SERVINGS

¼	cup olive oil
2	cloves garlic, peeled and minced
¾	teaspoon grated lemon zest
1	tablespoon lemon juice
	Salt
2	cups uncooked orzo
½	cup chopped mint
½	teaspoon freshly ground black pepper, or to taste

1. Heat the oil in a small skillet. Add garlic and cook over low heat for 2 minutes. Remove pan from heat and stir in lemon zest and juice. (Can be made several hours ahead and stored at cool room temperature.)

2. Bring a large pot of water to the boil. Add salt and the orzo and cook at a rapid boil for 8 to 10 minutes, or until pasta is al dente. Drain into a colander and toss with the garlic oil mixture and the mint; season with salt and pepper. Serve hot or tepid.

Grilled Summer Vegetables

The selection of vegetables here is very flexible. In lieu of or in addition to the types we suggest, you could grill thinly sliced eggplant, wedges of red onion, sliced fennel, or sliced sweet potatoes.

MAKES 6 SERVINGS

1	large red pepper
2	medium zucchini
2	medium yellow crookneck squash
1	large bunch scallions or 2 small bunches
6	tablespoons olive oil
	Salt and freshly ground black pepper to taste

1. Build a charcoal fire or preheat a gas grill.

2. Core and seed the pepper and cut into 1-inch strips. Slice zucchini and crookneck squash on the sharp diagonal to make pieces about 3 inches long and ¼ inch thick. Trim scallions and cut into 4-inch lengths. (Can be prepared up to 2 hours ahead.)

3. Brush vegetables generously with oil and cook over moderately hot coals for 3 to 5 minutes per side, or until nicely charred and somewhat softened. Watch the scallions carefully, as they will be done first.

4. Heap onto a platter, sprinkle with salt and pepper, and serve warm or tepid.

Raspberries with Cointreau Custard Sauce

This is one of our very favorite summer combinations. Rich and sweet enough to offset the raspberries beautifully, this Cointreau-spiked crème anglaise is also wonderful with just about any height-of-season fruit.

MAKES 6 SERVINGS

2	cups half-and-half
½	cup heavy cream
5	egg yolks
½	cup sugar
2	tablespoons Cointreau or other orange liqueur
1	teaspoon vanilla extract
4	cups raspberries
	Mint sprigs

1. Heat the half-and-half and cream in a heavy saucepan over medium heat until bubbles form around the edges.

2. Whisk the yolks and sugar together until the mixture is thick and light, about 2 minutes. Slowly whisk the hot cream into the yolks, return to the saucepan, and cook over very low heat, stirring constantly, until custard heavily coats the back of a spoon, about 10 minutes. Remove from the heat and stir in the Cointreau and vanilla.

3. Let cool. Refrigerate until ready to serve. (Can be made 2 days ahead.)

4. Divide sauce among 6 shallow dessert dishes or rimmed plates. Spoon berries over sauce and garnish with mint sprigs.

Brown Sugar Almond Wafers

These crisp, rich little cookies are scrumptious with any fruit dessert.

⅓ cup sliced almonds with skins
1 cup all-purpose flour
½ cup dark brown sugar
¼ cup granulated sugar
½ teaspoon baking powder
⅛ teaspoon salt
6 tablespoons (¾ stick) cold unsalted
    butter, cut into chunks
1 egg
½ teaspoon vanilla extract

1. Pulse the almonds in the work bowl of a food processor until they are chopped medium-fine. Add the flour, both sugars, baking powder, and salt and pulse until brown sugar is free of lumps. Distribute butter over sugar mixture and process until pieces of butter are about the size of corn kernels.

2. In a measuring cup, lightly beat the egg with the vanilla. With motor running, pour egg mixture through the feed tube and process until dough clumps together on top of the blade.

3. Turn out onto a sheet of plastic wrap and shape into a cylinder about 1¾ inches in diameter, using wrap to aid in making the roll even and smooth. Tuck ends under to seal and place in the freezer for about 30 minutes or in the refrigerator for at least 1 hour. (Can be made 1 day ahead or frozen up to 1 month.)

4. Preheat oven to 400° F. Working with half the cylinder at a time, slice into disks about ⅛ inch thick. Arrange 1 inch apart on lightly greased baking sheets, reshaping edges of cookies with your fingers if the rounds are less than perfect. Bake in preheated oven for 6 or 7 minutes, reversing the sheets halfway through the baking time, until cookies are pale gold in the center and light brown around the edges. Cool on a wire rack. (Can be stored in an airtight container for 3 days or frozen for 2 weeks.)

SUMMER WHITES

Cocktails in the Garden
FOR 40 OR MORE

Gin Rickeys   180
Full Bar (NO RECIPE)

~

Skewered Charred Moroccan Lamb and Melon   181
Cappelletti with Dill Sauce   182
Salmon Tartare Canapés   183
Summer Crudités with Raspberry–Thyme Dipping Sauce   184
Rosemary and Scallion Focaccia   185
Basket or Bowl of Plums (NO RECIPE)
French Cheeses on a Board or Lemon Leaves (NO RECIPE)
Toasted Macadamias (NO RECIPE)

WHAT BETTER SEASON than summer to give a big party? Nature, with its gorgeous greens and vivid colors, provides the perfect backdrop. The setting sun and long, lingering twilight create a magical mood that can't be manufactured at any other time of year. We love to take advantage of this free stage set to throw a large bash, inviting old friends, new friends, neighbors, coworkers (and the boss), as well as family.

The cocktail party format makes it very easy on the party-giver. There is no elaborate game plan, no real meal to cook, serve, or clean up after, and only glasses to rent.

So it is with pleasure that Brooke pens invitations that read "Come for Cocktails in the Garden, five-thirty until eight-thirty o'clock. RSVP." (Always include both start and finish times on a cocktail party invitation to make sure guests know that it isn't dinner!) Over the years the party has evolved into a full-scale, fancy affair faintly in memory of F. Scott Fitzgerald and his era of "summer whites."

The party begins in daylight, with a tape of Bobby Short piano music to set a Gatsbyesque tone. Two tables, a long one for a bar and a second round table for stationary food, are covered with pastel cloths. Potables are dispensed by a bartender and include a special "house drink" of the evening, this time a refreshing, tart gin rickey.

Big bouquets of summer flowers grace the tables and the irresistibly enticing aroma of grilling lamb draws guests to the hibachi set up in a corner of the garden. Pink salmon tartare canapés and fragrant herbed focaccia are passed from flat lacquered basket trays. Arrayed on the tables (and also passed intermittently) are a spectacular summer crudité, verdant dill-sauced pasta, and French cheeses displayed on shiny lemon leaves or a wooden board. Silver bowls of toasted macadamias and a huge basket or bowl of ripe red plums round out the menu.

As dusk gathers, the pace picks up along with the music, which usually segues into Pink Floyd. Guests drift from group to group, sampling tidbits from platters and forming new configurations. A teenage helper keeps the food flowing, with each new tray inspected and exclaimed over. As darkness falls, hurricane lanterns light the tables and lingering guests—who by now are rocking to the beat of Buddy Holly—feel the embrace of warmth, friendship, and the summer night.

In Advance

ORGANIZING a cocktail party is a breeze. The only dishes you need to worry about are large platters or basket trays, which you will want to have in good supply, even if it means renting a few for the occasion. You may also want to rent glasses. If so, order an all-purpose 12-ounce short-stemmed size (sometimes called a water goblet), since it works well for mixed drinks, wine, and sparkling waters, too. If you give large parties often, buy a supply of inexpensive glasses. Then, just get lots of pretty cocktail napkins, and that's it!

To make your work easier, do the nonfood preparation way ahead. If you are planning an outdoor setting, spruce up the garden and plant a few extra blooms for bright color. Also, order any rentals and hire your bartender and server. Take stock of the liquor supply and be sure to have plenty of soft drinks and sparkling waters for those who choose not to drink alcohol.

With the liquid refreshments under control, that brings us to the eternal party question—how much food? In Brooke's experience as a caterer, she found that the standard quantity of about 2 servings each of 7 or 8 hors d'oeuvres per person is a pretty reliable rule of thumb for this type of cocktail party. But she also learned that it is imperative to know your group, and to consider the occasion and the number of hours that the party will extend. Our recipes have, wherever possible, given yields of how many "bites" one can expect in order to help you plan, especially if you are gearing the numbers of dishes and the guests upward or downward.

Start food preparation up to a couple of weeks ahead by making and freezing the focaccia. A couple of days before the party,

you can make the dipping sauce for the crudités.

A day ahead, start the salmon tartare, marinate the lamb, and make the dill sauce. If you wish, you can also prepare the crudités now, too. Depending upon the weather forecast, set up outdoor tables.

On the morning of the party, thaw the focaccia, finish the salmon tartare, and cook the cappelletti. Then skewer the lamb and melon. Arrange the crudités and the cheese tray.

All that's left are the finishing touches and setting out the food—most of which can be done easily by the kitchen helper, who is also in charge of keeping the food flow smooth and even.

If Time Is Short …

☞   Use refrigerated pizza dough to replace homemade focaccia dough. Press or roll dough to approximately ¼-inch thickness and proceed with the recipe as directed.

☞   Limit your crudité assortment to 2 or 3 vegetables. In addition to being simpler, this can make a very dramatic statement, especially if you key off one particular color.

☞   You can always scale down by eliminating a couple of the more time-consuming recipes and making increased amounts of the simpler ones. Just be sure to keep a balance between vegetable, cheese, meat or fish, and bread.

Gin Rickeys

An old-fashioned highball that deserves revival, a rickey is a simple, refreshing blend of fresh lime juice, gin, and sparkling water, served over ice. John Mariani notes that the drink was probably concocted in the late nineteenth century and might have been named after a "distinguished Washington guzzler" of the period! Whether guzzled or sipped, it's a drink to be enjoyed! Make a pitcher to pour over ice if you prefer.

For each drink

1	tablespoon fresh lime juice
1½	ounces gin
	Seltzer or club soda
	Thin wedges of lime

Fill a tall glass or a 10- or 12-ounce stemmed glass with ice cubes. Add lime juice and gin and fill to the top with sparkling water. Stir well. Add a wedge of lime before serving.

Skewered Charred Moroccan Lamb and Melon

There is nothing quite as enticing to guests as the heavenly aroma of meat cooking on a grill. This marinade of exotic Moroccan spices and herbs is wonderful with the lamb.

MAKES ABOUT 60 HORS D'OEUVRES

Moroccan Marinade

6	tablespoons olive oil
¼	cup balsamic vinegar
2	cloves garlic, peeled and minced
¼	cup chopped fresh mint
1	teaspoon ground cumin
½	teaspoon cayenne
½	teaspoon ground coriander seed
1	teaspoon salt
1	teaspoon freshly ground black pepper

Lamb and Assembly

2	pounds lean lamb (leg or well-trimmed shoulder), cut in 1-inch cubes
About 60	1-inch chunks ripe but firm cantaloupe
60	6-inch bamboo skewers
	Branches of fresh mint for garnishing platter

1. For the marinade, combine the oil, vinegar, garlic, mint, cumin, cayenne, coriander, salt, and pepper in a bowl. (Can be made up to 2 days ahead. Cover and refrigerate.)

2. Place the lamb in a shallow dish. Pour marinade over meat, turning until well coated. Cover and set aside to marinate for 1 or 2 hours at room temperature or for up 12 hours in the refrigerator.

3. Soak the sixty 6-inch bamboo skewers in water to cover for at least 1 hour.

4. On each skewer, thread 1 piece of melon and then 1 piece of lamb. Spoon any extra marinade over the meat. (May be assembled 4 hours ahead. Wrap ends of skewers in damp paper towels. Cover and refrigerate.)

5. Light a charcoal grill or preheat a gas grill. Arrange skewers around the edges of the grill, making sure the handle ends are not directly over the fire. Cook over moderately hot coals until the meat is nicely charred on the outside but still pink inside. The melon should just heat through and caramelize slightly. If the bamboo is too hot to handle, use tongs to turn skewers.

6. Arrange on a platter and garnish with branches of fresh mint.

Cappelletti with Dill Sauce

Peanuts add an unusual and distinctive flavor to this sauce. Using store-brought cappelletti or tortellini makes the dish a breeze to prepare.

2	cups packed fresh parsley leaves, preferably Italian flat-leaf parsley
1⅓	cups packed fresh dill sprigs
½	cup (4 ounces) dry-roasted peanuts
2	cloves garlic, peeled
1½	cups olive oil
6	tablespoons red wine vinegar
½	teaspoon salt
½	teaspoon freshly ground black pepper
1½	pounds fresh or frozen cheese cappelletti or tortellini

1.   Purée parsley, dill, peanuts, and garlic in a food processor until mixture forms a paste. With machine running, pour oil and vinegar through feed tube. Add salt and pepper and pulse to mix. (Can be made 1 day ahead. Cover and refrigerate, but return to room temperature before using.)

2.   Cook cappelletti in boiling salted water according to package directions until al dente. Drain. (Pasta can be cooked about 3 hours ahead, tossed with about 2 tablespoons olive oil to keep moist, and stored, covered, at cool room temperature.) Shortly before serving, add sauce to pasta and toss gently to coat thoroughly.

3.   Serve at room temperature in a shallow bowl or on a platter, with wooden picks for spearing the pasta.

Salmon Tartare Canapés

An adaptation of an appetizer tasted while on a Hawaiian holiday, the salmon is "cooked" by the combination of salt and acid. Prepared in much the same way as Scandinavian gravlax, this is proof once again that cooking knows no geographical boundaries.

MAKES ABOUT 60 CANAPÉS

¾	pound skinned salmon fillet, cut into 1-inch pieces
⅓	cup coarse kosher or sea salt
3	tablespoons fresh lemon juice
1½	cups peeled, seeded, and chopped ripe meaty tomatoes (about 1¼ pounds)
1	large (about 8 ounces) sweet white or red onion, peeled and chopped
2	tablespoons vegetable oil
¼	teaspoon coarsely ground black pepper

About 60 thinly sliced buttered bread squares or triangles, from about 15 slices firm white bread

¼	cup very thinly sliced or minced scallion, white and green parts

1. In a nonaluminum bowl, combine the salmon, salt, and lemon juice. Mix to coat the fish completely. Cover and refrigerate 12 to 24 hours, stirring 2 or 3 times. The salmon will become very firm.

2. Put salmon in a colander and rinse very thoroughly under cold running water. Transfer to a mixing bowl, cover with cold water, and refrigerate 2 hours, changing the water once or twice. Drain salmon and pat very dry.

3. Chop salmon coarsely and place in a nonaluminum bowl along with tomatoes, onion, oil, and pepper. Use your hands to mix well and squeeze the salmon into very small pieces. Cover and refrigerate for at least 3 hours and up to 8 hours before serving.

4. To serve, drain off excess liquid and spoon about 1 teaspoon tartare onto each buttered bread square. Sprinkle with scallions. (Can be assembled up to 1 hour ahead. Refrigerate, lightly covered.) Or, set out a bowl of the tartare with the scallions sprinkled on top and let guests spoon it onto the bread themselves.

Summer Crudités
with Raspberry–Thyme Dipping Sauce

Crisp, fresh vegetables are exactly what many people want to eat in warm weather, and the beauty of the arrangement of contrasting colors and textures is unmatchable. If you have a favorite dipping sauce, by all means use it, but we love this simple mayonnaise flavored with pink raspberry vinegar and fragrant fresh thyme.

MAKES 35 TO 40 SERVINGS

Raspberry-Thyme Dipping Sauce
¼	cup raspberry vinegar
2	cups commercial mayonnaise
3	tablespoons minced fresh thyme
	Freshly ground black pepper
	Sprigs of thyme for garnish

Summer Crudités

TO BLANCH:

Sugar snap peas
Broccoli florets
Peeled asparagus
Cauliflower florets
Green beans

TO SERVE RAW:

Radishes
Pepper strips (in all colors)
Celery strips
Carrot sticks
Cherry tomatoes
Jicama slices

1.   In a small bowl, whisk the vinegar gradually into the mayonnaise. Stir in the thyme and season with black pepper to taste. Yield will be about 2½ cups. (Can be made 1 or 2 days ahead. Cover and refrigerate.)

2.   To blanch vegetables, bring a large pot of water to the boil. Add 1 teaspoon salt. Trim vegetables. Cook uncovered, at a rapid boil, 1 type at a time, until crisp-tender. (Time will vary from 1 minute for sugar snaps and skinny asparagus to 2 or 3 minutes for broccoli and cauliflower florets and beans.) Remove with a slotted spoon, drain in a colander, and refresh under cold running water to stop the cooking. Dry on paper towels, wrap well, and refrigerate. (Can be prepared 1 day ahead.)

3.   Prepare raw vegetables by trimming and slicing into manageable sizes. Wrap in damp paper towels and refrigerate in plastic bags. (Can be done up to 8 hours ahead.)

4.   To assemble crudités, arrange vegetables in one or two baskets or large platters, creating whatever beautiful patterns seem appropriate. Fill a glass bowl or, if you like, a hollowed-out cabbage or squash with the dip. Garnish dip with the sprigs of thyme and set in the center of the crudités. (Can be assembled up to 4 hours ahead. Cover with dampened paper towels, then wrap with plastic and refrigerate.)

Rosemary and Scallion Focaccia

Focaccia is to Genoa what pizza is to Naples. A simple, rustic, yeasty flatbread, this Italian snack can be seasoned with whatever herb is at hand. We happened to have an abundance of fresh rosemary and scallions along with an excess of ripe tomatoes one day, and here is the happy result. Because it goes fast (and freezes well) you might want to make two of these.

MAKES 60 TO 70 PIECES

Dough

3	cups all-purpose flour
1	package (2 teaspoons) active dry yeast (see Note)
1	teaspoon salt
2	tablespoons olive oil
1	cup warm water (110° F. to 115° F.)
1	tablespoon yellow cornmeal for the baking pan

Topping

1	large clove garlic, peeled and minced
¼	cup olive oil
1	cup (about 6 ounces) very thinly sliced, peeled, seeded, ripe but firm tomatoes
¾	cup thinly sliced scallion, including green parts
2	tablespoons grated Parmesan cheese
1	tablespoon minced fresh rosemary or 1 teaspoon dried

1. To make the dough, place the flour, yeast, and salt in the work bowl of a food processor and mix for a few seconds. With the motor running, pour in the oil and water and process until a dough forms on the blade. (If mixture is too wet to form a ball, add a bit more flour. If too dry, add a few drops water.) Continue to process for about 45 seconds to "knead" the dough.

2. Place in a lightly oiled mixing bowl and turn to oil the top. Cover lightly and let rise about 1 hour, or until doubled in bulk.

3. Meanwhile, steep the garlic in the ¼ cup olive oil. Preheat the oven to 425° F.

4. Sprinkle a large baking sheet with the cornmeal. Punch dough down and roll or pat on a lightly floured surface to an approximate 11- by 17-inch rectangle about ¼ inch thick and place in the prepared pan. Use your thumb to make several light dimples or indentations in the dough. Gently brush with 3 tablespoons of the flavored olive oil, then cover with a layer of thinly sliced tomatoes. Sprinkle with scallions, cheese, and rosemary. Dribble with remaining 1 tablespoon oil.

5. Bake in the lower third of the oven for 20 to 22 minutes, until focaccia is a rich golden brown and its edges are crisp. (Can be baked ahead, but underbake by about 3 minutes.) Immediately remove from pan. If serving right away, use a pizza cutter or sharp knife to cut into small squares. (If planning to freeze for up to 1 month and then serve, let cool completely on a rack, wrap in foil, and freeze in a single piece or in 2 pieces. To serve, thaw unwrapped on a rack, then bake for 5 to 8 minutes until golden brown and hot.)

Note: One package quick-rise yeast can be substituted. Rising time will be about half.

Ice Cream Social

A Fantasy Birthday Party
For 30

WHEN MELANIE was a child, her mother always asked what kind of birthday cake she wanted. One year her mother didn't even mention it. Although Melanie was a little disappointed, at least there was no agonizing decision between the two current favorites— spicy banana nut cake with clouds of seafoam frosting and dark, dark chocolate cake with fudge frosting.

The day dawned bright and sunny and she arrived home from school to a house so quiet that she wondered if everyone might have forgotten her birthday. That is, until she walked through the kitchen into the backyard.

Balloons floated from all the trees. A giant Happy Birthday banner hung from the swing set. Two picnic tables were pushed together to make enough space for what seemed like every cake she had ever dreamed about. But the only person in evidence was Bernice Cooper, who was quietly churning her big old ice cream maker. And then the whole neighborhood suddenly jumped out from nowhere and shouted, "Surprise!"

What a party it was! Calliope music filled the air, confetti and pastel curlicued ribbons bedecked the tables, and there were silly hats for everyone. The locally famous (and handsome) teenage magician did card tricks and the retired gentleman from next door dressed up like a clown and made dachshunds out of balloons.

Everyone sampled every cake, licked ice cream right off the dasher, slurped a juicy watermelon slice, and washed it all down with fizzy lemon-lime phosphates and cold milk.

This birthday party made such an indelibly delicious impression that the memory has been re-created many times since—at least once for each of the children and a couple of times as a theme for a church or school social. One summer, it became the basis for a neighborhood block party in which each family brought its best cake and there was an informal judging. Sometimes barbecued burgers, hot dogs, or sandwiches were added to the menu to make it a real lunch or supper, but the cake table ensured that we never lost sweet sight of why we were really there.

We think that this party is the answer to anyone's blahs, and could guarantee the success of the next world summit meeting.

In Advance

AS IMPRESSIVE as this array of desserts looks, putting the party together is not hard. Virtually everything can be made well ahead of time. All of the cakes—the chocolate layers, the banana layers, and the sponge roll—can be baked a couple of weeks ahead and frozen, unfrosted. To thaw cakes, leave them wrapped at room temperature for just about 1 hour before frosting.

Make the ice cream up to a week ahead, although it's also wonderful if freshly churned and served up immediately while it's still soft.

The lemon-lime syrup for the phosphates will keep for at least a week.

You can make the chocolate frosting a couple of days ahead, and store it in the refrigerator.

The day before the party, set up the tables and chairs. You can also fill and frost the chocolate layer cake.

On the morning of the party, assemble the fruit for the cobbler and mix and cut its biscuit topping. Make the seafoam frosting and frost the banana cake layers. Then make the sweetened whipped cream, fill and frost the sponge roll, and cut up the peaches. A couple of hours before you want to serve it, bake the cobbler.

Now, just cut the watermelon into slices, plug in the coffee, and then stand back and listen to the exclamations of delight!

If Time Is Short ...

☛ Buy the best vanilla ice cream available.

☛ Purchase a chocolate layer cake and a banana spice cake from a good bakery. You can also buy a whipped cream sponge roll, but you should dress it up with freshly sliced and sweetened peaches. The cobbler should be homemade, and don't skip the watermelon, for the fruit provides a needed balance.

☛ If you don't make the lemon-lime syrup for the phosphates, you can use frozen lemonade concentrate and dilute it with seltzer or sparkling water.

Decidedly Chocolate Layer Cake

This is the quintessential birthday cake—towering three layers high, with plenty of fudgy frosting, and enough chocolate to satisfy everyone.

MAKES ABOUT 12 SERVINGS

Chocolate Cake Layers

3½	ounces unsweetened chocolate, coarsely chopped
2⅔	cups sifted cake flour
1½	teaspoons baking soda
½	teaspoon salt
¾	cup (1½ sticks) unsalted butter, softened
1¼	cups granulated sugar
¼	cup packed light brown sugar
4	eggs, at room temperature
2	teaspoons vanilla extract
1	teaspoon powdered espresso dissolved in 2 tablespoons hot water
1½	cups buttermilk, at room temperature

Buttermilk Fudge Frosting

6½	ounces unsweetened chocolate, coarsely chopped
4	cups confectioners' sugar
⅓ to ½	cup buttermilk, at room temperature
4	teaspoons vanilla extract
10	tablespoons (1¼ sticks) unsalted butter, softened

Milk chocolate shavings for decoration (optional) (see Note)

1. To make the cake layers, preheat the oven to 350° F. Butter three 8-inch round cake pans and line bottoms with parchment or wax paper. Melt the chocolate in a double boiler over hot water, or in a microwave oven. Sift together the cake flour, baking soda, and salt.

2. In a large mixing bowl, cream the butter with the granulated and brown sugars until light and fluffy. Add the eggs 1 at a time, beating about 1 minute and scraping bowl after each addition. Beat in the vanilla, dissolved espresso, and melted chocolate. With mixer at low speed, add the buttermilk and the flour mixture alternately, beginning and ending with flour mixture. Transfer batter to prepared pans and smooth tops with a spatula.

3. Bake in the center of the oven for 25 to 30 minutes, until cakes are firm to the touch and a tester inserted in the center comes out clean.

4. Cool cake layers in the pans on a rack for 10 minutes, then turn out of pans, remove wax paper, and let cool completely on the racks. (Can be made up to 2 weeks ahead, wrapped well, and frozen.)

5. To make the frosting, melt the chocolate in a double boiler over hot water, or in a microwave oven. Set aside to cool slightly. Beat the confectioners' sugar, ⅓ cup buttermilk, and vanilla until smooth. Blend in the chocolate. Beat in the butter until light and fluffy. If frosting seems too thick to spread, beat in additional buttermilk a teaspoon at a time. (Can be made 2 to 3 days in advance. Cover and refrigerate; return to room temperature to use.)

6. To assemble, frost 2 cake layers with ½ to ¾ cup frosting each. Add third layer and frost top and sides with remaining frosting. Sprinkle

with chocolate shavings. (Can be assembled a day ahead. Refrigerate if kitchen is very warm. Return to room temperature to serve.)

Note: To make milk chocolate shavings, use a 6- or 8-ounce milk chocolate bar at room temperature. With a swivel vegetable peeler,

peel off shavings or curls from the long side of the chocolate bar, dropping them onto waxed paper. Refrigerate the shavings for at least 30 minutes or up to 2 days before sprinkling on the top of the frosted cake.

Mother's Banana–Walnut Spice Cake—Seafoam Frosting

Moist, lightly spiced, and with billows of old-fashioned, never-fail 7-minute seafoam frosting, this is a wonderful cake that Melanie's mother has made for years.

MAKES ONE 8- OR 9-INCH LAYER CAKE

Banana-Walnut Spice Cake

2	cups all-purpose flour
1	teaspoon baking powder
1	teaspoon baking soda
½	teaspoon salt
2	teaspoons ground cinnamon
½	teaspoon grated nutmeg
½	teaspoon ground allspice
¼	teaspoon ground cloves
¼	teaspoon powdered ginger
½	cup (1 stick) softened unsalted butter
1⅓	cups granulated sugar
3	eggs, separated
1	cup (about 3) mashed very ripe bananas
½	cup buttermilk (see Note)
¾	cup chopped walnuts or pecans

Seafoam Frosting

1½	cups light brown sugar
2	large-egg whites, unbeaten
⅓	cup cold water
1	tablespoon molasses
1	teaspoon vanilla extract
3	tablespoons chopped walnuts

1. To make the cake, preheat oven to 350° F. Grease two 8- or 9-inch round cake pans and line bottoms with parchment or wax paper. Sift together the flour, baking powder, soda, salt, cinnamon, nutmeg, allspice, cloves, and ginger.

2. Cream the butter and sugar together until light and fluffy, then add the egg yolks 1 at a time, beating about 30 seconds after each addition. Beat in the mashed bananas. Add the dry ingredients in 2 additions alternating with the buttermilk. Mix just until well combined. Stir in the nuts.

3. Beat the egg whites to stiff but not dry peaks. Stir about one-fourth of the whites into the batter to lighten, then fold in the remainder.

4. Turn into the prepared pans, smoothing the tops. Bake in the center of the oven for 30 to 35 minutes, until a cake tester inserted in center comes out clean.

5. Cool in pans on racks for 10 minutes,

[continued]

then turn out onto racks, peel off paper, and cool completely. (Can be made 1 day ahead and stored, well wrapped, at room temperature, or can be frozen up to 2 weeks.)

6.   To make the frosting, whisk together all ingredients except vanilla and walnuts in the top of a large double boiler or a stainless-steel bowl. Set the double boiler or bowl over simmering water. Using a hand-held electric mixer, beat at high speed for about 7 minutes, until soft peaks form and frosting has nearly quadrupled in volume. Remove top of double boiler from water and add the vanilla. Off the heat continue to beat for 2 or 3 minutes, until frosting has thickened to spreadable consistency.

7.   Use within an hour or so to sandwich the layers with about 1½ cups frosting; use the remainder to cover sides and top of cake generously. Sprinkle with 3 tablespoons chopped walnuts. (Cake can be frosted up to 6 hours ahead and kept at room temperature.) When ready to serve, cut slices with a serrated knife, since the cake is particularly tender.

Note: To substitute for buttermilk, stir 1 teaspoon lemon juice into ½ cup milk and let stand 15 minutes to clabber.

Wild Huckleberry Cobbler

We make this wonderful cobbler with huckleberries if we can find them, but we have found it to be equally delicious with blueberries, blackberries, or raspberries—even a combination of all three! Best served soon after baking, this dessert is no trouble for a party since the fruit and flavorings as well as the biscuits can be mixed together early in the day. An hour or 2 before serving, you need only arrange the biscuits atop the fruit and bake the cobbler.

MAKES ABOUT 16 SERVINGS

Fruit mixture

8	cups berries (huckleberries, blueberries, raspberries, blackberries, or a combination)
¾ to 1	cup sugar
1	teaspoon grated lemon zest
4	teaspoons lemon juice
1	teaspoon vanilla extract
1	tablespoon softened unsalted butter for greasing the dish

Shortcakes

2	cups all-purpose flour
3	tablespoons plus 2 teaspoons sugar
1	tablespoon baking powder
½	teaspoon salt
10	tablespoons (1¼ sticks) cold unsalted butter, cut in 20 pieces
¾	cup cold milk

Vanilla ice cream

1. Preheat the oven to 400° F.

2. In a large mixing bowl, gently toss together the berries, sugar, lemon zest, lemon juice, and vanilla. Generously grease a 9- by 13-inch or other 3-quart shallow baking dish with the 1 tablespoon softened butter. Spoon the berry mixture into the dish. (Can be prepared several hours ahead and refrigerated.)

3. To make the shortcakes, place the flour, 3 tablespoons of the sugar, baking powder, and salt in the work bowl of a food processor. Pulse 5 or 6 times to "sift." Distribute the butter evenly over the flour and pulse until mixture resembles small peas. With motor running, pour milk through feed tube. Process just until all ingredients are moistened.

4. Gather the dough into a ball and turn onto a floured surface. Roll to ½-inch thickness and cut out 16 to 20 biscuits with a 2-inch round cutter. Reroll scraps as needed. (Can be made 3 hours ahead. Place on a baking sheet and refrigerate, covered with plastic wrap.) Place the shortcakes close together atop the fruit in the dish. Sprinkle with remaining 2 teaspoons sugar.

5. Bake the cobbler for 25 to 30 minutes, until fruit is bubbly and shortcakes are golden brown. Let cool at least 30 minutes, then serve slightly warm or at room temperature with a scoop of ice cream on the side.

Note: In order to provide a dessert "sampling" in this menu, the biscuits have been cut rather small. If serving as the only dessert, use a 2½- or 3-inch cutter and make 12 to 16 biscuits. You may also cut the recipe in half for smaller parties. Bake in an 8- by 8-inch square dish or other 1½-quart shallow baking dish. Baking time will be the same.

Peaches and Cream Sponge Roll

The pure flavors of peaches and sweet cream shine through in this delectable summer dessert. The long cake roll heaped high with billows of whipped cream and decorated with peaches makes a most impressive display on a buffet table, yet it's simple and quick to make.

MAKES 12 TO 14 SERVINGS

Sponge Roll

5	eggs, separated
½	cup sugar
1	teaspoon grated lemon zest
1	teaspoon vanilla extract
¼	teaspoon salt
½	cup cake flour
3	tablespoons cornstarch

Filling and Topping

2	cups heavy cream
⅓	cup confectioners' sugar
1½	tablespoons rum
1	teaspoon vanilla extract
1½	cups peeled *diced* peaches
5	cups peeled *sliced* peaches
3 or 4	tablespoons sugar, depending on sweetness of peaches

1. Preheat oven to 375° F. and position a rack in the center. Grease a 10- by 15-inch jelly roll pan, line with parchment or wax paper, and lightly grease the paper.

2. Using an electric mixer, beat the egg yolks with ¼ cup of the sugar until light and lemon-colored, about 3 minutes. Beat in the lemon zest and vanilla.

3. Place the egg whites and salt in a large bowl and beat with an electric mixer until soft peaks are formed. Gradually add the remaining ¼ cup of sugar and beat until smooth and glossy.

4. Stir about one-third of the whites into the yolks to lighten them. Place the flour and cornstarch in a sieve set over a sheet of wax paper. Sift half the flour mixture over the yolks and fold in gently. Fold in half the remaining whites, then repeat with remaining flour and whites. Batter should be smooth and light.

5. Spread into prepared pan and bake in preheated oven for 10 to 12 minutes, until cake is pale golden, springs back to the touch, and the edges are beginning to pull away from the sides. Do not overbake.

6. Dampen a tea towel and wring out as much water as possible. Run a knife around pan to loosen edges of the cake, invert on the tea towel, and strip off paper. Use a large knife to cut off crisp edges and roll cake tightly in the towel, starting from a long side. Cool seam side down on a rack. (When cool, cake can be rerolled in plastic wrap and refrigerated well wrapped for a day, or frozen for 2 weeks.)

7. To make the filling, whip the cream with the confectioners' sugar to stiff peaks. Beat in the rum and vanilla. Remove one-third of the cream to another bowl, reserving remaining two-thirds to frost the top of the cake. Stir diced peaches into smaller amount of cream.

8. Unroll cake and spread peach cream filling over inside surface, coming to within ½ inch of edges. Reroll and place seam side down on a long platter or board. (See Note.) Insert

pieces of waxed paper under cake to protect board and frost cake with remaining whipped cream. Remove waxed paper. (Assemble at least 1 hour or as much as 5 hours ahead. Stick toothpicks into cake to protect it from wrap and loosely cover with plastic wrap. Refrigerate.)

9. Add the granulated sugar to the sliced peaches and place in a pretty bowl. (Can be done 4 or 5 hours ahead.) Dry a few peach slices on paper towels and use to decorate top of cake. Cut cake with a serrated knife and serve sliced peaches on the side.

Note: To make a serving board, cut a length of plank or heavy cardboard about 17 inches long. Cover with foil or freezer paper and arrange doilies down the center.

Bernice Cooper's Homemade Vanilla Bean Ice Cream

This is the first homemade ice cream that Melanie tasted, and she will never forget it! Bernice makes her vanilla ice cream every summer Sunday afternoon in an old-fashioned crank machine with farm-fresh eggs and cream. These days, we can buy premium-quality ice cream, but nothing can replace licking the paddle.

MAKES ABOUT 1¼ QUARTS

1	cup whole milk
¾	cup granulated sugar
	Pinch salt
1	whole vanilla bean
4	egg yolks, lightly beaten
2½	cups heavy cream

1. Bring the milk, sugar, salt, and vanilla bean to a simmer in a heavy saucepan. Whisk about half of the hot milk mixture into the eggs yolks to warm them, then return the mixture to the saucepan. Cook, stirring constantly over medium-low heat, for 8 to 10 minutes, until mixture is thick enough to coat the back of a spoon. Do not allow to boil. Strain into a mixing bowl and let cool 15 minutes. Stir in the cream, cover, and chill at least 3 hours until very cold. (Can be made 2 days ahead.)

2. Remove the vanilla bean from the custard, slit lengthwise, and use a small knife to scrape the seeds and pulp back into the custard. Discard the bean.

3. Freeze the custard in an ice cream maker according to manufacturer's directions. (Can be made a week ahead.)

Lemon–Lime Phosphates

Popular around the turn of the century before commercial soda pop was marketed, phosphates are an old-fashioned treat that deserve revival. A homemade lemon–lime simple syrup is diluted with sparkling water, served over ice, and garnished with thin slices of lemon and lime. Guests are curious to see how they're made, and love the refreshing result!

MAKES ABOUT 16 DRINKS

Lemon–Lime Syrup
¾	cup lemon juice
3	tablespoons lime juice
¾	teaspoon grated lemon zest
½	teaspoon grated lime zest
½	cup water
1½	cups sugar

Assembly
	Lemon-lime syrup
3	quarts seltzer or club soda
	Thin slices of lemon and lime

1. To make the syrup, combine all ingredients in a small saucepan. Bring to the boil, stirring to dissolve sugar. Simmer for 1 minute. Cool to room temperature and store in a covered container in the refrigerator for up to 2 weeks.

2. To make the phosphates, fill tall glasses with ice cubes. Spoon about 2 tablespoons of syrup into each glass, fill to the top with sparkling water, and stir well. Garnish with lemon and lime slices.

THE FAMILY REUNION

A Happy July Fourth Tradition
FOR 30 TO 35

ONCE EVERY couple of years the clan gathers. It is an occasion to celebrate recent momentous events such as the birth of a new cousin or the marriage of a niece. But it is also a time to remember and renew the closeness of a family scattered about the country. Because Melanie lives in a central location (and has the biggest backyard), the reunion has become a Connecticut tradition.

Invitations go out with the Christmas cards to give each family time to plan their route and sign up for vacation days. It also allows ample time to dust off the old recipe cards, for the highlight of this food-loving family's get-together is the traditional July Fourth picnic.

Though the main course, almost always fried chicken, is Melanie's responsibility, the rest of the meal is a communal effort. Some dishes arrive at the ready such as the sweet-and-sour watermelon pickles that Mary always brings from Florida, or the poppy seed rolls carried in the hand luggage on the plane from California. Marianne, on the other hand, makes her peach pie in Melanie's kitchen, but brings the peaches from home.

The menu always includes at least one new item to taste and talk about, such as the chocolate pecan pie invented in honor of a cousin who recently married a chocoholic. Open to new opinions, we added a splash of grenadine to the lemonade when preteen Jennie announced that pink was the "only" way to drink lemonade.

As with the cooking, the whole family contributes the decorations. The table can never be set until Aunt Dot arrives with the tablecloth that belonged to great-grandma's sister, and no one would dare hoist anything but our carefully mended 48-star flag.

The day starts early. Uncle Edwin gets up to take the kids to the beach while the young adults conduct a rather loose version of the triathlon, and the middle-agers go for a (short) game of volleyball and a (long) game of croquet. But come four o'clock, the entire family is always there for what is really important—the reunion supper that is the substance of the event and the real glue that sticks us together for another couple of years.

In Advance

THIS IS THE PERFECT "what can I bring?" menu, and we'd never look a gift horse in the mouth, but if you're doing it alone, here's how.

Start by baking the poppy seed pan rolls and stashing them in the freezer up to 2 weeks ahead.

Then make the pickles 2 weeks in advance and keep them in the refrigerator. The lemon syrup for the lemonade will keep, refrigerated, for a week. The dry coating mixture for the "fried" chicken can be stored airtight at room temperature for several days. The chervil vinaigrette for the bean salad can be made a couple of days ahead.

The day before the party, make the potato salad and mix up the lemonade. Blanch the green beans.

Early on the day of the party, make the pies. Then assemble the corn pudding and refrigerate it. Shake the chicken in its coating, arrange it on baking sheets, and refrigerate. Defrost the rolls.

A couple of hours before the guests are due, dress the bean salad, garnish the potato salad, bake the chicken, and slice the tomatoes. The corn pudding should be put in the oven about an hour before you want to serve it.

If Time Is Short ...

☛ Pink lemonade from frozen concentrate is fine if you add lemon slices, sliced strawberries, and mint to the pitcher.

☛ You can buy watermelon pickles in a jar.

☛ Though we love the idea of a groaning board of pies, unless you have some enthusiastic bakers in your group you might want to make friends with a good bakery.

☛ It's a bonus if that same bakery makes good soft dinner rolls.

☛ If you use purchased refrigerated rolled-out pie crusts, decrease the prebaking time to about 10 minutes.

Minted Pink Lemonade

A little grenadine syrup lends an elusive fruit flavor to this refreshing not-too-sweet lemonade—as well as turning it a pretty pastel pink. Double or triple this recipe if you are not serving other beverages.

MAKES 3 QUARTS (12 CUPS)

1¼	cups sugar
½	cup water
1½	cups lemon juice (from 8 to 12 lemons)
1	tablespoon grated lemon zest
4	teaspoons grenadine syrup
	Thin slices of lemon
8	small strawberries, hulled
	Mint sprigs

1.   In a small saucepan, bring the sugar and water to the boil, stirring until sugar is dissolved and syrup is clear. Remove from heat and add the lemon juice and lemon zest. Cover and chill. (Can be made 1 week ahead.)

2.   Transfer lemon syrup to a 1-gallon pitcher. Stir in 9 cups cold water and the grenadine. (Can be made a day ahead.)

3.   When ready to serve, add ice cubes to the pitcher and float lemon slices, strawberries, and mint sprigs in the lemonade. Serve in tall glasses.

Our Best "Fried" Chicken

As far as we are concerned, this is the only way to "fry" chicken these days. Unless you have 2 ovens, you will probably need to bake in successive batches.

MAKES 30 TO 35 PIECES

12	pounds cut-up chicken parts
1	cup vegetable oil
1¾	cups unseasoned dry bread crumbs
1	cup yellow cornmeal
½	cup all-purpose flour
1½	teaspoons salt
1	teaspoon freshly ground black pepper

1. Use a cleaver to cut the chicken breast halves in half again crosswise. If thighs are attached to drumsticks, use the cleaver to separate them.

2. Preheat the oven to 400° F. Place one-third of the oil in each of three 11- by 17-inch jelly roll pans or rimmed baking pans. Roll the chicken in the oil to coat all sides.

3. In a large plastic or paper bag, shake together the bread crumbs, cornmeal, flour, salt, and pepper. Add the chicken, a few pieces at a time, and shake to coat. Remove from bag, shaking off excess coating. Place in the jelly roll pans, skin side up, leaving a small space between pieces.

4. Bake about 45 minutes, until chicken is a rich golden brown and cooked through. (Can be baked 2 hours ahead and reserved at cool room temperature.)

5. Serve warm or at room temperature. (Leftovers can be refrigerated, but should be reheated in the oven to recrisp the coating.)

Aunt Annie's Picnic Potato Salad

This is Aunt Annie's perfected old-fashioned potato salad recipe that works beautifully every time.

MAKES 30 TO 35 SERVINGS

8	pounds waxy potatoes
	Salt
⅔	cup cider or white wine vinegar
⅔	cup vegetable oil
1½	teaspoons freshly ground black pepper, plus additional for finished salad
2½	cups thinly sliced celery
2	cups chopped red onion
3	cups mayonnaise
3	tablespoons Dijon mustard
½	cup milk or cream
5	sliced hard-cooked eggs
1½	cups thinly sliced radishes
½	cup chopped fresh herbs such as a combination of parsley and dill, basil, or chives

1. Bring a large pot of water to the boil. Cut the potatoes into 2-inch chunks. Add salt to the water and cook the potatoes over medium heat for about 15 minutes, until just fork-tender. Drain well. When cool enough to handle, peel and cut into ½-inch cubes. Toss warm potatoes with the vinegar, oil, 2 teaspoons salt, and pepper and set aside for 15 minutes. Add the celery and onion and toss to combine.

2. In a small bowl, whisk together the mayonnaise, mustard, and milk. Pour dressing over the potatoes and mix gently but thoroughly. Chill for at least 1 hour. (Can be made 1 day ahead.)

3. To serve, stir the salad again gently to redistribute dressing. Taste for seasoning, adding more salt and pepper if needed.

4. Serve in a shallow bowl garnished with sliced eggs and radishes and sprinkled with chopped herbs. Grind black pepper over top.

Bean, Yellow Pepper, and Bacon Salad

This marvelously colorful salad is equally delicious made with yellow beans and red peppers. Fresh chervil in the dressing adds a summery garden taste, but the final sprinkling of crumbled bacon is what really makes this salad special.

MAKES 30 TO 35 SERVINGS

Chervil Vinaigrette
½	cup plus 2 tablespoons red wine vinegar
1	tablespoon Dijon mustard
3	tablespoons sugar
1½	teaspoons salt, or to taste
1	teaspoon freshly ground black pepper
2	cups olive oil
⅓	cup chopped fresh chervil

Salad
5	pounds green beans, trimmed and cut in half
1	pound lean bacon
2	large yellow bell peppers, cored, seeded, and cut into thin strips
3	cups thinly sliced red onion
	Chervil sprigs if available

1. To make the dressing, whisk together the vinegar, mustard, sugar, salt, and pepper until the sugar is dissolved. Whisk in oil and stir in the chervil. (Can be prepared a day ahead. Cover and refrigerate.)

2. Cook the beans in a large pot of rapidly boiling salted water for 4 or 5 minutes, or until crisp-tender. Drain into a colander and refresh under cold water to stop the cooking. Blot dry with paper towels. (Can be cooked 1 day ahead. Wrap and refrigerate.)

3. Cook the bacon over medium-low heat until crisp. Crumble and reserve. (Can be cooked 4 hours ahead. Cover loosely and store at room temperature.)

4. Combine beans in a large bowl with the peppers and onions. Toss with dressing at least 1 hour before serving. (Can be prepared 4 hours ahead. Refrigerate.) Transfer to a large shallow platter, sprinkle with the bacon, stirring some into the salad, and garnish with chervil sprigs if available.

Beefsteak Tomatoes with Basil

Make this salad only when you can get really ripe, meaty tomatoes. Slicing parallel to the stem rather than across makes for neater, juicier slices.

MAKES 30 TO 35 SERVINGS

4   pounds (about 12) ripe tomatoes, cored
     Salt
     Coarsely ground black pepper
½   cup thinly sliced fresh basil leaves
     Whole basil sprigs for garnish

1.   Slice the tomatoes about ¼ inch thick, cutting parallel to the stem. Arrange slightly overlapping on a decorative platter. Sprinkle with salt, pepper, and the sliced basil. Garnish the platter with the basil sprigs. (Prepare up to 1 hour ahead of serving.)

2.   Serve at room temperature.

Pennsylvania Dutch Corn Pudding

This subtly seasoned custard is a wonderful foil for spicy summer foods. Add a small chopped red bell pepper for a colorful variation if you wish. Double the ingredients and bake in 2 dishes for this party.

MAKES ABOUT 16 SERVINGS

4   tablespoons (½ stick) unsalted butter
1   medium onion, peeled and chopped
¼   cup all-purpose flour
4   cups half-and-half
6   eggs
1½   tablespoons sugar
1   teaspoon salt
½   teaspoon freshly ground white pepper
⅛   teaspoon grated nutmeg
4   cups fresh or frozen corn kernels
1   cup thinly sliced scallions, including
        green tops (1 bunch)
2   cups (8 ounces) grated sharp Cheddar
        cheese

1.   Preheat oven to 350° F. Generously butter a 9- by 13-inch or other 3-quart shallow baking dish.

2.   In a large skillet, heat the butter and sauté the onion over medium-low heat for about 5 minutes, until softened. Stir in the flour and cook, stirring constantly, over medium heat for 1 minute. Slowly whisk in the half-and-half and cook, stirring constantly, until mixture thickens and comes to a boil. Remove from heat.

3.   Beat the eggs with the sugar, salt, pepper, and nutmeg. Whisk about half the sauce into the beaten eggs to warm them, then pour the egg mixture into the sauce. Whisk to combine well.

4.   In a large mixing bowl, toss together the corn, scallions, and cheese. Stir in the sauce. (Can be assembled 4 hours ahead and refrigerated. Remove from refrigerator 15 minutes before continuing.)

5. Pour the mixture into the prepared dish and place in the center of the oven. Bake 45 to 55 minutes, until the pudding is light golden brown and a knife inserted just off center comes out clean. If pudding has not begun to brown, run under a broiler for about 30 seconds to glaze the top.

6. Serve hot or warm, cut in squares.

Sweet-and-Sour Watermelon Pickles

These are among the easiest and certainly most economical of all pickles to make. If you want to "put them up" to enjoy during the winter, process in a boiling-water bath according to standard directions provided by manufacturers of canning jars.

MAKES ABOUT 1½ QUARTS

	Rind from ½ large watermelon
⅓	**cup salt**
2	**cups cider vinegar**
1½	**cups sugar**
1	**teaspoon whole cloves**
1	**teaspoon whole allspice**
1	**teaspoon whole black peppercorns**
2	**whole star anise**
1	**stick cinnamon, broken in half**
2	**thin slices fresh gingerroot**
2	**large strips lemon peel, colored part only**

1. Cut all of the pink flesh from the watermelon rind and discard. Cut the rind into ¾- to 1-inch cubes or ½- by 1-inch strips. You should have about 10 cups. Place in a large nonreactive bowl. Dissolve the salt in 6 cups of water and pour over the rind. If it is not completely submerged, weight it down with a plate. Let stand 6 hours at room temperature or overnight in the refrigerator.

2. Drain the rind in a colander and rinse thoroughly under cold running water. Place in a saucepan and cover with water. Simmer gently for about 20 minutes, until just fork-tender. Drain again.

3. In a large, nonreactive saucepan bring the vinegar, sugar, and ⅔ cup water to a boil, stirring to dissolve the sugar. Add the cloves, allspice, peppercorns, anise, cinnamon, gingerroot, lemon peel, and watermelon rind and stir gently. The liquid should just cover the cubes. If it does not, add a small amount of water.

4. Partially cover the pan and simmer over medium-low heat for 20 to 30 minutes, until the watermelon is tender and translucent. Let the pickles cool in the syrup, then chill at least 12 hours. (Can be made 2 weeks ahead and refrigerated.) If you like a very spicy pickle, leave the spices in the cooled liquid; discard them if you prefer milder pickles.

Poppy Seed Pan Rolls

These buttery pull-apart dinner rolls, baked in cake pans, emerge from the oven with a lovely puffed, domed shape.

<small>MAKES 48 ROLLS</small>

2	packages (4 teaspoons) active dry yeast (see Note)
½	cup plus 1 teaspoon sugar
½	cup warm water (about 105° F.)
2½	cups milk
14	tablespoons (1¾ stick) unsalted butter, melted
7	cups (approximately) all-purpose flour, preferably unbleached
2	egg yolks
3	teaspoons salt
2	egg whites, beaten until frothy with 2 tablespoons water
3	tablespoons poppy seeds

1. Dissolve the yeast and the teaspoon of sugar in the warm water until forthy.

2. In a large bowl combine the remaining ½ cup sugar, milk, butter, 4 cups of the flour, egg yolks, and salt. Add the yeast mixture and beat vigorously with a wooden spoon or the dough hook on a heavy-duty mixer to combine. Add 2 cups additional flour and knead on a well-floured board or in the mixer until dough is smooth and elastic, about 8 minutes. During the kneading process, add enough of the remaining flour to make a soft, workable dough.

3. Transfer to a greased bowl, cover, and let rise in a warm place until doubled in bulk, about 1½ hours.

4. Generously butter four 8- or 9-inch round cake pans. Punch dough down. Divide into 4 quarters, roll each out into a strand about 12 inches long, and cut each strand into 12 pieces. Shape each piece into a rough ball and arrange rolls 12 to a pan, leaving small spaces between each of them.

5. Cover loosely and let rise for 30 minutes. Preheat the oven to 375° F. Brush rolls with the beaten egg white and sprinkle generously with poppy seeds. Bake in the center of the oven for about 25 minutes, until rolls are a warm golden brown. Serve warm. (Can be baked and frozen 2 weeks ahead. Wrap in foil to reheat.)

Note: Quick-rise yeast may be substituted. Rising times will be about half as long.

Patty's Lemon Buttermilk Pie

This refreshingly sweet-tart buttermilk pie is less rich than some. Patty's secret is adding a little lemon zest to the crust, too. It's delicious topped with sliced fresh strawberries or blueberries.

MAKES 8 SERVINGS

Lemon Crust

1¼	cups all-purpose flour
½	teaspoon salt
½	teaspoon lemon zest
5	tablespoons cold unsalted butter
3	tablespoons cold vegetable shortening

Lemon Buttermilk Filling

¾	cup granulated sugar
1	tablespoon all-purpose flour
	Pinch salt
3	eggs
1	cup buttermilk
2	tablespoons lemon juice
1	teaspoon lemon zest
1	teaspoon vanilla extract
⅛	teaspoon grated nutmeg
5	tablespoons unsalted butter, melted

1.   For the crust, combine the flour, salt, and lemon zest in a food processor. Pulse to sift. Cut the butter and shortening into small pieces and distribute over the flour. Pulse until butter is about the size of small peas. With motor running, drizzle 3 tablespoons ice water through the feed tube, processing until dough just begins to clump together. Transfer to plastic wrap, gather into a ball, flatten to a disk, and wrap well. Refrigerate for at least 30 minutes. (Can be made 2 days ahead.)

2.   Remove dough from refrigerator about 10 minutes ahead. On a lightly floured surface, roll the dough out to a 12-inch circle. Ease pastry into a 9-inch pie plate. Trim edges and crimp. Prick with a fork all over and freeze for at least 30 minutes. (Can be made 2 weeks ahead.)

3.   Position oven rack to the lowest level and preheat to 425° F. Bake frozen shell for 15 minutes or until pale gold. If pastry puffs, press to flatten. Cool on a rack for 15 minutes. (Can be baked 1 day ahead. Store, covered, at room temperature.)

4.   Reposition oven rack to center and reduce temperature to 400° F. Make the filling: In a bowl, whisk together the sugar, flour, salt, and eggs until well blended. Whisk in the buttermilk, lemon juice, lemon zest, vanilla, nutmeg, and butter. Pour into the prepared pie shell and bake in the preheated oven for 10 minutes. Reduce heat to 325° F. and continue to bake for 30 to 35 minutes, until filling is slightly puffy and just set. A knife inserted 2 or 3 inches from the edge of the custard will come out clean.

5.   Cool on a rack. (Can be baked 8 hours ahead. Refrigerate when cool, but remove from refrigerator 1 hour before serving.)

Marianne's Spiced Peaches and Cream Pie

We think that this, our very favorite peach pie, is well worth the effort. Sealing the pastry with beaten egg white and starting the baking in the lower part of the oven are the secrets to a flaky, golden brown bottom crust. Vary the amount of sugar in the pie filling according to the sweetness of your peaches.

MAKES 8 SERVINGS

Crust

2¼	cups all-purpose flour
1	teaspoon salt
1	teaspoon sugar
½	cup (1 stick) chilled unsalted butter, cut into 12 pieces
5	tablespoons chilled lard or vegetable shortening, cut in 8 pieces
1	egg yolk
2	teaspoons cider vinegar
1	egg white, beaten until frothy

Filling

¾ to 1	cup sugar
2	tablespoons quick-cooking tapioca
¾	teaspoon ground cinnamon
¼	teaspoon grated nutmeg
¼	teaspoon ground mace
¼	teaspoon grated lemon zest
6	cups (about 2½ pounds) peeled and thickly sliced peaches (see Note)
1	tablespoon lemon juice
1	tablespoon dark rum
¼	cup cream

Glaze

1	tablespoon cream
1	teaspoon sugar

1.   Make the crust: Combine the flour, salt, and sugar in a food processor. Add the butter and lard and process until mixture resembles small peas. Beat the egg yolk, vinegar, and 3 tablespoons cold water in a small bowl. With machine running, add yolk mixture to processor and mix until dough just comes together. Gather dough into 2 balls, one slightly larger than the other. Flatten each into a disk, wrap in plastic, and refrigerate at least 30 minutes. (Can be prepared 2 days ahead.)

2.   Remove dough from refrigerator about 10 minutes ahead if it is very firm. Roll larger piece on a lightly floured surface to an 11-inch circle. Ease into a 9-inch pie plate. Brush bottom with beaten egg white. Roll the small piece of dough to a 10-inch circle. Place circle on wax paper on a baking sheet. Chill both doughs about 30 minutes while making the filling.

3.   To make the filling, combine the sugar, tapioca, cinnamon, nutmeg, mace, and lemon zest in a large mixing bowl. Add peaches, lemon juice, and rum and stir to combine well. Let stand 15 minutes.

4.   Preheat oven to 450° F.

5.   Spoon the filling into the chilled pie shell. Drizzle ¼ cup cream over filling. Cut the pastry circle into ½-inch-wide strips and use to weave a lattice top. Seal lattice to bottom crust by crimping decoratively.

6.   Glaze lattice by brushing with 1 tablespoon cream and sprinkle with 1 teaspoon sugar.

7.   Place pie in lowest rack of oven and bake 20 minutes. Remove from oven and lower

temperature to 350° F. Loosely cover edge of pie with strips of aluminum foil to prevent overbrowning. Replace pie in oven on the center rack and continue to bake for 25 to 30 minutes, until filling is bubbly and crust is golden brown. Let pie cool on a rack. (Can be baked 8 hours ahead and held at room temperature.)

Note: To peel peaches, plunge into boiling water for 20 seconds. Remove with tongs and peel off skins with a small knife or swivel peeler. Skins should slip off easily.

Aunt Dot's Blueberry Crunch Pie

Who can resist blueberry pie? Rolled oats add the nutty crunch in this crisp topping. And since the top crust doesn't need anchoring to the bottom here, we take the precaution of prebaking the bottom crust to ensure against sogginess. It makes a big difference.

MAKES 8 SERVINGS

Crust

1¼	cups all-purpose flour
¼	teaspoon salt
¼	cup (½ stick) chilled unsalted butter
¼	cup chilled vegetable shortening
1	teaspoon vanilla extract

Blueberry Filling

⅔	cup sugar
3	tablespoons all-purpose flour
	Pinch salt
5	cups blueberries
2	tablespoons lemon juice

Crumb Topping

⅔	cup all-purpose flour
3	tablespoons light brown sugar
2	tablespoons quick-cooking oats
⅛	teaspoon cinnamon
6	tablespoons (¾ stick) chilled unsalted butter

1. For the crust, combine the flour and salt in a food processor. Pulse to sift. Cut the butter into pieces and distribute it and the vegetable shortening over the flour. Pulse until butter is the size of small peas. In a measuring cup, combine 3 tablespoons ice water and vanilla. With the motor running, add the liquid through feed tube and process until dough just begins to come together. Turn out onto plastic wrap, shape into a flattened disk, and wrap well. Chill for at least 30 minutes. (Can be made 2 days ahead.)

2. Remove dough from refrigerator about 10 minutes ahead. On a lightly floured board, roll dough out to a 12-inch circle. Ease into a 9-inch pie dish. Trim and flute edges and prick crust all over with a fork. Freeze for at least 30 minutes. (Can be made 2 weeks ahead.)

3. Position rack in lowest third of the oven and preheat to 425° F. Place frozen pie shell on rack and bake for 15 minutes, until pale golden. If crust puffs up, press to flatten. Cool on a rack for 15 minutes. (Can be baked 1 day ahead. Cover and store at room temperature.)

4. For the filling, combine the sugar, flour, and salt in a large bowl. Add the berries and toss to coat. Add the lemon juice and toss gently to combine. Let stand while making the topping.

5. Reposition rack to the center of the oven and reduce temperature to 375° F. For the topping, combine the flour, brown sugar, oats, and cinnamon in the food processor. Pulse until oats are finely chopped. Cut the butter into small pieces and distribute over the flour. Pulse until mixture resembles coarse meal.

6. Heap blueberries into pie shell. Sprinkle crumb topping over fruit, pressing to make an even layer. Bake in preheated oven for 1 hour, or until fruit is tender and juicy and crumb topping is a rich deep brown.

7. Cool on a rack. (Can be baked 8 hours ahead and held at room temperature.)

Martha's Chocolate Pecan Pie

Devastatingly rich with chocolate and nuts, this pie should be cut in slim wedges. If you wish, top each serving with a dollop of whipped cream.

Pastry

1⅓	cups all-purpose flour
¼	teaspoon salt
5	tablespoons cold unsalted butter, cut into 8 pieces
3	tablespoons chilled vegetable shortening, cut in 5 pieces

Filling

3	eggs, lightly beaten
¾	cup light corn syrup
½	cup granulated sugar
2	tablespoons unsalted butter, melted
1	tablespoon bourbon
1	teaspoon vanilla extract
1½	cups pecan pieces
4	ounces (⅔ cup) semisweet chocolate chips

1.   To make the pastry, combine the flour and salt in a food processor. Distribute the butter and shortening over the flour and pulse to process until mixture resembles small peas. With the machine running, pour in ¼ cup ice water and process just until the dough begins to come together—only a few seconds. Gather dough into a ball, flatten into a disk, then wrap in plastic and refrigerate at least 30 minutes. (Can be made up to 2 days ahead.)

2.   When ready to roll the dough, remove from refrigerator about 10 minutes ahead if it is very firm. On a lightly floured surface, roll dough to an 11-inch circle. Ease into a 9-inch pie plate and flute edges in a decorative manner. Freeze at least 30 minutes. (Can be made 2 weeks ahead.)

3.   Preheat the oven to 425° F. Place rack in lower third of oven. Bake the pie shell, directly from the freezer, for 13 to 15 minutes, until it is very lightly colored. Let cool at least 15 minutes. (Can be baked a day ahead and stored at room temperature.)

4.   Lower oven temperature to 375° F. Reposition oven rack to center.

5.   To make the filling, in a large mixing bowl whisk together the eggs, corn syrup, and sugar until well blended. Whisk in the butter, bourbon, and vanilla. Stir in the pecans and chocolate chips.

6.   Pour the filling into the baked shell and bake 40 to 45 minutes, until edges of pie are firm and set but center still quivers slightly when moved.

7.   Cool on a rack. (Can be made 8 hours ahead and held at room temperature.)

Autumn

Homecoming

The Garden Harvest

Halloween for Adults Only

A New England Thanksgiving

Homecoming

A Tailgate Picnic
FOR 8 TO 10

Zinfandel (NO RECIPE)

Country Terrine with Ham and Currants   220
Sourdough Toasts   221

Autumn Bisque   221

Game Hens with Crabapple–Thyme Glaze   222
Chippewa Wild Rice Salad in Radicchio   223
Roasted Broccoli and Sweet Peppers   224
Poppy Seed Breadsticks (NO RECIPE)

Free-form Pear and Ginger Tarts   224

THE INVIGORATING snap of a crisp autumn day, a milling crowd of old friends, the air of pregame excitement—the mix of all these elements creates a palpable party atmosphere. This is homecoming.

There was a time when our tailgate picnics consisted of giant deli sandwiches, bags of chips, and a keg. But then we graduated and came back for homecoming. We found that, along with the diploma, a great deal had changed about the way we looked at college and football games. For one thing, we wore tweeds and plaids instead of jeans and T-shirts. In the same way, the old menu just didn't seem appropriate any longer. Our taste buds had apparently matured a bit.

These days, our tailgate parties are more genteel, comfortable, and rather adult affairs.

First of all, we bring a folding table, chairs, and even a real tablecloth, silverware, and china serving platters. Then we arrive with food that is definitely a cut above our former menus, but still planned to be easy and portable, since our days now are no less busy than when we were undergraduates.

A spicy Zinfandel is just right with the rich terrine. Then, after a mug of hot, golden cream of carrot bisque, the main course is set out on the table. And what a colorful, inviting, and sophisticated edible picture it is, with a plate of crisp-skinned, lightly glazed game hen quarters, elegant wild rice salad spooned into ruby-red radicchio cups, and a composition platter of earthy roasted vegetables. Slices of buttery, free-form pear tarts are the delicious segue to the kickoff.

In Advance

FOR A PICNIC, "in advance" is a given. Equally important is thinking about how you're going to pack and transport the food. Gather all silverware, paper goods, serving pieces, and utensils well in advance.

Several days ahead, make the terrine, the sourdough toasts, and prepare the tart pastry.

One day ahead, make the carrot bisque base, cook the wild rice, and make the glaze for the hens and the dressings for the salads. Cut up the vegetables for roasting and refrigerate them overnight.

On the morning of the picnic, first bake the tarts. Then roast the game hens and the vegetables and finish the wild rice salad and the bisque. Then pack everything as directed.

Enjoy the day, the friends, and the game.

If Time Is Short ...

☛ Buy a high-quality country-style pâté and melba toasts from a good retail food shop.

☛ If that same good take-out shop sells homemade squabs or roast chicken you could buy them, too.

☛ You can use purchased refrigerated rolled-out pie crusts for the tarts. They'll probably need to be rolled out a little larger; also, decrease the baking time by a few minutes, since they have a tendency to burn.

☛ Pear or apple tarts from a bakery could substitute for the homemade ones.

Country Terrine with Ham and Currants

Don't be daunted by the long list of ingredients. This is one of the easiest pâté recipes we've found, with most of the mixing done right in the food processor. We get raves on it every time!

MAKES ABOUT 20 SERVINGS

Terrine

¼	pound smoked ham, cut in ½-inch cubes
½	cup dried currants
1	cup port or Madeira
½	pound sliced bacon
2	eggs
½	cup heavy cream
2	tablespoons brandy or Cognac
2	teaspoons minced garlic
2	teaspoons dried thyme
2	teaspoons salt
¾	teaspoon freshly ground black pepper
½	teaspoon ground allspice
¼	teaspoon grated nutmeg
1¾	pounds lean ground pork
½	pound chilled fresh pork fat, coarsely chopped

Garnishes

	Coarsely ground black pepper
1	small jar cornichons, sliced lengthwise
6	radishes, thinly sliced
	Sourdough Toasts (recipe follows)

1. Combine the ham and currants in a small bowl with the port or Madeira. Set aside to macerate for 1 hour.

2. Preheat the oven to 300° F. Completely line an 8-cup loaf pan or pâté mold with the bacon strips, reserving some strips for the top.

3. In a 2-cup measuring cup, beat the eggs lightly with the cream and brandy. Add the garlic, thyme, salt, pepper, allspice, and nutmeg. Drain ham and currants and add the port soaking liquid to the egg mixture.

4. Place the pork and chopped pork fat in the work bowl of a food processor. (This will need to be done in two batches unless you are using the large-capacity processor.) Process with long pulses until well combined. With the motor running, pour the egg mixture through the feed tube. Process until smooth and pastelike. Transfer to a mixing bowl and combine well with the reserved ham and currants.

5. Spoon meat mixture into the prepared pan, pressing it smooth to eliminate any air pockets. Lay strips of bacon over the top to enclose meat. Cover tightly with foil, place in a larger baking pan, and half fill the larger pan with hot water. Bake for 2 hours. Remove foil and bake for another 30 minutes, or until a meat thermometer registers 160° F.

6. Remove terrine from water bath and cool for 1 hour. Cover with foil. Place another slightly smaller pan on top of foil and fill it with heavy cans to weight the terrine so that it is compressed to an even, sliceable texture. (Refrigerate overnight or for up to 4 days.)

7. To serve, scrape or peel off bacon and discard. Place terrine on a platter and sprinkle the top heavily with coarsely ground pepper. Garnish with the pickle spears and sliced radishes. Serve cut into thin slices and quartered to place on toast rounds.

Sourdough Toasts

These elegant little toasts are nice to have on hand for serving with cheeses as well. They keep well for a few days at room temperature or can be frozen.

MAKES 30 TO 40 TOASTS

1   thin baguette, preferably sourdough

Preheat the broiler. Cut the loaf into scant ½-inch slices. If the loaf is larger than about 3 inches in diameter, cut slices in half. Arrange in a single layer on baking sheets and toast under the broiler until very pale golden. Turn with tongs and toast second side. Cool. (Can be stored in sealed plastic bags for 2 or 3 days at room temperature, or frozen.)

Autumn Bisque

A single ladleful of this rich yet delicate and lightly textured golden carrot bisque is a delightful way to begin a tailgate picnic.

MAKES 8 TO 10 FIRST-COURSE SERVINGS (ABOUT 12 CUPS)

6	tablespoons olive oil
2	large onions, peeled and chopped
3	pounds carrots, peeled and chopped or thinly sliced (about 10 cups)
1	tablespoon grated fresh ginger
2	teaspoons grated orange zest
½	teaspoon ground coriander
5	cups chicken broth
2	cups light cream
1	cup heavy cream
	Salt and white pepper to taste
½	cup minced parsley

1.   Heat the oil in a large saucepan and cook the onions and carrots, covered, over low heat for 5 minutes, stirring once or twice. Add the gingerroot, orange zest, and coriander. Add enough broth to barely cover the vegetables, about 2 cups. Simmer, covered, over medium-low heat for about 30 minutes, until carrots are very tender.

2.   Purée in a food processor in batches. (Can make 1 day ahead. Cool and refrigerate.) Shortly before serving, bring the soup just to a simmer. Stir in remaining broth and the light and heavy creams. Reheat gently, but do not boil. Taste and season with salt and pepper. (If canned broth is used, no salt may be needed.)

3.   Transport soup in a large thermos and serve in small glass cups. Sprinkle with parsley.

Game Hens with Crabapple–Thyme Glaze

Cut into quarters and burnished with a tart-sweet thyme-scented glaze, these game hens make a beautiful presentation for a picnic. Serve at room temperature.

MAKES 8 TO 10 SERVINGS

Crabapple-Thyme Glaze
½	cup crabapple or apple jelly
3	tablespoons dry white wine
1	tablespoon chopped fresh thyme, or 1 teaspoon dried
1	clove garlic, peeled and minced
2	teaspoons Worcestershire sauce

Hens
4 or 5	Cornish hens, cut in quarters (see Note)
5	tablespoons olive oil
	Salt and freshly ground black pepper
	Thyme sprigs for garnish (optional)

1. To make the glaze, combine the jelly, wine, thyme, garlic, and Worcestershire in a small saucepan. Heat to the simmer and cook, stirring, for 1 minute. Remove from heat. (Can be made a day ahead. Reheat to melt again before using.)

2. Preheat the oven to 375° F. Brush the quartered hens on both sides with oil and sprinkle lightly with salt and pepper. Arrange skin side down on racks in two shallow baking pans. Roast for 20 minutes.

3. Brush chicken pieces with glaze, turn to skin side up, brush with glaze, and return to the oven. Continue to roast for 20 to 25 minutes more, brushing once more with glaze and the pan juices, until a thigh tests done.

4. Heat the broiler. Place hens about 5 inches from the element and broil for about 1 minute to crisp and brown skin. Remove to a platter and garnish with thyme sprigs if available. Serve warm or cool. If packing for a picnic, arrange in serving dish, cover lightly, and transport in a cooler. (If serving cool, hens can be baked 2 or 3 hours ahead and held at cool room temperature.)

Note: Ask a butcher to quarter the hens; or you can do it quite easily at home with a cleaver or poultry shears. Cut around the backbones and discard.

Chippewa Wild Rice Salad in Radicchio

We love the rich, almost grassy flavor of native wild rice, but brown rice would also be wonderful in this salad.

MAKES 8 TO 10 SERVINGS

Creamy Vinaigrette

⅓	cup mayonnaise
3	tablespoons white wine vinegar
6	tablespoons olive oil
½	teaspoon salt
½	teaspoon freshly ground black pepper

Salad

2	cups wild rice
2	cups chicken broth
½	teaspoon salt
2	cups seedless grapes, preferably a combination of red and green
1	cup toasted walnut pieces (see Note)
1	cup thinly sliced celery
1	cup chopped red onion
½	cup minced parsley
1 or 2	heads radicchio, separated into leaves to make "cups"

1. To make the dressing, whisk together all the ingredients in a small bowl. Cover and refrigerate. (Can be made 2 days ahead.)

2. To make the salad, rinse the rice under cold water. Bring the broth and 3 cups water to a boil in a large saucepan. Add salt and the rice and cook, covered, over very low heat for 45 to 55 minutes, until grains are softened and most have split. If there should be any excess liquid, drain it off. (Can be cooked 1 day ahead. Refrigerate.)

3. In a large bowl combine rice with the grapes, walnuts, celery, onion, and parsley. Toss with the dressing and taste for seasoning, adding more salt and pepper if needed. Spoon into the radicchio cups and arrange on a serving platter. (Can be filled 2 to 3 hours ahead or at the picnic.)

Note: To toast nuts, spread on a baking sheet and place in a 350° F. oven for about 7 minutes, or toast in a microwave for 4 or 5 minutes, stirring twice.

Roasted Broccoli and Sweet Peppers

An assortment of colorful roasted vegetables with their charred edges is beautiful and easily transportable. Drizzle with the vinaigrette just before serving.

MAKES 8 TO 10 SERVINGS

Vinaigrette

¼	cup olive oil
2	tablespoons lemon juice
1	tablespoon white wine vinegar
1	teaspoon Dijon mustard
¾	teaspoon grated lemon zest
¼	teaspoon salt
¼	teaspoon freshly ground pepper

Vegetables

1	large bunch (about 1½ pounds) broccoli
2	red bell peppers
2	yellow bell peppers
7	tablespoons olive oil

1.   To make the vinaigrette, whisk together all ingredients. (Can be made 1 day ahead. Cover and refrigerate. Return to room temperature to serve.) Transport to the picnic in a tightly covered container.

2.   To make the vegetables, preheat the oven to 500° F. Trim the broccoli and divide into florets, each with 2 to 3 inches of thin stem. Cut the bell peppers into 1½-inch strips. Lightly brush the broccoli and peppers on both sides with the olive oil. Place in a single layer on 2 rimmed baking sheets. Roast, turning vegetables once and alternating pan positions in the oven, for 8 to 10 minutes, until vegetables are crisp-tender and lightly charred. (Can be made up to 4 hours ahead. Let stand at cool room temperature.)

3.   Arrange vegetables on a platter or transport in jars.

4.   To serve, shake or whisk the vinaigrette to reblend. Drizzle over the vegetables.

Free-form Pear and Ginger Tarts

Two smaller free-form tarts are both prettier and easier to transport to a picnic than 1 large unwieldy piece of pastry. So, for this party, simply double the ingredients and make 2 tarts. The larger quantity of pastry will still fit in a standard food processor and the filling can be mixed in a large bowl.

Pastry

1¼	cups all-purpose flour
½	teaspoon grated lemon zest
½	teaspoon salt
½	cup (1 stick) chilled unsalted butter, cut into 12 pieces
½	tablespoon lemon juice

Filling

1½	pounds ripe, firm pears such as Bosc or d'Anjou
2	teaspoons lemon juice
2	teaspoons Poire William or brandy
2	teaspoons finely chopped crystallized ginger
¼	cup sugar
1	teaspoon all-purpose flour
¼	teaspoon powdered ginger
½	teaspoon grated nutmeg
3	tablespoons chilled unsalted butter

Confectioners' sugar

1. To make the pastry, blend the flour, lemon zest, and salt in the work bowl of a food processor. Add butter and process with on/off turns until butter is the size of small peas. Combine 3½ tablespoons water and the lemon juice. With motor running, pour liquid through feed tube and process just until dough begins to come together. Gather into a ball, flatten into a disk, and cover in plastic wrap. Refrigerate at least 30 minutes or freeze 10 minutes before rolling. (Can be made 2 days ahead and refrigerated or frozen up to 1 month.)

2. To make the filling, peel and core the pears, then cut into ¼-inch-thick slices. Place in a mixing bowl and toss gently with lemon juice, Poire William, and crystallized ginger. In a separate bowl, stir together the sugar, flour, ground ginger, and nutmeg. Add to pears and toss to combine.

3. Preheat oven to 425° F.

4. On a lightly floured surface, roll the pastry disk to a 13-inch circle. Do not trim edges; they are supposed to be raggedy. Transfer the round to a large rimmed baking sheet. Patch any tears in pastry by pressing together with fingers. Place the pear mixture on the pastry round, mounding slightly higher in the center and leaving a 2-inch border all around. Dot the fruit with the 3 tablespoons butter. Fold border in to make an uneven rustic edge of about 1½ inches.

5. Bake 15 minutes, then reduce oven temperature to 375° F. and bake until pastry is golden brown and filling bubbles, about 35 minutes longer. (Don't worry if some juices begin to seep out. That's why you used a rimmed sheet.)

6. Using 2 large spatulas, transfer the tart to a rack to cool. Dust edges liberally with confectioners' sugar. Serve slightly warm or at room temperature. (Can be made 6 hours ahead. Store at room temperature.) To transport, place cooled tarts on platters or shallow baskets and cover lightly with foil. If desired, take a shaker of confectioners' sugar to the picnic to freshen up the dusting.

THE GARDEN HARVEST

An Early Autumn Dinner
FOR 6 TO 8

Prosciutto and Figs   230

~

Tomato, Mozzarella, and Crostini Salad   231

~

Lemon-grilled Swordfish   232
Fennel Herb Butter   232
Capellini Nests with Sauce Niçoise   233
Whole Wheat Breadsticks (NO RECIPE)

~

Plum Custard Tart   234

~

French Roast Coffee (NO RECIPE)

No, we don't bale hay or mow down the cornstalks, but our backyard gardens do yield a bountiful harvest, albeit on a relatively small scale. This is the time of year when the beds overflow with zucchini growing about an inch every hour, bushy basil plants sending out heady fragrance, eggplants gleaming like giant gemstones, and, of course, the luscious tomatoes that are the real highlight of every home garden. One of the greatest joys for those who love to till the soil is to reap these last rewards, since the late harvest is the prime time to savor the ripest and best of the season, even if your garden is the local produce stand.

Since we believe that you can never be too rich in tomatoes, they star in the elegant first course composed salad with mozzarella and crostini, then play a supporting role in the niçoise sauce for the pasta. The lovely flavor interplay of prosciutto-wrapped, fresh early autumn figs makes a simple yet memorable hors d'oeuvre.

These days fish is often our main course choice. Firm steaks such as swordfish, tuna, salmon, or halibut can be grilled with ease, and their meaty texture will convert even the most dedicated carnivores. Here we cap the grilled fish steaks with a simple but heady fennel butter to further play out the Provençal theme of the menu.

Small purple plums, which make a brief but prolific appearance in the early autumn, star in the rich, cardamom-scented custard tart. Dark French roast coffee is just the right ending to this meal.

For people who love to cook, the last of the harvest may well be the best season of all.

In Advance

EVEN WITH SMALL DINNERS, we follow our own advice and do most of the preparation in advance, but with a party of this size, we don't mind doing a *little* cooking at the last minute, as long as it doesn't require following a lengthy recipe.

If you wish, you could make and freeze the pastry for the tart.

Two days before the dinner, make the fennel herb butter.

A day ahead, make the niçoise sauce and the salad dressing. Bake the tart shell.

Then, in the afternoon before the dinner, make the tart, wrap the figs with prosciutto, toast the crostini, and prepare the other salad ingredients. Marinate the fish.

Shortly before serving, assemble the salad plates. During the first course, boil the water for the pasta, reheat the sauce, and be sure the fire is ready for the fish. After the first course, grill the swordfish and cook the pasta.

If Time Is Short …

☛ In place of the plum tart, buy a fruit tart from a bakery.

Prosciutto and Figs

Fresh figs are one of the glories of this season. For this recipe, you can use either the green or black variety. The figs should be ripe, but not so soft that they're too pulpy to pick up.

MAKES 6 TO 8 SERVINGS

6 to 8	ripe but firm figs, any variety
⅛	pound prosciutto, sliced paper-thin

1. Cut the figs into quarters.

2. Cut prosciutto into strips about ¾ inch wide and 2½ inches long. Wrap ham around fig segments and place on a platter, seam side down. (Can be made 2 hours ahead. Wrap and refrigerate.)

Tomato, Mozzarella, and Crostini Salad

This salad, inspired by Tuscan panzanella, should be made with the best oil, vinegar, and bread.

MAKES 6 TO 8 SERVINGS

Balsamic Vinaigrette

¾	cup olive oil
¼	cup plus ½ tablespoon balsamic vinegar
1	clove garlic, peeled and minced
½	teaspoon salt
½	teaspoon freshly ground black pepper

Salad

6	ounces French bread baguette
1	clove garlic, peeled and cut in half
2	pounds (about 6) ripe, firm tomatoes
8	ounces fresh mozzarella cheese
1	sweet white or red onion, peeled
⅓	cup lightly packed fresh basil leaves
6 to 8	small sprigs basil for garnish

1. To make the vinaigrette, whisk together the oil, vinegar, garlic, salt, and pepper. (Can be made a day ahead. Cover and refrigerate.)

2. Preheat the oven to 400° F. Cut the bread into ½-inch slices. Place in a single layer on a baking sheet and toast in the oven for 5 minutes. Turn and toast 4 to 5 minutes more until pale golden. Rub one side of the toasts with the cut side of the garlic. (Toasts can be prepared several hours ahead and stored at room temperature.)

3. Peel and seed the tomatoes, then cut into ¼-inch slices. Thinly slice the cheese. Chop the onion and the basil leaves. (Can prepare 3 hours ahead. Refrigerate separately.)

4. When ready to serve, overlap the tomatoes and cheese in a circular flower-petal fashion on individual plates. Surround with the toasts, tucking them under the tomatoes and cheese slightly. Sprinkle with the chopped onion and basil. Whisk the vinaigrette to reblend, then drizzle over the salads, including the toasts. Garnish each salad with a basil sprig.

Lemon-grilled Swordfish

Swordfish is wonderful cooked on the grill. Its mild, firm flesh holds up just beautifully to the intense heat and is enhanced by the fire's smokiness.

¼   cup olive oil
2   teaspoons lemon juice
2 or 3   pounds swordfish, cut 1 inch thick (see Note)
        Salt and freshly ground black pepper

1. Build a barbecue fire or light the gas grill.
2. Combine the oil and lemon juice and brush over the fish. Sprinkle with salt and pepper and let stand for at least 10 minutes. (Can be prepared 2 hours ahead. Refrigerate.)
3. Cook fish on a hot grill for about 5 minutes per side. Serve on warm plates topped with a medallion of the fennel herb butter.

Note: Adjust amount of fish to the number of guests. It could also be cooked in the stove broiler.

Fennel Herb Butter

This lovely green butter, flavored with just a hint of anise, is also delicious melted over steamed vegetables.

MAKES 6 TO 8 SERVINGS

½   cup packed parsley leaves
2   tablespoons minced chives
½   teaspoon fennel or anise seed
½   teaspoon Dijon mustard
⅛   teaspoon cayenne
½   cup (1 stick) unsalted butter, softened

1. On a board or in a food processor, chop the parsley, chives, and fennel seed together until parsley is finely minced and fennel seeds are bruised to release their oil. Combine in a bowl with the mustard and cayenne. Add the butter and combine until well mixed.
2. Transfer to a sheet of plastic wrap and use the wrap to help shape the butter into a log about 6 inches long. Refrigerate for at least 1 hour, or for up to 3 days. (Can be frozen for 1 month.)
3. To serve, cut off ½-inch medallions of the butter and place atop hot fish or vegetables.

Capellini Nests with Sauce Niçoise

Capellini pasta can be easily twirled into neat little "nests" to hold this colorful and intensely flavored sauce inspired by the last of our summer harvest combined with the flavors of Provence.

MAKES 6 TO 8 SERVINGS

Sauce Niçoise

5	tablespoons olive oil
1	large onion, peeled and chopped
2	cloves garlic, peeled and minced
1	medium or 2 small zucchini (about 8 ounces), chopped
1	small eggplant (about 12 ounces), peeled and cut in ¼-inch dice (about 3 cups)
1	green bell pepper, cored, seeded, and cut in ¼-inch dice
1½	pounds plum tomatoes, peeled, seeded, and chopped (about 3 cups)
1	cup white wine
½	cup chicken broth
½	cup pitted niçoise olives, halved
2	teaspoons drained capers
2	teaspoons chopped fresh rosemary, or 1 teaspoon dried
½	teaspoon freshly ground black pepper
¼	teaspoon dried red pepper flakes
3	tablespoons chopped parsley

Pasta

12	ounces capellini or other thin-strand pasta
1	tablespoon olive oil

1.   To make the sauce, heat the oil in a large skillet. Add the onion and cook over medium heat until it begins to soften, about 5 minutes. Add garlic, zucchini, eggplant, and green pepper. Cover skillet and cook over medium-low heat, stirring occasionally, for 20 minutes.

2.   Add tomatoes, wine, and broth and simmer uncovered for 15 more minutes, until eggplant is tender and sauce is thickened. Stir in olives, capers, rosemary, black pepper, and red pepper flakes and cook for 5 minutes. Sauce consistency should be similar to ratatouille, but a little juicier. (Can be made a day ahead. Cover and refrigerate.)

3.   When ready to serve, reheat and stir in the parsley. Add broth or wine if sauce is too thick.

4.   To cook the pasta, bring a large pot of water to the boil. Add salt and the capellini and cook at a rapid boil for about 4 minutes, or until pasta is al dente. Drain into a colander, return to the pot, and toss with oil.

5.   Using about ¾ cup of pasta for each serving, place on dinner plates and swirl with your forefinger to create a neat nest with a cavity for the sauce. Spoon about ½ cup of the sauce into the center.

Note: You will probably have leftover sauce, but it's great reheated the next day or used as a cold salad. It will keep in the refrigerator for about a week.

Plum Custard Tart

Small Italian prune plums, which come into season at the end of summer, have a wonderful texture and flavor for baking. This tart makes sophisticated use of these lovely plums by baking them in a crisp, brown-sugar pastry covered with a rich brandy- and cardamom-scented custard.

MAKES 6 TO 8 SERVINGS

Brown Sugar Pastry

1¼	cups all-purpose flour
1	tablespoon brown sugar
¼	teaspoon salt
½	cup (1 stick) chilled unsalted butter, cut into small pieces

Filling

12	ounces fresh Italian prune plums
5	tablespoons sugar
2	egg yolks
1	tablespoon all-purpose flour
1	tablespoon brandy
½	teaspoon vanilla extract
¼	teaspoon ground cardamom
⅔	cup heavy cream

Confectioners' sugar

1.   To make the pastry, mix the flour, brown sugar, and salt in a food processor. Dristribute the butter over the flour and process until butter is the size of small peas. With the motor running, drizzle 3 to 4 tablespoons ice water through feed tube and process until dough begins to come together. Gather into a ball, flatten into a disk, wrap in plastic, and refrigerate for at least 30 minutes or up to 2 days.

2.   Roll the dough out on a lightly floured surface to about an 11-inch round. Transfer to a 9-inch tart pan with a removable bottom. Press dough into sides of pan and trim edges. Place in the freezer for at least 30 minutes, uncovered, or cover and freeze up to 2 weeks.

3.   When ready to bake, preheat oven to 425° F. Bake tart shell, directly from the freezer, for 13 to 15 minutes, until light golden. (If pastry puffs, press to flatten.) Cool completely on a rack. (Can be baked a day ahead. Store at room temperature.)

4.   To make the filling, preheat the oven to 350° F. Pit the plums and cut the fruit into quarters or sixths, depending upon the size. (You should have about 2 cups cut-up fruit.) Arrange the fruit, overlapping slightly, in concentric circles to form a single layer covering the bottom of the tart shell. Sprinkle with 2 tablespoons of the sugar. Bake for 20 minutes, until fruit is beginning to soften.

5.   In a bowl, whisk together the remaining 3 tablespoons sugar, egg yolks, flour, brandy, vanilla, and cardamom. Whisk in cream until blended. Pour the custard evenly over the partially baked plums. Return to oven and bake an additional 25 minutes, until the custard is just pale gold and set in the center.

6.   Serve warm or at room temperature. (Can be baked 3 hours ahead and held at cool room temperature.) Just before serving, dust lightly with confectioners' sugar. Refrigerate leftovers.

HALLOWEEN FOR ADULTS ONLY

A Caribbean "Day of the Dead" Party
FOR 12 (OR 13)

CIDER, DOUGHNUTS, and bobbing for apples are just fine with us. But after years of trekking through the neighborhood trick-or-treating with the tykes, we think it is high time to celebrate the festival for adults only.

The idea for this party comes from several vacations in the Caribbean, where we were introduced to the exotic flavors and customs of the islands south of the border. There, rather than highlighting Halloween, the people focus on the Day of the Dead (All Souls Day), November 2. Instead of mourning, they celebrate happy memories of relatives and friends with parties and even picnics in the cemeteries. We think it is the perfect excuse for a colorful, whimsical, macabre, joyous, funny, and exotic Caribbean banquet.

For decorations, use some traditional Halloween accoutrements including cardboard skeletons and pumpkins, but add the brilliant colors of the Caribbean in tablecloths of azure blue and napkins of sunshine yellow and flamingo pink. The buffet centerpiece is a huge display of tropical fruits and vegetables surrounding a gorgeous, gaudy, and deliciously edible pan de muertos—bread for the Day of the Dead—decorated with the customary crossbones and teardrops made of dough.

Our menu draws freely from all parts of the region, beginning with a potent rum drink, colorful marinated shrimp, spicy grilled chorizo tidbits, and addictive fried plantain chips. The main course consists of platters of the lip-searing Jamaican classic "jerked" pork and chicken, traditional allspice-scented rice and beans, a refreshing contemporary vegetable and fruit salad, and a big basket of golden sweet potato biscuits. As condiments, put out as many bottles of exotic tropical hot sauces as you can find.

Recorded reggae music playing throughout the party is also the rhythmic inspiration for the limbo dancing contest using 2 stepladders and a wooden pole.

After all the back-breaking postdinner exercise, soothing coconut bread pudding, an array of tropical fruit slices, and a cup of java spiked with Tia Maria are just the right antidotes.

Yes, cider and doughnuts and bobbing for apples are just fine with us. But the Day of the Dead party is so much fun that we may make it our new Halloween tradition—for adults only.

In Advance

THIS DAY OF THE DEAD party requires some planning, but if you get yourself well organized, the "execution" is relatively painless.

Two weeks ahead, make the bread and freeze it. The biscuits can also be baked and frozen if you wish. This is the time to plan your costume and to think about house decorations.

The day before the party, make the salad dressing, cook the shrimp, and precook the chorizo. Marinate the pork and chicken and make the base for the rice. You can also make the zombie mix if you like.

On the morning of the party, thaw and glaze the bread. Make the shrimp marinade and skewer the chorizos. Assemble the bread pudding and cut up the salad ingredients and the tropical fruits. Fry the plantain chips.

In the afternoon, whip the cream for the coffee. Bake the rice, then the chicken and pork, and finally the bread pudding. Make the biscuits if you have not done so earlier. Then combine the shrimp and the marinade.

Just before serving, grill the chorizo, reheat the rice, and run the pork and chicken under the broiler.

Caramelize the top of the bread pudding before putting it out with the fruit and the coffee.

Limber up for the limbo contest!

If Time Is Short ...

☛   Fried plantain chips can be purchased from some Spanish groceries.

☛   Ask the fish market to cook the shrimp for you.

☛   The sweet potato biscuits could be replaced with store-bought biscuits or bread.

☛   If you can locate a Spanish bakery, buy the pan de muertos or another similar sweet yeast bread.

Zombies!

The original was supposed to have been made with 5 kinds of rum. This version has 3, if we stretch it, and it's plenty potent! Be judicious; more than one zombie could turn you into one of the walking dead. If you have palm tree stirrers, they look great in this drink.

MAKES 1 DRINK, BUT CAN BE MULTIPLIED

For each cocktail

1½	ounces white rum
1½	ounces dark rum
½	cup pineapple juice
3	tablespoons orange juice
2	tablespoons lime juice
½	ounce 151-proof dark rum (optional)

1. Stir or shake together the white and dark rums, pineapple juice, orange juice, and lime juice. You can easily multiply the amounts and mix in a blender or a pitcher. (Can be made a day ahead.)

2. Pour over ice in a glass and float the optional 151-proof rum on top.

Grilled Chorizo Brochettes with Sweet Mustard

Spanish chorizo is a wonderful, highly seasoned link sausage that is readily available in specialty shops and Latin groceries. If you can't find it, use hot Italian sausage or garlicky kielbasa. Purchased sweet mustard is fine, but if you wish, you could make our Wild Thyme Honey-Mustard Sauce on page 94.

MAKES 12 SERVINGS

1   pound Spanish chorizo sausage or hot Italian sausage links
1   cup hearty red wine (such as Spanish Rioja or Italian Barolo)
About 48 bamboo skewers, each about 6 inches long
     Sweet mustard sauce

1.   Place sausages in a single layer in a 9-inch skillet. Pour wine over sausage and bring to a boil. Reduce heat, partially cover skillet, and simmer gently, turning once, until sausages are cooked through, about 12 minutes. Remove from pan and cool. (Can be prepared 1 day ahead. Cover and refrigerate.)

2.   Soak the bamboo skewers in water for at least 30 minutes before using. Cut the sausages into ½-inch slices and place a piece of chorizo on the end of a wet skewer. (Can assemble several hours in advance and refrigerate with ends of wooden skewers wrapped in wet paper toweling to keep them moist.)

3.   When ready to cook, build a medium barbecue fire or preheat the broiler. If grilling outdoors, place skewers with empty ends toward outside of grill and cook, turning once, for 4 to 5 minutes until hot and charred. If cooking indoors, place skewers on a broiler pan, empty ends toward outside, and broil about 4 inches from the heat source for 2 to 3 minutes, until hot and charred.

4.   To serve, spoon mustard into a small bowl and place in the center of a platter. Arrange skewers around outside.

Shrimp "Janga"-style

Janga are tasty Jamaican crawfish, but shrimp are a perfect substitute in this refreshing and colorful preparation. Scotch bonnet chilis are small, hot, and similar to jalapeños.

MAKES 12 SERVINGS

Shrimp

2	teaspoons salt
3	peppercorns
2	slices lemon
1½	pounds (about 48) medium shrimp

Marinade

1	cup white vinegar
1½	tablespoons sugar
½	cup olive oil
1 to 2	Scotch bonnet or jalapeño peppers, minced
1	red onion, peeled, thinly sliced, and separated into rings
1	green bell pepper, cored, seeded, and thinly sliced into strips
1	lemon, thinly sliced
1	large clove garlic, peeled and minced

1.   To prepare the shrimp, bring a large pot of water to the boil. Add salt, peppercorns, lemon, and the shrimp. Cook for about 3 minutes, or until shrimp turn pink. Drain into a colander and run under cold water to stop the cooking. Peel and devein. Transfer to a bowl, cover, and refrigerate. (Can be prepared a day ahead.)

2.   To prepare the marinade, whisk together the vinegar and sugar until sugar dissolves. Then whisk in the olive oil. Stir in remaining marinade ingredients. (Can be made 6 hours ahead and refrigerated.) Add the shrimp. Cover and refrigerate, stirring several times, for at least 2 hours and up to 4 hours before serving.

3.   To serve the appetizer, drain off about half the marinade, then spoon remaining marinade and the shrimp and vegetables in a shallow rimmed dish and provide toothpicks for spearing the shellfish.

Plantain Chips

Although they look like large bananas, plantains are never eaten raw. Cut into thin slices and fried, they will make potato chips seem mundane! Instead of using large quantities of oil, we shallow-fry our plantain chips in a skillet. Use green plantains for this recipe, for they slice and fry better.

MAKES 12 SERVINGS

3   **large firm green plantains**
     Vegetable oil
     Salt

1.   Use a small knife to peel the skin from the starchy flesh of the plantains. Cut the plantains into very thin slices, no more than ¹⁄₁₆ inch thick.

2.   In a large skillet or electric frypan, heat about ½ inch oil to about 375° F. (Test with a cube of bread—it will brown in about 30 seconds.) Add enough plantain slices to fill but not crowd the pan. Fry about 4 minutes, turning once or twice with a slotted spoon, until rich golden brown and crisp. Remove with a slotted spoon and drain on paper toweling. Sprinkle with salt while still hot. Continue to fry all chips.

3.   Serve immediately or prepare about 6 hours ahead and hold on a baking sheet at room temperature. Shortly before serving, rewarm in a 350° F. oven for a few minutes. Serve in a napkin-lined basket.

Jerked Pork and Chicken

The story is that the first European settlers in Jamaica learned this cooking method from the Arawak Indians, who would pierce meat (or "jerk" it), stuff the holes with spices, and then smoke it in a pit lined with hot rocks. In contemporary Jamaica the technique has evolved into first immersing or rubbing pork or chicken with a hot/sweet/sour/spicy marinade before cooking it either on the grill or in the oven. Jerked meat should be searingly spicy, but you can adjust it to your taste by varying the amounts of chilis and cayenne.

MAKES 12 SERVINGS

Jerk Marinade

¾	cup olive oil
⅓	cup white vinegar
⅓	cup orange juice
3	tablespoons lime juice
3	tablespoons sugar
½	cup minced scallions, including green tops
4	cloves garlic, peeled and minced
1 or 2	Scotch bonnet, jalapeño, or serrano peppers, minced
2	teaspoons dried thyme
1½	teaspoons dried leaf sage
1	teaspoon ground allspice
1	teaspoon ground cinnamon
1	teaspoon salt
1	teaspoon freshly ground black pepper
¾ to 1	teaspoon cayenne

12 to 16 boneless pork loin chops (approximately 3½ pounds), about ½-inch thick
12 to 16 boneless chicken breasts and/or thighs (approximately 3½ pounds), with skin on (see Note)

1.   To make the marinade, combine all ingredients in a bowl, whisking to dissolve sugar. (Can be made a day ahead.)

2.   Place pork and chicken in large bowls or glass baking dishes. Pour marinade over meat, lifting up chicken skin to rub some marinade beneath the skin. Cover and refrigerate for at least 3 hours or for as long as overnight.

3.   Preheat the oven to 375° F. Arrange meat close together or slightly overlapping in a single layer in shallow baking pans or jelly roll pans, with chicken skin side up. Bake uncovered for about 25 minutes, or until cooked through, brushing once with the marinade and pan juices. (Can be baked 2 or 3 hours ahead and held, covered, at cool room temperature.)

4.   To finish, preheat the broiler. Brush meat again with pan juices and spoon out any excess drippings so they don't burn. Broil about 5 inches from the heat source until pork is browned and chicken skin is crisp and lightly charred, 2 to 3 minutes. Arrange on platters to serve.

Note: Ask the butcher to bone the chicken, leaving the skin intact. The meat may also be grilled over moderately hot coals until cooked through, basting 2 or 3 times with marinade.

West Indian Peas and Rice

This spicy dish is eaten all over the Caribbean. In Jamaica, where it's usually made with red beans,
they call it "rice 'n peas," whereas on other islands the same dish, made with one of a number of other
dried beans, is known as "peas 'n rice." We like this version with both red and black beans.

MAKES 12 TO 15 SERVINGS

1½	cups shredded coconut, either sweetened or unsweetened
5	tablespoons vegetable oil
2	cups chopped onion
2	cloves garlic, peeled and minced
1 or 2	Scotch bonnet or jalapeño peppers, minced
2½	cups raw long-grain rice
3	cups chicken broth
2	tablespoons chopped fresh thyme, or 1 tablespoon dried
1	teaspoon ground allspice
½	teaspoon cayenne
½	teaspoon salt
½	teaspoon freshly ground black pepper
1	1-pound can red beans (either pink beans or kidney beans), drained and rinsed
1	1-pound can black beans, drained and rinsed
1	cup chopped scallions, including green tops
	Thyme sprigs for garnish, if available

1.   Place the coconut in a bowl, pour 2½ cups boiling water over it, and set aside to steep for 40 minutes. Strain through a sieve, pressing hard on the coconut to extract as much flavor as possible. Discard coconut and reserve liquid.

2.   Heat the oil in a large skillet. Sauté onion over medium-low heat until softened and lightly browned, about 10 minutes. Add garlic, minced peppers, and rice and cook for 1 minute, stirring so that rice is coated with oil. Transfer rice to a 4-quart baking dish or divide among two 2-quart dishes. (Can be made 1 day ahead. Cover with foil and refrigerate.)

3.   Preheat the oven to 350° F. Measure the coconut liquid (you should have about 2 cups) and add enough water to make 3 cups. Heat in a large saucepan along with the chicken broth, thyme, allspice, cayenne, salt, and pepper. Pour over the rice, dividing equally if using two dishes, add the beans, stir to combine, and cover tightly with foil. Bake 2 smaller dishes for 40 to 50 minutes, and the larger baking dish for 60 to 70 minutes, until rice is tender and most, but not all, of the liquid is absorbed. The dish should be somewhat soupier than regular rice. (Can be baked up to 4 hours ahead. Reheat in a 350° F. oven for about 20 minutes, or, if you have used the smaller dishes, in the microwave, adding a little more liquid if it seems dry.)

4.   Just before serving, stir in the scallions and taste for seasoning, adding salt and black pepper if necessary. Garnish with the thyme sprigs if you are using them.

Tropical Salad with Cilantro–Curry Vinaigrette

A wonderfully colorful array of exotic tropical vegetables and fruits, this composed salad is dressed with a vinaigrette flavored with cilantro and a touch of curry.

MAKES 12 SERVINGS

Cilantro-Curry Vinaigrette

3	tablespoons white wine vinegar
1	tablespoon lime juice
1	teaspoon Dijon mustard
1	teaspoon honey
⅔	cup olive oil
½	teaspoon curry powder
½	teaspoon salt
½	teaspoon freshly ground black pepper
3	tablespoons chopped fresh cilantro

Tropical Salad

2	red bell peppers
1	green bell pepper
1	large barely ripe mango or papaya
1	large or 2 small avocados
1	cup chopped red onion
	Sprigs of cilantro for garnish

1. To make the dressing, whisk together the vinegar, lime juice, mustard, and honey. Slowly whisk in the oil and season with the curry powder, salt, and pepper. (Can be made a day ahead.) Stir in the cilantro before using.

2. For the salad, halve the peppers, remove the seeds and ribs, and thinly slice into half-rings. Spread out onto one or two large platters. Peel the mango or papaya with a vegetable peeler, cut into slices, stack the slices, and cut into thin julienne strips. Scatter over the peppers. (Can be made 6 hours ahead. Cover and refrigerate.)

3. Shortly before serving, peel and slice the avocado and fan it out over the top of the salad. Sprinkle with the chopped red onion. Drizzle salad with the dressing and garnish with cilantro sprigs.

Sweet Potato Biscuits

Mashed sweet potato adds moistness and flavor to these tender biscuits. Serve them with butter or jalapeño jelly.

1	large or 2 small (about 12 ounces total) sweet potatoes
6	tablespoons milk
2	cups all-purpose flour
1	tablespoon baking powder
1	tablespoon light brown sugar
1	teaspoon salt
¼	teaspoon freshly ground pepper
¼	cup (½ stick) chilled unsalted butter, cut in bits
2	tablespoons chilled vegetable shortening, cut in bits

1. Prick the sweet potatoes, then cook in a microwave oven for about 8 minutes, or bake, wrapped in foil, in a conventional oven for about 1 hour at 375° F. until very tender. Let cool, then peel and mash with a fork to make 1 cup. Blend the milk into the mashed sweet potatoes and set aside. (Can prepare 1 day ahead. Cover and refrigerate.)

2. Preheat the oven to 425° F.

3. In a large mixing bowl, sift or whisk together the flour, baking powder, brown sugar, salt, and pepper. Cut in the butter and shortening until mixture resembles small peas. Using a fork, gently beat in the mashed sweet potato mixture to make a soft but manageable dough.

4. Turn dough onto a lightly floured surface and knead about 5 times. Roll or pat to ½-inch thickness and cut with a 2-inch biscuit cutter. Reroll and cut scraps once. Place biscuits about 2 inches apart on a large greased baking sheet. (Can be prepared 3 hours ahead. Cover lightly and refrigerate on baking sheet.)

5. Bake in the center of the oven for 14 to 17 minutes, until golden brown and well risen. (Biscuits can be served immediately or within a few hours, or they can be baked ahead and frozen. Thaw, then reheat for a few minutes in an oven set at any temperature between 350° F. and 425° F.)

Coconut–Rum Bread Pudding

The top of this rich, rum-spiked custard is covered with shredded coconut, which caramelizes as the pudding bakes to make a beautiful golden brown crust. Use your most attractive baking dishes, as the dessert is served right from the oven.

MAKES 12 SERVINGS

12	ounces day-old French bread
6	tablespoons (¾ stick) unsalted butter, melted
6	eggs
3	egg yolks
1	cup sugar
½	cup cream of coconut (see Note)
1	quart half-and-half
2	cups milk
¼	cup rum, either light or dark
1	tablespoon vanilla extract
¾	cup shredded sweetened coconut

1. Cut the bread into ½-inch slices and arrange in 2 layers in one 3½- to 4-quart shallow baking dish or two 2-quart dishes. Drizzle bread with melted butter.

2. Preheat the oven to 325° F. In a large bowl, whisk together the eggs, egg yolks, sugar, and cream of coconut. Stir in the half-and-half, milk, rum, and vanilla. Pour egg mixture over the bread, pushing bread down into the liquid to make sure it is well soaked. The dish will be quite full. (Can be assembled several hours ahead. Cover and refrigerate.)

3. Bake in the preheated oven for 20 minutes. Sprinkle with the shredded coconut and return to the oven for 25 to 30 minutes for the smaller dishes, 35 to 45 minutes for the larger pan. The pudding is done when it is puffed and golden and a knife inserted 2 inches from the edge comes out clean. The center should still be slightly wobbly since it will continue to cook a bit after being removed from the oven. Pudding will sink as it cools. (Cool on a rack and serve warm, or bake 3 hours ahead and serve at room temperature.)

4. When ready to serve, preheat the broiler. Place pudding about 5 inches from the heat source and broil for about 30 seconds, until the top is an even, deep golden brown. Cut into squares and serve with fruit.

Note: Cream of coconut is a canned sweetened coconut cream, best known as an ingredient in piña coladas. Be sure to buy plain cream of coconut, not the piña colada mix.

Caribbean Fruits

This platter of cut-up exotic fruits goes perfectly with the rich bread pudding. The whole fruits—and some tropical vegetables—flanking the pain de muertos will then be your gorgeous edible centerpiece.

MAKES 12 SERVINGS

A selection of some of the following:

> Pineapple spears
> Banana slices
> Papaya slices
> Mango slices
> Kiwi slices
> Pink grapefruit sections

Centerpiece
> **Whole tropical fruits**
> **Chile peppers**
> **Avocados**
> **Any other colorful and interesting tropical fruits or vegetables such as plantains, gourds, and the like**

Arrange cut-up fruit on a platter. (All but the bananas can be sliced early in the day. Cover and refrigerate.) Surround with whole fruits and vegetables to make a colorful tropical display, with the decorated bread in the center.

Jamaican Java

This is almost dessert all by itself!

MAKES 12 SERVINGS

¾   cup heavy cream
10   cups freshly brewed hot coffee
8 to 12   tablespoons Tia Maria or Kahlúa to taste
       Ground cinnamon

1. Whip the cream and reserve. (Can be whipped 4 hours ahead. Cover and refrigerate.)
2. Combine the coffee with the Tia Maria. Pour into cups and top each serving with a dollop of whipped cream and a sprinkling of cinnamon. Serve immediately.

Pan de Muertos (Bread for the Day of the Dead)

The Day of the Dead, or All Souls Day, on November 2 is celebrated throughout Latin America with festivals and all kinds of memorabilia. Pan de muertos is a round, sweet, orange-scented loaf sold in Caribbean and Mexican bakeries. Decorated with dough skulls, crossbones, and teardrops to commemorate deceased relatives, the baked bread is often iced and sprinkled with pink-colored sugar. Here we use it, along with an array of tropical fruits and vegetables, as a dramatic edible centerpiece.

MAKES 1 LOAF SERVING ABOUT 12

Bread Dough

½	cup milk
¼	cup plus 1 teaspoon sugar
4	tablespoons (½ stick) unsalted butter
1	teaspoon salt
1	package (2 teaspoons) active dry yeast (see Note)
¼	cup lukewarm water (105° F. to 115° F.)
3½ to 3¾	cups all-purpose flour
1	tablespoon grated orange zest
1	teaspoon orange flower water
2	eggs
1	egg beaten with 2 teaspoons water

Decoration

¾	cup confectioners' sugar
½	teaspoon orange flower water
	Pink-colored sugar crystals

1.   To make the bread dough, heat the milk, ¼ cup sugar, the butter, and salt until very warm and butter is nearly melted. Stir to dissolve sugar, then let cool to lukewarm. Dissolve the yeast in the lukewarm water and remaining 1 teaspoon sugar. Let stand 5 to 10 minutes until frothy.

2.   Place 3½ cups flour in the work bowl of a food processor or in a large mixing bowl, preferably one with a dough hook. Add the orange zest, orange flower water, eggs, milk mixture, and yeast mixture. Process or beat to make a soft and slightly sticky but workable dough. If too sticky, add the additional flour. Process for 45 seconds or knead with a dough hook or by hand on a lightly floured surface for about 5 minutes until smooth and elastic. Place in a greased bowl, turn to grease top, then cover lightly and let rise in a warm place for 1 to 1½ hours until doubled in bulk.

3.   Punch down and place on a lightly floured surface. Pull off a piece of dough about 2 inches in diameter. Form remaining dough into a ball and place on a greased baking sheet. Flatten slightly to make a circle about 7 inches in diameter. From the 2-inch ball of dough, pinch off small pieces and form into about twelve 1½-inch strips, each about ¼ inch wide. Form remaining dough into about 10 small balls about ½ inch in diameter. Paint bottoms of 8 of the strips with egg glaze, then crisscross them on the top of the bread to make 4 crosses. Taper the ends of the remaining strips to simulate teardrops. Paint bottoms of these strips and the small dough balls, then stick them randomly onto the bread as well. (Reserve remaining glaze.) Cover the dough lightly with a tea towel or greased plastic wrap and let rise in a warm place for about 45 minutes until nearly doubled in bulk.

4. Preheat the oven to 375° F. Gently brush the risen dough with some of the remaining egg wash. Bake in the center of the oven for 30 to 35 minutes, until rich golden brown and loaf sounds hollow when tapped. Remove to a rack to cool completely. (Bread can be made 2 weeks ahead, wrapped well, and frozen. Decorate after thawing.)

5. To make the decoration, mix together the confectioners' sugar, the orange flower water, and enough water (3 or 4 teaspoons) to make a thick drizzling consistency. Drizzle randomly, then immediately sprinkle with the colored sugar. Let stand at least 30 minutes to allow icing to set. (Bread can be iced several hours ahead.)

Note: Quick-rising yeast can be used. Rising times will be about half.

A New England Thanksgiving

A Composite of Our Favorite Recipes
FOR 8 TO 10

Relish Tray of Iced Radishes, Celery, and Carrots (NO RECIPE)

~

LIVING IN New England includes the privilege of feeling a special connection to Thanksgiving. After all, the first Pilgrim feast was held right in our "neighborhood" more than 370 years ago and has continued practically without a break ever since.

We know that when the Wampanoag Indians came to help the settlers of the Plymouth Colony celebrate their first harvest with a 3-day feast, they brought many of their own dishes with them. Though there is doubt about whether they ate roast turkey that first year, records list oysters, eel, venison, cornbread, succotash, leeks, berries, and plums for sure. Two years later turkey, pumpkin pie, and cranberries were definites, and the unbroken tradition began.

Because most of these are familiar foods, readily available and well loved in our part of the world, for us it's a natural process to gather many of these same ingredients together each year, creating a feeling of being part of a New England Thanksgiving continuum. Our molasses-glazed turkey highlights one of the few sweeteners available to the first settlers. It makes a beautiful, shiny roasted bird. The cornbread stuffing uses both native American maize and the hearty green kale that has become a favorite of the substantial Portuguese communities that endure along the New England seacoast. Brilliant ruby-red cranberries grew wild in early New England, and root vegetables such as potatoes, parsnips, and winter squash were customarily stored by thrifty householders, whether Indian or Pilgrim.

We like to begin our meal with a relish tray, probably a tradition brought with the settlers from their English homeland. Chowder, that most famous of New England soups, can be made with fish, clams, or, as we do here, with oysters. Though the seafood is variable, the soup base is not. New England chowder always uses salt pork, milk or cream, and potatoes. (Never, never tomatoes!)

No Thanksgiving feast would be complete without a pie. Our personal favorite is an old-fashioned apple, with a flavor intensity that comes from boiled-down cider. As for cider, it is worth looking for the best and freshest, preferably from a local cider mill, for the flavor is far superior to the pasteurized supermarket kind. There are many small cheese makers throughout New England, especially in Vermont, and a slim wedge of sharp Cheddar is a delightful accompaniment to a slice of apple pie. To go with the pie, we love this light baked pumpkin custard, especially when dolloped with whipped cream and sprinkled with toasted walnuts.

Happy Thanksgiving!

In Advance

IN THE BEST of all possible worlds, Thanksgiving dinner should be the community effort that it was on that first holiday. In that case, you might certainly ask guests to bring the desserts, the vegetables, the rolls, or the cranberry sauces. But these days, when families are no longer likely to live on the same block, it is entirely possible that you will be the orchestrator of the dinner. This is not a fate to be equated with the Salem witch trials. In fact, if you follow our detailed step-by-step preparation list and parcel out the jobs among your houseguests, your freedom is guaranteed.

Make your grocery list, order the turkey (we like fresh turkeys), and polish the silver a couple of weeks ahead. The Parker House rolls and the pie crust disks can be made now and frozen.

Two days ahead, make both cranberry sauces and the cornbread for the stuffing. Set the table and shop for fresh ingredients to avoid the day-before-Thanksgiving crunch in the supermarket.

One day ahead, make the turkey stuffing, peel the potatoes and parsnips, cut the acorn squash, and make the chowder base. Make the giblet broth and also the gravy, if you are using the do-ahead gravy instructions.

On Thanksgiving morning, make the pie and the pumpkin pudding, then cut up the vegetables for the relish tray and refrigerate them wrapped in wet paper toweling.

About 5 hours before dinner, stuff and roast the turkey. Microwave and glaze the squash rings, then make the succotash. Make the butter mixture for the potatoes and parsnips.

About 1 hour ahead, cook the potatoes and parsnips, begin to heat the chowder base, and put the cranberry sauces on the table.

While the roasted turkey is resting, make the gravy and mash together the potatoes and parsnips. Heat the rolls. Add the oysters to the chowder and broil the squash rings.

Give thanks and then feast!

While basking in the afterglow, you might want to announce that though cooking is indeed your strength, you have never been very good at doing dishes.

If Time Is Short …

☞ Prevail upon your guests to bring some of the vegetable dishes and desserts.

☞ Buy the Parker House rolls from a bakery.

☞ You could substitute packaged cornbread for homemade in the stuffing.

☞ Order apple and pumpkin pies from a bakery.

☞ Call your mother and tell her that you've had a power failure and that everyone is coming to her house instead.

Wellfleet Oyster Chowder

Though there are literally hundreds of known oyster varieties, this chowder is named after a favorite native to the Wellfleet, Massachusetts, area waters. However, our variation on a real New England classic is wonderful made with any small, fresh oyster. We have added wine to the base to make it even more festive. Common crackers, available all over New England and in specialty food stores in other parts of the country, are customarily served with chowder. But oyster crackers or other hard biscuits are acceptable, except to diehard Cape Cod folks.

MAKES 8 TO 10 FIRST-COURSE SERVINGS
(10 CUPS)

⅔	cup diced salt pork
1	large onion, peeled and chopped (about 1¼ cups)
2	ribs celery, chopped (about 1¼ cups)
3	cups (1 pound) peeled and diced russet potatoes
1	cup white wine
1	cup bottled clam juice
1½	tablespoons chopped fresh thyme, or 1½ teaspoons dried
½	teaspoon freshly ground white pepper
⅛	teaspoon grated nutmeg
1	bay leaf, broken
5	cups half-and-half
1½	pints (24 to 30) shucked small oysters with their liquor
	Salt and additional white pepper, if needed
3	tablespoons butter
¼	cup chopped parsley

Common crackers or oyster crackers

1. In a heavy 4-quart saucepan, fry the salt pork over medium-low heat for about 10 minutes, stirring often, until pork is rich golden brown and fat is rendered. Remove salt pork with a slotted spoon, drain on paper toweling, and reserve.

2. Add onions and celery to drippings in pan. Sauté over medium-low heat, stirring often, for about 5 minutes, until vegetables are softened. Add potatoes, wine, clam juice, ½ cup water, thyme, pepper, nutmeg, and bay leaf, and bring to a boil. Cover pan, lower heat, and simmer for about 10 minutes, until potatoes are tender. Add half-and-half and bring to a simmer. (Can be done a day ahead. Remove bay leaf, cool, and refrigerate. Return to a simmer before proceeding.) Add oysters with their liquor and simmer for 2 to 3 minutes until edges of oysters begin to curl. Taste and season with salt and additional white pepper, if needed.

3. To serve, ladle broth and about 3 oysters into shallow soup bowls. Place 1 teaspoon butter in center of each serving and sprinkle lightly with parsley. Serve with common crackers or oyster crackers on the side.

Molasses-glazed Roast Turkey

Inspired by an idea in Anthony Dias Blue and Kathryn K. Blue's wonderful book, Thanksgiving Dinner *(HarperCollins, 1990), we use molasses here to glaze our bird. It gives the skin a shiny, mahogany–brown sheen and a hint of bittersweet molasses flavor.*

MAKES 10 SERVINGS, WITH PLENTY OF LEFTOVERS

1	15-pound turkey, preferably fresh
About 10 cups Sage and Kale Cornbread Dressing (recipe follows)	
3	tablespoons unsalted butter
	Salt and freshly ground black pepper
1	tablespoon molasses
1	teaspoon red wine vinegar

Kale leaves and branches of sage if available, for garnish

1.   Preheat oven to 325° F. Rinse turkey under cold water and dry inside and out with paper towels. Pull off and discard any large pieces of fat around the body cavity.

2.   First stuff the neck cavity, using a metal skewer to secure skin to body. Then stuff the body cavity, tucking the legs back under the precut band of skin or metal lock to secure them. Tuck wing tips back under the shoulders of the bird.

3.   Put any unused stuffing in a baking dish, sprinkle with 2 to 4 tablespoons of broth, cover with foil, and refrigerate. Bake during the last 45 minutes of the turkey's roasting time.

4.   Place turkey, breast side up, on a rack in a shallow roasting pan. Rub with 2 tablespoons of the butter and sprinkle with salt and pepper.

5.   Roast in the preheated oven for approximately 17 minutes per pound (approximately 4½ hours for a 15-pound bird), basting with the pan drippings every 20 to 30 minutes.

6.   Thirty minutes before turkey is due to be done, combine the remaining tablespoon butter, molasses, and vinegar in a small saucepan and heat gently until butter is melted. Brush glaze all over turkey skin. Baste with glaze twice more as turkey finishes roasting. Use an instant-read thermometer to test for doneness. It should register 185° F. in the thigh.

7.   Remove bird to a board or platter and let rest for 20 minutes before carving. Garnish with kale leaves and sage branches if desired.

Sage and Kale Cornbread Dressing

Kale adds color and its pleasantly bitter edge to this rich cornbread stuffing. In New England, the favored brand of poultry seasoning is Bell's, sold since 1867. The formula was concocted in Revere, Massachusetts, by Willie Bell and his mother from herbs grown in their garden. Other poultry seasonings from reputable spice companies can substitute, but if you can find Bell's in its beautiful yellow and red cardboard box with the turkey on the front, do try it.

MAKES ENOUGH FOR A 15-POUND TURKEY

7	tablespoons unsalted butter
2	cups chopped onion
1½	cups chopped celery
6	cups slivered kale leaves (see Note)
3	tablespoons chopped fresh sage, or 1 tablespoon dried leaf sage
1	tablespoon good-quality poultry seasoning
¾	teaspoon salt
½	teaspoon freshly ground black pepper
1	egg, lightly beaten
1	cup chicken or turkey broth
7	cups coarsely crumbled day-old Black Pepper Cornbread (recipe follows) (see Note)
4	cups day-old bread cubes, from good-quality white bread (see Note)

1. Melt the butter in a large skillet. Add onion and celery and cook over low heat until softened, about 15 minutes. Add kale and cook for 5 minutes, stirring often until kale is wilted. Stir in sage, poultry seasoning, salt, and pepper. Combine the egg and broth in a small bowl and add to vegetable mixture.

2. Place crumbled cornbread and white bread cubes in a large bowl. Add the vegetable mixture and toss gently but thoroughly with a large fork until well combined. To taste for seasoning, make a small flat patty and sauté over medium heat until cooked through. Taste and adjust seasonings if necessary. (Cool thoroughly. Can be made a day ahead. Cover and refrigerate.)

3. Use dressing to stuff both cavities of a 15-pound turkey. If not all is used, put remainder in a buttered baking dish, cover with foil, refrigerate, then bake along with the turkey for the last 45 minutes of roasting. Add up to ¼ cup broth as necessary if dry.

Notes: Save some nice-looking outside kale leaves to garnish turkey if desired. You may substitute unseasoned packaged cornbread cubes and white bread cubes, but add up to 1 cup more broth to compensate for dryness.

Black Pepper Cornbread

Baking this cornbread batter in a larger pan makes for more browned crust per square inch—a plus when making the dressing. To eat the cornbread on its own, bake in an 8- by 8-inch pan, increasing the baking time by a few minutes.

MAKES ABOUT 7 CUPS CRUMBLED CORNBREAD

¾	cup all-purpose flour
¾	cup yellow cornmeal
1½	tablespoons sugar
1	tablespoon baking powder
½	teaspoon salt
½	teaspoon freshly ground black pepper
1	egg
¾	cup milk
2	tablespoons vegetable oil

1. Preheat the oven to 400° F. Grease a 7- by 11-inch baking pan.

2. In a mixing bowl, combine the flour, cornmeal, sugar, baking powder, salt, and black pepper. Stir with a whisk to lighten and combine.

3. In a small bowl, whisk together the egg, milk, and oil.

4. Pour the liquid ingredients into the dry and stir just until all the flour is moistened. Do not overmix. Pour batter into the prepared pan, smoothing out as evenly as possible. Bake in preheated oven for 15 to 17 minutes, until bread is an even, pale golden brown.

5. Cool in the pan for 5 minutes. Cut into quarters and remove with a spatula. Let cool completely. Crumble into large (¾-inch) crumbs. Spread onto jelly roll pan and leave to dry uncovered overnight at room temperature.

Note: If also using fresh bread for crumbs, tear into cubes and dry on the baking sheets at the same time that you dry the cornbread.

Giblet Gravy

Finely chopped giblets contribute flavor and richness and sherry lends a sophisticated flair to this traditional gravy. If there are guests who are not giblet-lovers, just remove some gravy from the pan before adding the giblets. We have made enough here to provide an ample amount of leftover gravy.

MAKES ABOUT 5½ CUPS

Giblet Broth

	Turkey giblets, including neck (reserve liver for adding later)
1	small onion, peeled and halved
1	rib celery, with tops, coarsely chopped
1	teaspoon fresh sage, or ½ teaspoon dried
4	black peppercorns
½	teaspoon salt

Giblet Gravy

6	tablespoons turkey drippings
7	tablespoons flour
5	cups turkey or chicken giblet broth (see Note)
⅓	cup dry sherry
	Turkey juices from roasting pan and carving board
	Salt and black pepper to taste
	Turkey giblets (excluding neck), finely chopped

1. To make giblet broth, place all giblets except liver in a saucepan, cover with 4 to 5 cups cold water, and add onion, celery, sage, peppercorns, and salt. Bring to the boil, skim any foam that rises to the surface, reduce heat, and simmer, partially covered, for about 1½ hours, until gizzard is tender. Rinse liver, add to the broth, and simmer for about 5 minutes until just cooked through.

2. Strain, reserving broth and discarding vegetables and neck. Trim gizzard and chop giblets finely. (Can be made a day ahead. Refrigerate broth and chopped giblets.)

3. Make the gravy. After turkey has been transferred to a carving board, remove rack from the pan. Pour all drippings into a large glass measuring cup and let settle for 5 minutes. Spoon 6 tablespoons fat from the top of the measuring cup and return it to the roasting pan. Spoon off and discard remaining fat in the cup, reserving juices.

4. Set roasting pan over 2 burners on the stove over medium heat. Stir in flour, and cook, stirring with a wooden spoon, for 2 minutes to brown lightly. Gradually whisk in broth and sherry and bring to the simmer. Cook and stir over medium heat for 1 minute. Add reserved turkey juices, including any that have accumulated on the carving board, and season to taste with salt and pepper. Stir in chopped giblets.

Note: To make gravy a day ahead, buy a couple of pounds of inexpensive turkey parts, roast them, and use their drippings and juices to make the gravy. Use any combination of turkey giblet broth and/or chicken or turkey broth to make the gravy.

Whipped Potatoes and Parsnips

Potato purists will not detect parsnips here. They will simply think that these are the best whipped potatoes ever. We think the mild onion flavor also contributes to make them the tastiest we have had since grandma stopped digging and storing her own roots.

MAKES 8 TO 10 SERVINGS

4	pounds white russet or other starchy potatoes
1½	pounds parsnips
½	cup (1 stick) unsalted butter
1	clove garlic, peeled and minced
½	cup chopped scallions, white and green parts
1⅓ to 1½	cups whole milk
	Salt and freshly ground pepper

1.   Peel the potatoes and parsnips and cut both in approximate 1½-inch chunks. (Can be done 12 to 24 hours ahead; cover with cold water and refrigerate separately. Boil the potatoes in a large pot of lightly salted water for 8 minutes, then add parsnips and boil another 12 to 15 minutes until both vegetables are tender. Drain and return pot to low heat for about 1 minute to dry out the vegetables.

2.   While the vegetables are cooking (or up to 2 hours earlier in the day), heat the butter in a medium saucepan and sauté the garlic and scallions over low heat, stirring, for 1 minute. If using immediately, add milk and bring just to a simmer. If doing ahead, add milk and simmer just before mashing potatoes.

3.   Mash the potatoes and parsnips with a ricer, a potato masher, or an electric mixer. Slowly add the butter and milk mixture, beating until smooth. Blend in salt and pepper to taste. Serve immediately or hold for up to 30 minutes, then rewarm briefly in a microwave oven.

Narragansett Succotash with Red Pepper

Introduced to colonial cooks by Rhode Island Indians, succotash (probably made with shell beans or cranberry beans) was almost certainly served at the first Thanksgiving. Nowadays almost always made with more readily available lima beans, succotash has been further updated here by the addition of some colorful chopped sweet red bell pepper.

MAKES 10 SERVINGS

1	pound (3 cups) frozen or fresh lima beans (regular or baby)
1	pound (3 cups) frozen or fresh corn kernals
1	cup finely diced red pepper
1	cup heavy cream
½	teaspoon salt, or to taste
½	teaspoon freshly ground black pepper, or to taste
½	teaspoon sugar
2	tablespoons minced parsley

1. Cook the lima beans in salted water for 6 to 8 minutes, until almost tender. Add the corn, bring to the simmer, and add the red pepper. Cook for 2 minutes. Drain well, return to the saucepan, and add the cream. (Can be made 3 hours ahead.)

2. When ready to serve, bring to the simmer and cook, uncovered, for 2 minutes. Season with the salt, pepper, sugar, and parsley.

Maple-buttered Acorn Squash Rings

After much experimentation, we decided that we like the microwave cooking method best for this recipe, though conventional cooking instructions are also provided. Cut into rings, the squash cooks quite evenly in a microwave and is also as decorative as it is delicious.

MAKES 8 TO 10 SERVINGS

4	acorn squash (about 4 pounds total weight)
2	tablespoons unsalted butter
3	tablespoons maple syrup
	Salt and freshly ground pepper

1. Trim the ends from the squash and cut each crosswise into ½-inch slices. You will get about 4 slices from each squash. Use a biscuit cutter slightly larger then the seeded center of each slice to punch out the seeds, leaving a neat and attractive circle in each slice. Alternately, use a sharp knife to cut out a circle, discarding seeds and fiber. Place squash rings, overlapping, in a 9- by 13-inch or other shallow 3-quart microwave-safe baking dish. Cover with plastic wrap. (Can be done a day ahead, covered well, and refrigerated. Return to room temperature before proceeding.)

2. Melt the butter with the maple syrup. (Can be done several hours ahead. Remelt if necessary.)

3. Microwave the squash on high for about 10 minutes, moving slices around once during cooking time, until squash is tender. Let stand 5 minutes, then drain off any liquid from bottom of dish. Rearrange slices, if necessary, so that they are slightly overlapping. Sprinkle with salt and pepper. (Can be prepared 2 hours ahead and kept at room temperature.)

4. Preheat the broiler. Brush squash liberally with maple butter. Broil about 3 inches from the heat source for 1 to 2 minutes until glazed. Brush with any remaining maple butter.

5. Serve directly from baking dish or arrange slices, overlapping, on a decorative platter.

Note: To bake conventionally, preheat oven to 400° F. Arrange squash as directed above, cover with foil, and bake 12 to 15 minutes, until nearly tender. Glaze and broil as directed above. Or glaze and continue to bake about 10 minutes more.

Parker House Rolls

Made famous at the Parker House hotel in Boston in the nineteenth century, these dinner rolls start with a dough very similar to many other buttery yeast doughs. The only difference is in their distinctive shape. They are also sometimes known as "pocketbook rolls" because of their purselike folding.

MAKES ABOUT 2½ DOZEN ROLLS

1	package (2 teaspoons) active dry yeast (see Note)
¼	cup plus ½ teaspoon sugar
¼	cup warm water (about 105° F.)
1¼	cups milk
7	tablespoons melted unsalted butter
3 or 4	cups all-purpose flour, preferably unbleached
1	egg yolk
2	teaspoons salt
4	tablespoons (½ stick) unsalted butter, melted

1. Dissolve the yeast and the ½ teaspoon sugar in the warm water.

2. In a large bowl, combine the ¼ cup sugar, milk, butter, 2 cups of the flour, egg yolk, and salt. Add the yeast mixture and beat vigorously with a wooden spoon to combine. Add 1 cup additional flour and knead on a well-floured board or with a dough hook in a heavy-duty mixer until dough is smooth and elastic, about 8 minutes. During the kneading process, add enough of the remaining flour to make a soft, workable dough.

3. Transfer to a greased bowl, cover, and let rise in a warm place until doubled in bulk, about 1½ hours.

4. Grease 2 baking sheets. Punch dough down and divide into 2 parts. Roll out 1 part on a lightly floured board to approximately ⅜-inch thickness. Using a 2½- to 3-inch biscuit cutter, cut out rounds of dough. Repeat with second half of dough, rerolling and cutting scraps once. Brush rounds lightly with melted butter, and, using a chopstick or knife handle, make a deep crease across the diameter of each round. Fold rounds in half, pressing together gently to seal slightly.

5. Arrange no more than ½ inch apart on baking sheets and brush with melted butter. Cover loosely with plastic wrap and let rolls rise for 30 to 40 minutes, until almost doubled in bulk.

6. Preheat oven to 375° F. Bake rolls in the preheated oven for 18 to 22 minutes, until a rich golden brown. Brush hot baked rolls with melted butter again and remove to a rack to cool. (Store at room temperature for a few hours or freeze in plastic bags for up to 2 weeks.)

7. Reheat thawed rolls in a 350° F. oven for 5 minutes before serving.

Note: Quick-rise yeast may be substituted. Rising times will be about half as long.

Cranberry–Kumquat Relish

This uncooked cranberry relish sparked with chopped kumquats is a refreshing and contemporary contrast in a traditional Thanksgiving feast. Use only fresh cranberries for the best texture.

MAKES ABOUT 3 CUPS

1	12-ounce package fresh cranberries (about 3 cups)
10	fresh kumquats, quartered
1	cup granulated sugar
3	tablespoons currants

1. Put the cranberries, kumquats, and sugar in a food processor and pulse to process until the fruits are finely chopped. Stir in the currants

2. Let stand at room temperature for 1 hour or refrigerate up to 2 days before using in order to allow flavors to blend fully and sugar to dissolve.

Gingered Cranberry and Port Sauce

A wonderful combination of sweet port and tart fruits, this is also a fine condiment for a dinner featuring roasted duck or goose.

MAKES ABOUT 3 CUPS

1	12-ounce package fresh or frozen cranberries (about 3 cups)
⅔	cup port wine
¾	cup sugar
2	tablespoons finely chopped candied ginger
1	tablespoon grated orange zest

1. In a nonreactive saucepan, combine the cranberries, port, and sugar. Bring to a boil, stirring to dissolve sugar. Stir in ginger and zest. Lower heat and simmer, stirring often, for about 10 minutes, until berries have popped and sauce is lightly thickened. (Sauce will thicken more as it cools.)

2. Serve chilled or at room temperature. (Can be made up to 2 days ahead.)

Double Crust Cider Apple Pie

Old-time Yankee pie bakers lament the disappearance of good, really flavorful local pie apples from the markets. These days, most supermarket produce departments seem to stock only 3 or 4 nationally available types. If you can't find tart and tasty local apples, use this trick of Yankee ingenuity. Simply get some good cider, boil it down, and add the potent, natural apple concentrate to your pie.

MAKES 8 TO 10 SERVINGS

Pie Crust

2½	cups all-purpose flour
1	teaspoon salt
1	teaspoon sugar
½	cup (1 stick) chilled unsalted butter, cut in 12 pieces
6	tablespoons chilled vegetable shortening, cut in 8 pieces
1½	teaspoons cider vinegar

Cider–Apple Filling

2	cups good quality apple cider
5 or 6	Granny Smith apples (about 2 pounds)
1	Golden Delicious apple (about 8 ounces)
¾	cup sugar
3	tablespoons all-purpose flour
½	teaspoon cinnamon
¼	teaspoon ground mace
⅛	teaspoon salt
1	tablespoon lemon juice
2	tablespoons unsalted butter, cut in bits

1. For the crust, combine the flour, salt, and sugar in a food processor. Add the butter and shortening and process until mixture resembles small peas. Mix the vinegar and 5 tablespoons water. With machine running, add vinegar mixture to processor and mix until dough just comes together. If dough seems too dry to come together, add 1 tablespoon more water. Gather dough into 2 balls. Flatten each into a disk, wrap in plastic, and refrigerate at least 30 minutes. (Can be prepared 2 days ahead. Let stand at room temperature 15 to 20 minutes until workable before continuing.)

2. For the filling, boil the cider over medium heat for 20 to 30 minutes until reduced to ½ cup. Let cool completely. (Can be prepared 2 days ahead and refrigerated.)

3. When ready to bake pie, preheat oven to 425° F. Set rack in lower third of oven.

4. Peel, core, and slice all the apples about ¼ inch thick. You should have 8 cups. In a large mixing bowl, stir together the sugar, flour, cinnamon, mace, and salt. Add apples and toss to coat. Stir in reduced cider and the lemon juice. Set aside.

5. On a lightly floured surface, roll 1 pastry disk to a 12-inch circle. Ease into a 9-inch pie plate. Roll remaining pastry disk to 11-inch circle. Spoon filling and all juices into pie shell. Dot with butter. Cover with remaining pastry, seal, and flute edges, then make several slashes in top pastry for steam vents.

6. Bake 20 minutes, then reduce temperature to 350° F. and bake 35 to 45 minutes more, until pastry is rich golden brown and filling is bubbly. (If pastry edges begin to brown too much, loosely cover them with strips of foil.) Cool pie on a rack. Serve slightly warm or at room temperature.

Baked Spiced Pumpkin Pudding

Like a pumpkin pie without the crust, this fragrant baked custard is a lovely Thanksgiving dessert, especially with a dollop of lightly sweetened, walnut-studded, rum-spiked whipped cream. Black walnuts used to be common in New England. Though they are harder to find these days, use them if you can, for they lend a distinctive, rich, pleasantly bitter contrast to sweet baked goods.

MAKES 8 TO 10 SERVINGS

Pudding

2	cups half-and-half
4	eggs
⅓	cup granulated sugar
⅓	cup golden brown sugar
¼	cup molasses
1	teaspoon ground cinnamon
1	teaspoon powdered ginger
½	teaspoon grated nutmeg
¼	teaspoon salt
⅛	teaspoon ground cloves
1	1-pound can (about 1¾ cups) pumpkin purée (not pie filling)

Walnut Cream

1	cup heavy cream
2	tablespoons confectioners' sugar
1	tablespoon dark rum
½	cup toasted chopped walnuts, preferably black walnuts (see Note)

1. Preheat the oven to 325° F. Butter a shallow 2-quart baking dish such as a standard 9- by 9-inch or 7¾- by 11½-inch dish or another decorative baking and serving dish.

2. Heat the half-and-half until bubbles appear around the edge. In a large mixing bowl, whisk together the eggs, both sugars, and the molasses. Whisk in the cinnamon, ginger, nutmeg, salt, and cloves. Then whisk in the pumpkin purée and the warm half-and-half.

3. Pour into the prepared baking dish. Set dish in a larger pan and pour enough hot water in large pan to come halfway up the sides of the baking dish. Bake in the center of the oven for 40 to 45 minutes, until a knife inserted halfway between edge and center comes out clean. Center of custard will still be soft but not liquid, and will continue to cook a bit after it is out of the oven. Remove baking dish from water bath and set on a rack to cool. (Can be made several hours ahead.)

4. To make the walnut cream, whip the cream with the confectioners' sugar until soft peaks form, then whisk in the rum. (Can be made about 4 hours ahead and refrigerated. Whisk again before serving if cream begins to separate.) Just before serving, fold in most of the walnuts. Spoon cream into a serving dish and sprinkle with remaining nuts.

5. Serve the pudding warm, at room temperature, or lightly chilled. Spoon a portion of pudding onto each dessert plate and dollop some walnut cream onto each serving. Refrigerate leftovers.

Note: Walnuts may be toasted while pudding bakes. Place in a single layer on a baking sheet and toast in 325° F. oven for about 8 minutes, stirring once or twice, until browned and fragrant.

Index

Crab cakes, tiny, with tarragon
    mayonnaise, 147
Cranberry
    -kumquat relish, 265
    -pecan pound cake, 14
    and port sauce, gingered, 265
    -Riesling good intentions, 42
Crawfish, andouille, and duck
    jambalaya, 46
Cream, peaches and
    pie, Marianne's spiced, 210
    sponge roll, 194
Cream cheese
    lemon frosting, carrot cake
        with, 138
    lemon-scallion, lox on small
        bagels with, 8
    pastry, for Brooke's apple-
        mincemeat turnovers,
        34
Crème brulées, cherry, 84
Crostini, mozzarella, and tomato
    salad, 231
Croustade, mustard greens and
    bacon, 44
Crudité assortment with roasted
    garlic sauce, 133
Crudités
    cherry tomato and broccoli,
        with Russian dip, 7
    summer, with raspberry-thyme
        dipping sauce, 184
Cumin vinaigrette, toasted, sliced
    oranges on romaine
    with, 109
Curaçao, sliced tangerines in,
    49
Currant(s)
country terrine with ham and,
    220
    sage-glazed corned beef, 10
Curried cashews, 162
Curry-cilantro vinaigrette,
    tropical salad with, 246
Custard
    sauce, Cointreau, raspberries
        with, 174
    tart, plum, 234
    vanilla nutmeg chantilly, 49

D

Damson plum jam, Irish oat
    scones with, 120
Decidedly chocolate layer cake,
    190
Desserts
    apple-mincemeat turnovers,
        Brooke's, 34
    apricot almond tart, 167
    bars
        chocolate almond
            macaroon, Carol's, 35
        Toni's citrus, 30
        brownies, spiced chocolate
            pecan, 111
    cake
        brandied caraway seed, 75
        carrot, with lemon cream
            cheese frosting, 138
        cheesecake, candied orange
            ricotta, 99
        chocolate layer, decidedly,
            190
        mocha bûche de Noël, 24
        peaches and cream sponge
            roll, 194
        pound, cranberry-pecan,
            14
        shower, coconut raspberry,
            123
        spice, Mother's banana-
            walnut, with seafoam
            frosting, 191
        wedding memory, 154
    candied orange ricotta
        cheesecake, 99
    Caribbean fruits, 249
    cherry crème brulées, 84
    cookies. *See* Cookies
    custard
        sauce, Cointreau,
            raspberries with, 174
        tart, plum, 234
        vanilla nutmeg chantilly,
            49
    exotic fruit platter, 74
    fudge, Mamie's famous, 15

    ice cream
        butterscotch sauce for, real,
            63
        hot fudge sauce for, double
            decadent, 64
        vanilla bean, Bernice
            Cooper's homemade,
            195
    lemon tartlets in walnut
        pastry, 121
    Margarita mousse, 110
    mousse
        Margarita, 110
        strawberry meringue, 152
    orange ice ring, 6
    peaches and cream sponge roll,
        194
    pear and ginger tarts, free-
        form, 224
    pie
        blueberry crunch, Aunt
            Dot's, 212
        chocolate pecan, Martha's,
            213
        lemon buttermilk, Patty's,
            209
    peaches and cream, Marianne's
        spiced, 210
    pudding
        bread, coconut-rum, 248
        pumpkin, baked spiced,
            267
    pyramid of winter fruits and
        nuts, 16
    raspberries with Cointreau
        custard sauce, 174
    rum-soused pineapple and
        raspberries, 63
    tangerines in Curaçao, sliced,
        49
    tart
        apricot almond, 167
        pear and ginger, free-form,
            224
        plum custard, 234
    trifle, Laurel's winter berry, 26
    wild huckleberry cobbler, 193
Dill sauce, cappelletti with, 182
Dinner rolls, 152

INDEX

Tomato(es) (*cont.*)
    mozzarella, crostini, and,
        231
    and sweet onions with
        Gorgonzola vinaigrette,
        137
Toni's citrus bars, 30
Tortilla chips, fresh, 106
Trifle, Laurel's winter berry, 26
Tropical salad with cilantro-
    curry vinaigrette, 246
Turkey
    molasses-glazed roast, 257
    smoked, whole, on a bed of
        kale, 11
Turnip and potato galettes, lacy,
    82
Turnovers, apple-mincemeat,
    Brooke's, 34

V

Vanilla
    bean ice cream, Bernice
        Cooper's homemade,
        195
    nutmeg chantilly custard, 49
Vegetable(s)
    spears, Cheddar and ale
        fondue with, 56
    summer
        and chicken mosaic, 164
        grilled, 173
Vinaigrette
    Gorgonzola, tomatoes and
        sweet onions with, 137

mint-parsley, for couscous
    garden salad, 151
mustard-honey, for lucky
    black-eyed pea and
    pepper salad on mâche,
    47
toasted cumin, sliced oranges
    on romaine with, 109
Vinegar, balsamic
    beurre rouge, broiled poussin
        on radicchio with, 81
    -honey vinaigrette, for corn,
        black bean, and red
        pepper salad, 107
    tomatoes with oil, chives, and,
        152
Violets, candied, 122

W

Wafers
    benne seed coins, 43
    brown sugar almond, 175
    chocolate-dipped pistachio,
        Judy's, 33
    mocha, 124
Walnut(s)
    -apricot bran muffins, 73
    -banana spice cake, Mother's,
        with seafoam frosting,
        191
    pastry, lemon tartlets, 121
Wassail bowl, spiced cider, 23
Watercress, tea sandwiches with
    smoked chicken, chutney,
    and, 119

Watermelon pickles, sweet-and-
    sour, 207
Wedding memory cake, 154
Wellfleet oyster chowder, 256
West Indian peas and rice, 245
Whipped potatoes and parsnips,
    261
White Christmas fruit punch, 6
White sangria, 104
Whole smoked turkey on a bed
    of kale, 11
Wild huckleberry cobbler,
    193
Wild rice salad, Chippewa, in
    radicchio, 223
Wild thyme honey-mustard
    sauce, 94
Wine
    blush wine punch, 116
    cranberry-Riesling good
        intentions, 42
    white, sangria, 104
Winter spinach salad bowl, with
    orange buttermilk
    dressing, 61

Y

Yellow rice, 60
Yogurt frappés, raspberry, 92

Z

Zombies!, 240